Video Editing with Avid

Media Composer, Symphony, Xpress

Roger Shufflebottom

Focal Press

OXFORD AMSTERDAM BOSTON LONDON NEW YORK PARIS
SAN DIEGO SAN FRANCISCO SINGAPORE SYDNEY TOKYO

Focal Press
An imprint of Elsevier Science
Linacre House, Jordan Hill, Oxford OX2 8DP
225 Wildwood Avenue, Woburn, MA 01801-2041

First published 2001
Reprinted 2002

British Library Cataloguing in Publication Data
Shufflebottom, Roger
    Video editing with Avid: Media Composer, Symphony, Xpress
    1. Avid Xpress (Computer file)   2. Media Composer (Computer
    file   3. Symphony (Computer file)   4. Video tapes – Editing –
    Data processing
    I. Title
    778.5′93′0285′5369

Library of Congress Cataloguing in Publication Data
A catalogue record for this book is available from the Library of Congress

For information on all Focal Press publications visit our website at
www.focalpress.com

Trademarks/Registered Trademarks
Computer hardware and software brand names mentioned in this book
are protected by their respective trademarks and are acknowledged

ISBN 0 240 51678 8

Composition by Genesis Typesetting, Rochester, Kent
Printed and bound in Great Britain by MPG Books Ltd, Bodmin, Cornwall

Video Editing with Avid

Contents

Introduction

Avid Technology was one of the pioneers of the wave of digital non-linear editing systems that have transformed the video post-production world. I had been a film editor for a number of years before I first sat in front of an Avid system (version 3, I recall), in 1992. I had read about computer-based editing and seen a few systems at trade shows but nothing prepared me for the speed and flexibility of this new toy. From that day on, I hardly touched film again and have spent the subsequent years editing with Avid, writing about Avid and teaching editors, journalists, directors and producers how to use Avid systems.

Why another book about Avid? There are other books – some strong on the film side, some excellent on advanced features – but so far, no one book moving from the beginner to intermediate level, covering Media Composer, Xpress and Symphony, with the similarities and differences explained. From my experience as a trainer, I have formed strong ideas about what information a new user needs, and when they need it. This is not specifically a training book (I hope it comes across as a good read, too) but by working through the text, a reader will be able, by the end, to complete an Avid project competently, enjoy themselves along the way, and learn some efficient and powerful working techniques.

If you compare the length of this book with the hefty volumes which come with an Avid system, you may wonder how I can fit it all in . . . well, I can't and I haven't. There are usually several ways to do anything on an Avid and I mention what I consider to be the most useful, intuitive and productive. Avid experts may well find a favourite technique missing but the book would have been twice as long if I'd included everything.

What's not covered? This is a book aimed at video editors, both offline and those finishing projects on Avid. Specific film editing features are not covered, neither is Script Integration, the Paint and Animatte options or the advanced Symphony features such as motion stabilization and motion tracking, advanced colour correction or the real-time Ultimatte keyer. The book assumes that the reader has the use of a working system – there is no step-by-step guide to assembling the components from a stack of boxes; this is covered in depth in Avid's documentation.

This book is not a primer about video in general – it will be a great help to know the difference between a frame and a field, between PAL and NTSC, and between component and composite. On the other hand, editors shouldn't need to be computer experts, so the first chapter includes some Mac OS and Windows information aimed at Avid users.

Avid editing systems – an overview

'Non-linear' describes the way in which the editing proceeds compared with the linear way of a two- or three-machine tape editing suite. With tape, the new edited master tape is built up by having shot after shot recorded in a linear way, from the beginning to the end. If a change needs to be made, other than simply replacing one section with another of the same length, problems arise. Either part of the programme has to be re-edited from scratch or the recorded material has to be dubbed again, resulting (usually) in a loss of quality.

In a digital non-linear system, material (from tape, CD, microphone, graphics or whatever) is digitized by the computer, with the resulting data stored on large, fast disk drives. The digitizing process converts the signal from the tape into a digital format and (usually) compresses the video (i.e., some of the information is discarded). Once stored on disk, the editor can rapidly assemble a programme and make as many changes or alterations as required. The assembly, or sequence, can be shortened, lengthened and quickly made into new versions. Video effects and titles can be added and the audio can be mixed and balanced.

The early non-linear systems had poor picture quality and were only used for offline work. In offline, the editing decisions are made using copies of the source material, with the final edit carried out (usually) in a high-quality tape suite using the master tapes. Information is carried from the offline to the online in the form of an Edit Decision List (EDL) usually on a computer disk.

Current versions of Avid systems offer extremely high picture quality and the output from the computer is routinely used for broadcast. The video compression is now so low that it is difficult to tell that the material has been edited, unless the same piece has been redigitized several times (something to be avoided). The down-side of the ability to work with high-quality images is the amount of disk storage required. One hour of uncompressed video on the latest systems needs around 72GB of storage. One hour of video at Avid's highest compressed resolution (2:1) would need around 30GB of storage. For this reason, programmes are still offlined on Avid systems at a high compression rate (low quality). Working at a typical offline resolution, that same 30GB would give around 15–20 hours of storage. Editors will frequently offline and online on the same Avid system, possibly keeping all the original audio and simply replacing the pictures with higher quality images. All audio on Avid systems is digitized or input at a high quality from the start.

Systems covered in this book

This books covers Avid Media Composer, Symphony and Xpress systems. Table A shows the various releases covered, and the computer platforms they use. For years, Avid systems used Apple computers but, in 1998, Symphony was released,

Table A Avid releases and their computer platforms

Model	Apple Mac	Windows NT	ABVB video	Meridien video
Media Composer v7	Yes	No	Yes	No
Media Composer v8	Yes	Yes	No	Yes
Media Composer v9	No	Yes	No	Yes
Media Composer v10	Yes	Yes	No	Yes
Xpress v2	Yes	No	Yes	No
Xpress v2.1	No	Yes	No	Yes
Xpress v2.5	Yes	No	No	Yes
Xpress v3.x	Yes	Yes	No	Yes
Xpress v4.x	Yes	Yes	No	Yes

running on IBM computers using Windows NT. This was the first Avid system to offer uncompressed video. In 1999, Media Composer was released on Windows NT in addition to Mac and has uncompressed video either as standard or as an option.

Another Avid product is the Film Composer, which offers additional features enabling the editor to track film key numbers right through the edit and allowing a cut list to be made for the negative cutter. Most editing procedures on Film Composer are identical to those on Media Composer.

Avid Xpress is a less expensive system with fewer editing features than Media Composer but still offering high quality images. Xpress is available for both Mac and NT systems. A variation is Xpress DV, cheaper still, purely for editing native DV footage. This is the only Avid editing product available as software only; Xpress DV users will find much useful information in this book although this model is not dealt with explicitly. Table A also gives information on two video boards used by Avid systems – ABVB and Meridien. These will be described in Chapter 1.

Version 10 of Media Composer runs on both Mac OS and Windows NT and this book applies equally to both systems; the features are the same on both platforms with occasional differences noted where required. Media Composer version 7 ran only on Mac OS and used different video boards – see Chapter 2. Versions 8 and 9 are also described here. Basic editing on Symphony is done in the same way as on Media Composer – all Symphony systems run on NT only. The editing workflow on Avid Xpress is very similar to that on Media Composer and important differences will be pointed out in these pages. Avid Xpress versions 2–4 are covered. Illustrations are a mixture of Mac and NT, with both platforms shown where there are differences.

Current Media Composer models include the Offline XL and two online systems, the 1000 XL and 9000 XL. The 9000 XL has 3D effects, real time multicamera editing and many other features. Some of these features are options on the other models. Avid Xpress is currently available as either the Plus, the Deluxe or the Elite, with an increasing number of features, mostly on the effects side, from model to model. Symphony is available as a high-end finishing system or as the Symphony Universal that has support for 24P (24 fps progressive or non-interlaced) resolutions and the ability to output multiple versions of a sequence in different formats. These features are beyond the scope of this book.

Typical system components

Media Composer and Symphony use two large computer monitors to display the Composer window (where the editing is done), the Timeline (which gives a graphical representation of the edit), the various tools (such as the Audio and Digitize tools) and the bins that contain the clips. An additional video monitor is used to view the edited material. The video monitor may be a cheap television for offline but will need to be a calibrated broadcast monitor for critical finishing work. Two self-powered audio speakers are usually supplied, although these are often upgraded for critical work. Avid Xpress is supplied with one computer monitor although a second monitor can be added. Figure Intro.1 shows typical Media Composer components (Mac v7) and Figure Intro.2 shows typical Xpress components (Windows NT v4). Figures Intro.3a and Intro.3b show a typical Media Composer monitor display; Figure Intro.4 shows a typical Xpress monitor display.

The internal hard disk in the computer holds the system software, Avid application, any other installed programs and the files for the Avid projects. These files contain information about the various clips logged or digitized, the tape numbers and timecodes, and the edited sequences. The computer can be used to store and run other programs such as word processors or graphics applications.

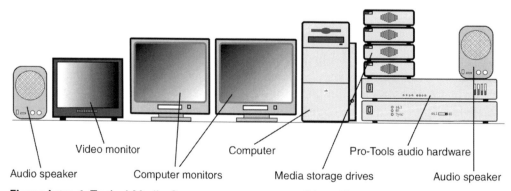

Video monitor   Computer   Pro-Tools audio hardware

Audio speaker   Computer monitors   Media storage drives   Audio speaker

Figure Intro.1 Typical Media Composer components (Mac v7)

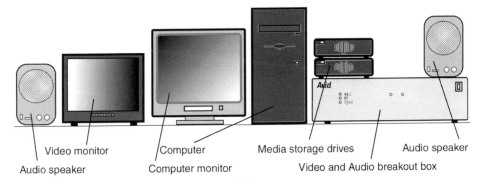

Video monitor   /Computer   Media storage drives   Audio speaker

Audio speaker   Computer monitor   Video and Audio breakout box

Figure Intro.2 Typical Xpress components (NT)

None of the digitized audio and video is stored on the internal drive – all the MediaFiles (as they are known) are stored on high capacity fast external disk drives (or in the case of Xpress DV, extra internal drives). In the early days these may have been 1.5 or 2GB (which seemed massive a few years ago) and were very expensive. Nowadays 18GB, 36GB and 73GB drives are available and the cost has dropped. These drives are often grouped together in a process known as drive striping – data is written to and read from several drives simultaneously, which can double or quadruple the data throughput. This is essential for reliable playback of the highest video resolutions.

Workflow

Let's take a look at the workflow on a typical job. First, the editor (or director or producer) will log the source tapes, identifying the best sections. This can be done away from the Avid, thus saving time and money. Next the chosen sections are digitized into the computer, at either a low or high resolution depending on the length of the job and the storage available. Each shot that is digitized is known as a clip and is stored in a bin (the computer equivalent of the trims bins found in a film cutting room). The editor works with the clips, which can be named and organized in any way the editor desires. The clips are linked to the media files that are stored on the external drives. When the editor chooses a clip for playback, the system finds the media files that are linked to the clip and the audio and video are played back from the media drives.

During the editing process, the editor creates one or more sequences, which consist of a series of clips, or parts of clips, strung together. The media is never actually cut or changed, the sequence is simply a list of instructions to play one clip followed by another clip. This means that it is very easy to duplicate a sequence to

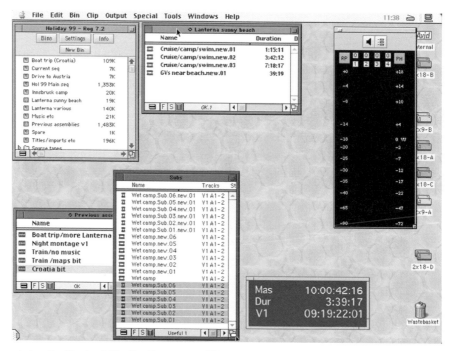

Figure Intro.3a Typical Media Composer Bin monitor display (Mac v7)

try alternative versions. Sections of the edited programmes can be shortened, lengthened and moved about with great speed and flexibility.

After the cut is agreed, video effects can be added, the audio can be balanced and further sound effects, commentary and music added. Titles can be added at this stage. All the tools needed to finish a programme (within certain limits) are available on the Avid system. At this point the programme will be output to tape (a process called Digital Cut) and the edit is complete. If the programme was being edited at an offline resolution, the project information can be taken from an offline Media Composer or Xpress to an online Media Composer or Symphony and the job completed. The edited sequence contains a lot of information apart from the actual edits, including audio levels and equalization, information about titles, colour grading, effect details and much more. Alternatively an EDL may be made and the online carried out in a conventional tape editing suite.

When the job is complete, the project information will be backed up to floppy disk, Zip cartridge or some other medium and the media drives cleared ready for the next job.

Figure Intro.3b Typical Media Composer Edit monitor display (Mac v7)

Figure Intro.4 Typical Xpress monitor display (NT v4)

1 Computer basics

Before starting to edit on the Avid, let's take a look at the two computer systems users will encounter: Apple computers with the Mac operating system and IBM computers running the Windows NT operating system. Not all the versions of Avid software run on the same hardware; Appendix 1 lists the recent history of Avid software and the matching hardware. The following information is designed to help Avid editors who are new to Mac or Windows; it is not a definitive run-down of every feature on each operating system! Editors shouldn't need to be computer experts but some basic knowledge is very useful.

Apple Mac

Avid Media Composer (Mac) software versions 7, 8 and 10 and Xpress v2–v4 run on the Apple Macintosh computer. Media Composer v9 was not released for Mac OS. Media Composer v8 and v10 and Xpress v2.5, v3 and v4 use the same video hardware (the Meridien system) as Symphony, Media Composer and Xpress on NT. Media Composer v7 and Xpress v2 used different hardware, described below.

ABVB systems

These systems are mostly based on the Apple PPC 9500 or 9600, which have six PCI expansion slots inside. Five of these slots will be occupied, as follows:

- a Digidesign audio board, to deal with audio input and output;
- an Avid Broadcast Video board. This deals with video input and output at the ITU R-601 video standard. This board has either a Betacam input (offering analogue component and composite I/O) or a serial digital interface;
- a JPEG video compression board, which is directly linked to the ABVB;
- an ATTO fast SCSI board, for connecting the external disk drives used for storage;
- a graphics board to drive a second computer monitor.

The sixth slot may be used for a second ATTO card or an internal board for 3D effects.

Cables are connected to the ABVB to link it to the VTR used for digitizing and recording back to tape. On basic systems with the Digidesign Audiomedia card, audio connections are made directly to RCA (phono) sockets on the board. Better-specified systems have the Digidesign SA4 board, which is linked to a Digidesign Pro Tools 442 or 888 rack-mounted audio interface. The modem port on the computer is used for controlling the VTR.

During the life of Media Composer v7 and Xpress v2, Apple stopped making the six-slot PPC 9600 and introduced the first phase of beige G3 computers, which only had three PCI slots. To accommodate the various boards needed (see above) Avid supplied their systems with a PCI expansion chassis (a large metal case which could be rack mounted).

Meridien systems

Media Composer versions 8 and 10 (and Xpress v2.5, v3 and v4) use different hardware. The computer (usually a beige or blue G3 or graphite G4) is linked to an external breakout box (the 'BOB') for the video and audio connections and uses Avid's Meridien board set, which offers new video resolutions and the uncompressed video option. The BOB makes it much easier to connect video and audio equipment to the Avid and is more versatile than earlier hardware. Taking a current G4 Mac system as an example, the computer will have connectors for one computer monitor (the Bin monitor; see later), serial ports for controlling VTRs, USB ports for the keyboard and other accessories and a port for the ribbon cable that links to the expansion chassis. The expansion chassis has a connector for the system cable leading to the Meridien breakout box and SCSI connectors for the media drives.

Inside the computer is the Central Processing Unit (the CPU), banks of Random Access Memory (RAM), a floppy disk drive (not on the later G3 and G4), a CD ROM drive, possibly a Zip drive and an internal fixed or hard disk drive. The internal fixed disk (usually called the Avid drive) contains the Avid application, any other programs and applications loaded on to the computer, the computer's system software and the Avid project folders and files. The actual digitized media files are stored on external disk drives connected via a SCSI or Fibre Channel interface.

On the latest G4 systems, an external floppy disk drive will be attached to a USB hub that is connected to the computer. All systems described here also have an Avid hardware key or 'dongle', usually connected to the keyboard cable or USB hub. Without the dongle, the computer will run but no editing can be done. Dongles are very valuable and should be looked after.

The amount of video and audio storage is governed by the size of the disk drives linked to your computer. It is unlikely that you will run out of room on your internal drive but the length of programme you can edit is governed by the storage capacity of your external drives.

Jo Coleman

Information Update Service

Butterworth-Heinemann

FREEPOST SCE 5435

Oxford

Oxon

OX2 8BR

UK

Keep up-to-date with the latest books in your field.

Visit our website and register now for our FREE e-mail update service, or join our mailing list and enter our monthly prize draw to win £100 worth of books. Just complete the form below and return it to us now! (FREEPOST if you are based in the UK)

www.bh.com

Please Complete In Block Capitals

Title of book you have purchased:..

....

Subject area of interest:...

Name:...

Job title:...

Business sector (if relevant):..

Street:..

Town:... County:...

Country:.. Postcode:...

Email:...

Telephone:..

How would you prefer to be contacted: Post ☐   e-mail ☐   Both ☐

Signature:.. Date:...

☐ Please arrange for me to be kept informed of other books and information services on this and related subjects (✔ box if not required). This information is being collected on behalf of Reed Elsevier plc group and may be used to supply information about products by companies within the group.

FOR OFFICE USE ONLY

Butterworth-Heinemann,
a division of Reed Educational
& Professional Publishing Limited.
Registered office: 25 Victoria Street,
London SW1H 0EX.
Registered in England 3099304.
VAT number GB: 663 3472 30.

BUTTERWORTH HEINEMANN

A member of the Reed Elsevier plc group

Starting a Mac system

Power up the system in the following sequence: first turn on the external disk drives, then turn on the other hardware (expansion chassis, monitors, BOB, Digidesign 888 interface and USB power supplies if fitted). Allow 20 seconds or so for the external drives to spin up to speed before starting the Mac. If you don't do this, the computer will not recognize their presence. Start the computer by pressing the large key at the top right of the keyboard (some G4 systems with USB keyboards may need to be started using the button on the front of the computer). The computer can be started without switching on the breakout box, 888 and media drives but these must be turned on before launching Avid.

When the computer is running, the disk drives appear as icons on the right-hand side of the startup monitor (normally the left of the two on a Media Composer – see Figure Intro.3a). The top icon (normally named 'Avid'), is the internal hard disk in the Mac. This will contain a folder called 'Avid Projects' or 'Composer Projects', depending on the software version. All information about the projects you work on will normally be stored in this folder. The external drives, usually with names such as 'Media 1' or 'Media B', are displayed below this. At the bottom of the screen is the trash or wastebasket icon.

If you have large external drives or groups of drives, it is possible that more than one icon per drive will be displayed. This will be because the drives have been partitioned (divided into sections). On the other hand, several striped drives may only appear as one large volume. It is always helpful to know which drives match which icons on the desktop.

The Finder and the Desktop

To examine the contents of a drive or folder, move the mouse pointer over an icon and double-click. A window will open up displaying the contents. The external drives normally contain only the media files containing the digitized video and audio to play your clips. If you double-click on the icon for an external drive or partition, you should see only one folder, named OMFI (Open Media Framework Interchange) MediaFiles.

When you are moving around at desktop level, the Mac is actually running a program called the Finder. It has its own icon (a monitor symbol or the Mac OS symbol). Look at the top right-hand corner of the menu bar to see the Finder icon. This changes to a Media Composer or Xpress icon when you are editing. By clicking on this icon it is possible to hide or swap between running applications. Figure 1.1 shows typical locations of key files and folders on a Mac system.

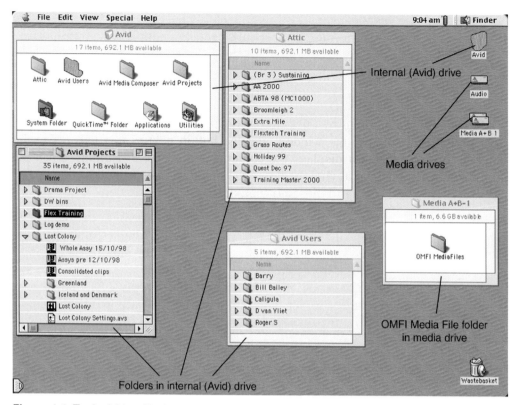

Figure 1.1 Typical Mac file layout

Moving, copying and deleting files

Although the Avid will automatically save your work (see Chapter 13), you need to know how to move files around the system. For instance, it is advisable to back up your project information regularly.

To move a file from one folder to another, simply click on the file's icon and, holding the mouse button down, drag the icon to a destination folder. If you wish to move more than one file (or folder), click on the first item then release the mouse button, hold down the shift key on the keyboard and select more items by clicking (known as 'shift-clicking'). All the items selected become highlighted on the screen. If you wish to select every item in a window, go to the Edit menu and click on 'Select All'. There is a keyboard shortcut for this: Cmd (⌘)+A. This means hold down the Command (also known as the Apple key) and simultaneously press 'A'. There are many other useful shortcuts that work both at Finder level and within applications. Once you have selected your items, click on one to drag them all to the destination folder.

If you click and drag items to a different location on the same disk, the Finder simply moves the items. If you wish to copy the items, hold down the option key (sometimes marked 'alt') while you carry out the operation. Dragging items to a different drive (or floppy) automatically copies them. To delete files or folders, drag them to the Trash, then empty the Trash from the Special menu. Objects are deleted in a different way when working within Avid (see later).

Mac windows are closed by clicking on the button at top left. The extreme top right button will collapse the window and the button next to this will resize the window to a size that just displays the contents and no more. Holding down the option key when opening a window closes the previous one as the new one opens. Option+⌘+W is a shortcut to close all windows.

Removable disks

If you insert a floppy disk (or a Zip cartridge or CD) into the computer, an icon appears on the desktop. You can now copy items to and from a floppy or Zip as described above. Jaz cartridges are often used for moving audio media files to a digital audio workstation for dubbing.

If the computer cannot read the disk, it will display a message asking if you wish to initialize or format it. A utility called PC Exchange enables the Mac to read, write and format DOS (IBM compatible) format disks as well as Mac disks. Use HD (1.4MB) Mac disks or Zip cartridges to back up your projects. Use DD (720KB) DOS disks to save Edit Decision Lists (EDLs).

To back up your project after working, first make sure that your work is saved to the Avid drive (this is done automatically when you quit). In the Finder, double click on the Avid drive icon, then on the Composer (or Avid) Projects folder, until you can see your project folder. Drag this to the floppy or Zip disk icon. If you have already backed up your work to this disk, a message will inform you that an item of the same name exists and asks if you wish to replace it. The answer is yes! Large folders can be compressed using a utility such as Stuffit or Compact Pro (included on some systems).

If you wish to restore a project from floppy, or move your project to a different computer, the process is reversed. Insert your floppy disk and drag your project folder into the Composer (or Avid) Projects folder on the Avid drive of the computer. Do not open a project or bin from a floppy – always copy the project to the Avid drive on the computer first.

You can also save and copy your user settings. User settings are kept in a folder called Avid Users on the Avid drive. By putting a copy of your settings on a floppy, you can begin work quickly on another machine. Do not use settings from one version of the software on a different version as the results may be unpredictable. Always make new settings when a software upgrade is released.

Apple Menu Items Folder

In the System folder is a folder called Apple Menu Items. Click on the Apple symbol at the left-hand end of the menu bar to see the contents. It can contain files or folders but often contains aliases – pointers to applications that may be hidden away in folders (similar to a Windows shortcut). The normal way to launch Avid is from an alias in the Apple menu or on the desktop. The Apple menu contains some useful items:

Chooser allows the user to control the computer's connection to such external devices as printers and networks. AppleTalk should normally be off when using Avid unless your system is linked to Avid Unity Medianet. In this case, use the Chooser to link to your workspace.

Key Caps gives access to extra keyboard characters. This useful when working with the Title Tool (see Chapter 12).

Vantage is a text editor bundled with Avid and is useful to check EDLs or shot logs.

Control Panels

Many aspects of the Mac can be modified using the Control Panels. The Control Panels folder is in the System folder, but is usually accessed via the Apple Menu. The following are useful:

Date & Time allows the user to set date and time of computer's clock and set the time display in the menu bar. Make sure this is correct as all files are date-stamped when made or modified.

Memory allows the user to check and change memory settings – keep the cache size as small as possible, no RAM disk and virtual memory off for Avid.

Monitors and Sound allows the user to modify monitor settings such as resolution and colour depth and set sound options. Check your release notes for specific settings for the version you are using as getting this wrong may have surprising results.

Extensions Manager lets you decide which extensions are loaded at startup and save sets for different situations. Avoid loading non-essential extensions that a) will take up RAM unnecessarily and b) may conflict with Avid. See the current release notes for details.

ATM (Adobe Type Manager) allows Postscript fonts to appear anti-aliased (non-jaggy) on the screen. Almost essential for use with Title Tool.

Energy Saver should be set to never shut down the system.

Shutting down

When you have finished work, choose 'Quit' from the File menu and shut down the computer by going to 'Shutdown' in the Special menu. By doing this, the Mac updates its files and closes down any running application in a controlled way.

Windows NT

On Windows systems, Avid usually supplies IBM computers running the Windows NT4 operating system. All NT systems (Symphony v1–v3, Media Composer v8–v10 and Xpress v2.1–v4), use the Meridien boardset and breakout box as described in the Mac section. Xpress DV also runs on NT but doesn't use the external hardware.

To start a typical system, power up the external drives, the breakout box and any other hardware, then press the 'On' key on top of the computer. After various startup messages, you are invited to press the Ctrl+Alt+Del keys to log on. After this, you need to key in a Windows user name and password – just press 'Return' on most systems. Some installed systems may have specific users and passwords set – this is advisable as the system administrator will be able to prevent inexperienced users from meddling with the Windows NT settings. The computer will attempt to start up from a floppy disk left in the A drive so you may see the 'Not a system disk' error message (or worse) if you inadvertently leave a disk in the drive.

To see the drive icons look for the 'My computer' icon on the desktop (Figure 1.2). Double-click this and a window opens showing the storage drives and other things including the Control Panel. The internal hard disk on NT systems is normally partitioned; drive C: contains the Windows files and drive D: contains the Avid Projects folder and other files and folders accessed by the user. Double-click on a drive icon to see the contents (NT doesn't indicate whether there is a floppy disk inserted; double-click on the appropriate icon to check).

You can decide globally whether your existing window closes as another one opens or whether window after window opens on the desktop. Set this by right-clicking on the View button at the top of the folder window and choose Folder

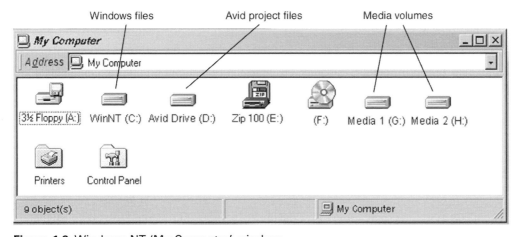

Figure 1.2 Windows NT 'My Computer' window

options. This setting is on or off until changed for all windows, but the actions can be reversed by holding down Ctrl when switching. To close a window, press Alt+f4 or click the small × button, top right. To minimize a window, click the small minus button, top right. A minimized application is still running and can be brought back by clicking on the name in the taskbar. To close all the windows back to the root of one drive, press shift+Alt+f4.

At the bottom or the side of the monitor display is the Windows taskbar. This shows any running applications and open windows, enabling the user to swap between programs. This can be resized or removed (to claim extra desktop space). Right-click on the taskbar and choose 'Properties'. Deselect 'Always on top' to gain space for the Avid display.

The normal way to start Avid will be from a Shortcut on the desktop (double-click with the left mouse button).

Moving, copying and deleting files

Although Avid will automatically save your work for you (see Chapter 13), you need to know how to move files around the system. For instance, it is advisable to back up your project information regularly.

To move a file from one folder to another, left-click on the file's icon and, holding the mouse button down, drag the icon to a destination folder. To move files around from folder to folder on the same drive, simply drag them (going from folder to folder on the same drive moves files; going to a different drive copies them, as on the Mac). To copy files, you can Ctrl+drag them to the destination folder, or right-click on the file (or folder) with the mouse and choose 'Copy'. Now right-click in the destination folder and use 'Paste' and the copied file appears in the folder.

If you wish to move more than one file (or folder), click on the first item then release the mouse button, hold down the control key on the keyboard and select more items by clicking. If one item in a list (of files for example) is selected, and another item is selected with the shift key held down, all items in between will be selected also. All the items selected become highlighted on the screen. If you wish to select every item in a window, hold down Ctrl+A. Once you have selected your items, drag them all to the destination folder. To delete files, right-click and choose 'Delete' from the menu or select the object and press the small 'Del' key on the keyboard; deleted files are sent to the Recycle Bin. To empty the Recycle Bin, right-click on it and choose 'Empty Recycle Bin'.

Removable disks

If you insert a floppy disk into the computer, double-click on the floppy disk icon (Drive A) in the 'My Computer' window to see the contents. If the computer cannot read the disk, it will invite you to format it. A utility is included by Avid to enable the PC to read Mac format disks as well as DOS disks. Use HD (1.4MB) disks to back up your projects. Use DD (720KB) DOS disks to save EDLs.

To back up your project, first make sure that your work is saved to the Avid (normally D:) drive (this is done automatically when you quit). In the 'My Computer' window, double click on the Avid drive icon, then on the Avid Projects folder, until you can see your project folder. Copy this to the floppy. If you have already backed up your work to this disk, a message will inform you that a item of the same name exists and asks if you wish to replace it. The answer is yes! Large folders can be compressed using WinZip, which is usually included on the system.

If you wish to restore a project from a floppy, or move your project to a different computer, the process is reversed. Insert your floppy disk, double-click on the icon, and copy your project folder into the Avid Projects folder on the Avid (usually D:) drive of the computer.

You can also save and copy your user settings. User settings are kept in a folder called Avid Users on the Avid drive. By putting a copy of your settings on a floppy, you can begin work quickly on another machine using your own settings. Do not use settings from one version of the software on a different version as the results may be unpredictable. Always make new settings when a software upgrade is released.

Changing the Windows display

With the monitors set to a high resolution, the text in the menus is very small. Avid supply a display scheme with purple window bars that can be changed by using the Control Panel in the 'My Computer' window (or 'Settings' from the Start button). Choose 'Display', then choose 'Appearance'. Move down to the 'Item' box and change some of the font sizes. Candidates are 'Active Title Bar', 'Inactive Title Bar', 'Menu', 'Selected Items' and so on; try bold text or a slightly larger point size. The display scheme can be saved and named. If you hate grey, then change the desktop and application backgrounds to a more pleasant colour.

Note that Windows NT sees the two monitors on a Media Composer or Symphony as one big monitor (alert messages appear across both, for instance). The monitor resolution should not be set to less than 2048 × 768 pixels on Media Composer or Symphony, or less than 1024 × 768 on Xpress.

File structure

Figure 1.2 shows the contents of the 'My Computer' window on a typical NT system. The files and folders on NT systems are stored in a similar way to those on Mac systems (Figure 1.1). This shows Mac windows in detail but gives a good idea of what to look for in the D: drive of an NT system (Figure 1.3). Depending on the

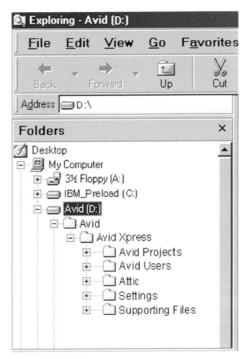

Figure 1.3 Typical file locations – Windows NT

installation, some items may not be where you expect; check for the location of the Avid Projects and Attic folders, for instance. Possible locations for the Avid Projects folder are: D:\Avid\Avid Projects, or D:\Avid\Media Composer\Avid Projects or even D:\Program Files\Avid\Media Composer\Avid Projects. You may find the project and user folders on the C: drive on some installations (replace Media Composer with Xpress or Symphony as appropriate).

When you have finished work, quit Avid [Ctrl+Q] and shut down the computer by going to 'Shutdown' under the Start button. By doing this, the computer updates its files and closes down any running application in a controlled way. Do not switch off until prompted to do so. When the computer is off, switch off the external drives and other peripherals.

General points

Every time the computer manufacturers bring out a new model, or Avid release a new software version, extensive testing is done to make sure that everything works smoothly together. Always check the Release Notes from the version you are working on, particularly if things don't work in the way you'd expect. This book is not the place to go deeply into troubleshooting routines, but one simple step you can take if things aren't right is to create a new user setting and try again. If this fails, make a new project and try that (see Chapter 2). Often quitting from Avid and relaunching, or restarting the computer will put things right.

Windows NT users have the use of a two-button computer mouse. Right-clicking on a window when editing will bring up a context-sensitive menu; try this on bins, the Composer window, the Timeline and so on. Current Mac systems often come with a two-button mouse but the right button doesn't do anything. To see context-sensitive menus in Media Composer v10 and Xpress v4 (Mac), hold down Shift+Ctrl and click with the left button. Happy editing!

2 **Getting started**

In the pages that follow, some illustrations show Mac windows, and some NT. Where there are considerable changes from version to version, or from system to system, extra illustrations are included. Features are identical unless specifically noted. For many functions and shortcuts, two keys are used; on the Mac they are the Command key (⌘) also known as the Apple key, and the option key (which may be marked 'alt'). On NT, the Control key and Alt key are used (although they don't always translate exactly). Keyboard shortcuts and other variations for NT are in [square brackets]. Whenever functions or procedures for Media Composer, Symphony and Xpress are the same, the text will simply refer to 'Avid'.

Projects, bins and clips

Our first step is to make a new project. A project may encompass as little as a short commercial or as much as a multi-part series. The project will contain all the information about clips, timecodes, tape names, edited sequences, titles, sound levels and so on. Launch Avid (either from an alias (Mac) or a shortcut [NT]) and

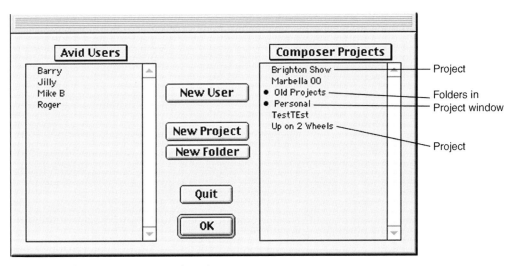

Figure 2.1 Choosing a user and project

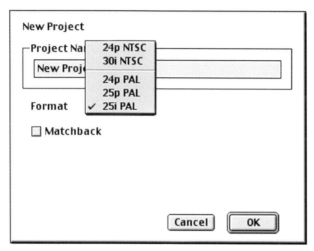

Figure 2.2 New Project dialogue

choose 'New Project' when the first dialogue box appears (Figure 2.1). Normally you will see 'Avid Projects' ('Composer Projects' on some systems) at the top of the right-hand column. It is possible to make folders within the Avid Projects folder, perhaps to organize projects by date or editor. Folders are indicated by a black dot (Mac) or asterisk [NT] next to the folder name. Projects have no dots or asterisks. Make sure that you have started your project in the correct folder, if there are any. Choose PAL or NTSC and Interlaced or Progressive if available (Figure 2.2) (working with progressive projects is not covered here). Type a name for your project, then 'OK', and the new project is created.

If you are new to this system, choose 'New User', too, and enter your name when prompted. Settings that you create and modify in Avid will be saved under your name – when you return to the system, select your name and your settings are restored. Click 'OK' and you can begin work.

Create your bins

When a new project opens, the Project window, which displays your bins and settings, appears on the monitor (Figure 2.3). First, create one or more bins to hold your clips. All master clips, subclips, sequences and effect clips such as titles must be stored in bins – the computer equivalent of the fibre trims bins found in film cutting rooms. As an editor, you have complete control over how you name your bins and clips so choose a sensible scheme that will help you work efficiently. Consider what might happen if another editor has to take over; would they be able to understand your arrangement? In a large project, bins can be organized into folders within the project window. Click on the fast menu (looks like a hamburger

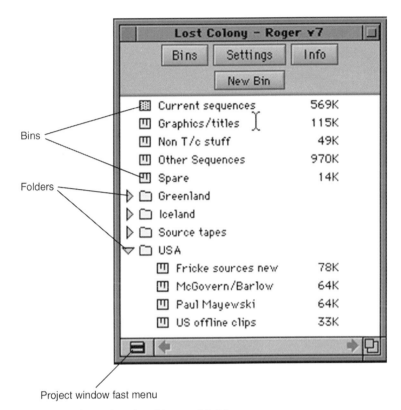

Bins

Folders

Project window fast menu

Figure 2.3 Project window showing bins and folders

– Figure 2.4) at the bottom left of the project window to make a new folder. The project window also has its own Trash – deleted bins end up in here and can be removed via a command in the fast menu.

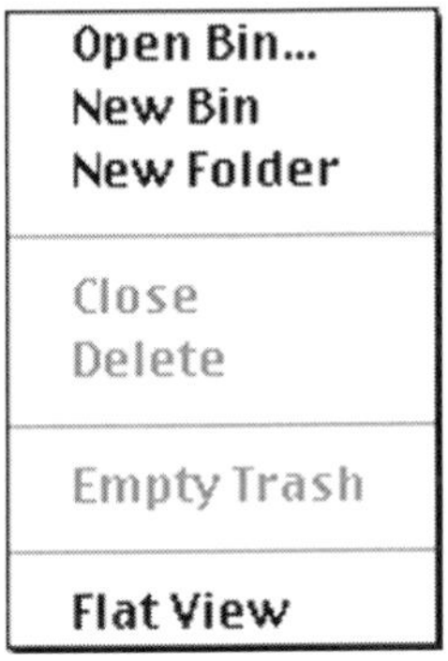

Figure 2.4 Fast menu choices

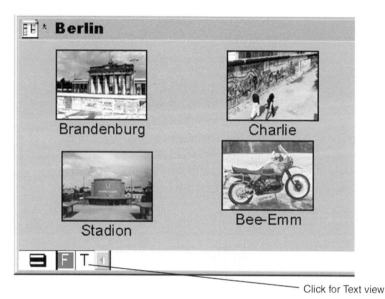

Click for Text view

Figure 2.5 Xpress v3 Bin in Frame view

If you know the material, you may be able to create sensible bins from the start: 'Scene 1', 'London interviews' and so on. If you are faced with a mass of tapes and don't know what you'll find, use bins such as 'Tapes 1–5', 'Tapes 6–10'and so on and digitize clips from those tapes into those bins.

Bin views

You can control how your bin information is displayed. Beginners often opt for frame view (F at the bottom left corner of the bin) but this takes up quite a lot of space if you have many clips (Figure 2.5). Text view (T) can be more useful (Figure 2.6), particularly if you know the material and can relate to the clip names, as more information is displayed.

When a new bin is created it displays with an untitled Custom view (text), with no columns. A standard Statistics view can be selected by clicking in the window immediately to the right of the 'T' at the bottom of the bin (this normally reads 'Untitled').

S gives you a Script view (not on Xpress v3 and earlier), which displays a frame, some statistical information, and a window in which lines of script or annotation can be entered (Figure 2.7).

See Chapter 4 for more information on working with bins.

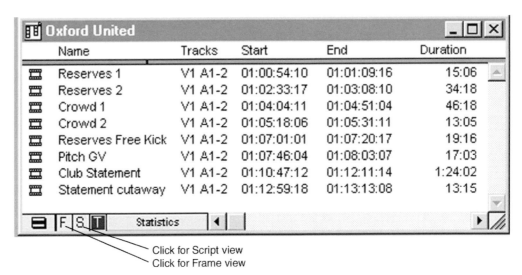

Figure 2.6 Bin in Text view

Using Settings in the Project window

If the 'Settings' button is pressed in the Project window (Figure 2.8), the list of Bins disappears and a list of settings associated with the current user and project appears. Most of the settings reflect the personal preferences of the current user (editor) and can be used on any other project that the editor works on. Others (such as the General setting) are associated with the current project. A few (such as Deck

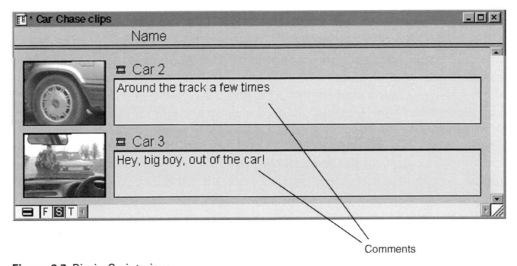

Figure 2.7 Bin in Script view

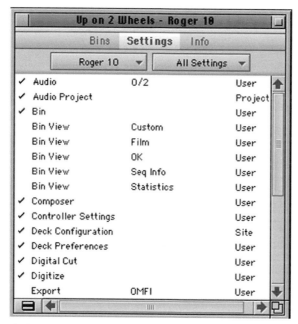

Figure 2.8 Project window showing settings

Configuration) belong to the Site, i.e., this particular computer and hardware. Site settings are the same for all users and all projects.

To change a setting, double-click on the appropriate word and a dialogue box opens. Some useful settings are:

The **Audio Project** setting, which allows the user to determine the current audio settings (digital or analogue input, sample rate and so on). See Chapter 3.
The **Audio** setting, which allows the user to set the default audio pan and adjust scrub settings (see Chapters 5 and 9). In some earlier versions, Audio and Audio Project settings are combined into one setting (Audio).
The **Bin** setting, which controls how frequently the system automatically saves work as the editing progresses and what happens when a clip is loaded (see Chapters 5 and 13).
The **Composer** settings (not Xpress), which allow the user to have more or less information displayed in the Composer window and allow modification of some editing buttons (see Chapter 5).
The **Deck Configuration** and **Deck Preference** settings, which govern how the system communicates with tape decks (see Chapters 3 and 16).
The **Digitize** setting, which controls events during the digitizing process (see Chapter 3).

The **General** setting, which allows the user to set the default start timecode for sequences, audio file type for the project and to govern which disks are used for media storage.

The **Keyboard** setting, which allows customization of the keyboard (see Chapter 8).

The **Timeline** setting, which modifies the behaviour of some Timeline functions (see Chapter 7).

Other settings will be described as they are encountered (and see Chapter 8).

3 **Digitizing**

- Levels of compression and storage considerations
- Preparing to digitize
- Tape numbering
- Video and audio line-up
- Methods of digitizing
- Capturing non-timecoded material

Video resolutions (compression ratios)

Before digitizing you need to choose a video resolution. Your choice will depend on whether you are offlining or onlining, how much material you have and how much storage is available on your system. Avid's resolutions are described differently depending on whether you are using an Avid Broadcast Video Board (ABVB) system (Media Composer v7 and Xpress v2) or the Meridien hardware (later versions).

Mac systems with ABVB

On ABVB systems, video resolutions are split into three groups (not all resolutions will be available on all systems):

1 *Single-field resolutions* (AVR2s, 3s, 4s, 6s, 8s and 9s)
2 *Two-field resolutions* (AVR12, 70, 75, and 77)
3 *Multicam resolutions* (AVR2m, 3m, 4m and 6m – not Xpress)

Resolutions can be mixed within each family, but not between families, i.e., 3s and 8s can be mixed in one sequence, but 3s and 70 cannot.

Resolutions 2s to 6s are offline resolutions. Many long projects are edited at AVR3s, which is a reasonable compromise between clarity and storage. AVR8s and 9s, even though they are single-field, are not really 'offline' resolutions but are high quality/low compression for use when a good single-field image is required.

AVR70 is the resolution used by Avid's Mac-based Newscutter and by the first Editcam. AVR75 offers around 3:1 compression with frame rates up to 240KB/ frame while AVR77 is around 2:1 compression with frame rates up to 360KB/ frame. AVR12 is a two-field offline resolution compatible with the other two-field resolutions; this is useful for editing new footage into an AVR77 sequence. If many graphics are needed, AVR12 could be chosen as the offline resolution with the graphics imported at AVR77 from the start (graphics cannot be batch imported on ABVB systems).

The 'm' resolutions are designed for use with Avid's Hardware Multicam option, which allows simultaneous playback of up to four sources. These resolutions can be mixed except when playing back as a four-way split (see Chapter 8).

Mac and NT systems with Meridien hardware

Resolutions on the Meridien systems fall into the following groups (not all resolutions will be available on all systems):

1 Single-field resolutions (2:1s, 4:1s, 15:1s)
2 Two-field interlaced resolutions (2:1, 3:1, 10:1, 20:1)
3 Multicam resolutions (4:1m, 10:1m – from Media Composer v10 and Symphony v3 only)
4 Uncompressed interlaced (2-field): (1:1)

Resolutions can be mixed within each family, but not between families, i.e., 2:1s and 15:1s can be mixed in one sequence, but 2:1s and 20:1 cannot. 15:1s is an offline resolution offering good storage efficiency. 2:1s, even though it is single-field, is not really an 'offline' resolution but is higher quality/lower compression for use when a good single-field image is required. The Meridien single-field resolutions are not sampled in the same way as the ABVB single-field resolutions, and can't be directly compared.

The two-field resolutions 2:1 and 3:1 are often used for broadcast. The uncompressed resolution (1:1) gives the best possible images but cannot be mixed with other resolutions. 10:1, even though it is regarded as an offline resolution, offers reasonable quality images for non-broadcast or approval copies.

20:1 (two-field) is useful for mixing offline images with 2:1 or 3:1 online resolutions.

Preparing to digitize

Make sure the tape deck is wired to the Avid correctly. Mac ABVB systems normally come with a Betacam top (daughterboard) fitted to the Avid Broadcast Video Board that deals with video I/O. The alternative is a Serial Digital interface. The Betacam board allows input and output of analogue component video and composite video. The SDI board offers digital I/O but gives a composite feed for a monitor. Meridien systems offer composite, analogue component, S-video and SDI as standard on Media Composer and Symphony (SDI is an option on Xpress).

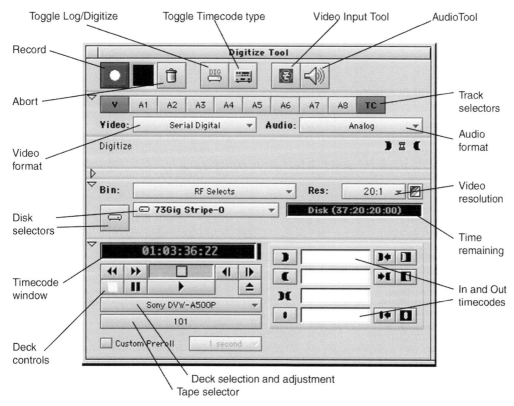

Figure 3.1 Digitize Tool

The Digitize Tool

Select the bin into which you plan to digitize and choose the Digitize Tool from the Tools menu. On Media Composer and Symphony an alternative is to choose 'Go To Capture mode' (⌘+B) [Ctrl+B] from the Bin menu. The Digitize Tool (Figure 3.1) lets you control the deck, select sections to log and digitize, choose the media drive and set the resolution. Some of the functions (FF/REW, Stop, Play and marking In and Out) can be done on the keyboard, too. In Media Composer v10, Symphony v3 and Xpress v4, the J-K-L keys will allow tape shuttling from the keyboard, as when editing (see Chapter 5). In these versions it is also possible to select video and audio inputs from the Digitize Tool.

Using the resolution pop-up, choose the video resolution or compression. Remember that you can only mix resolutions within each 'family' (single, multicam or two-field). At an offline resolution you can work with a single media drive but higher resolutions have greater data demands. There are now so many combinations of drives, software versions and possible video resolutions that it is advisable to

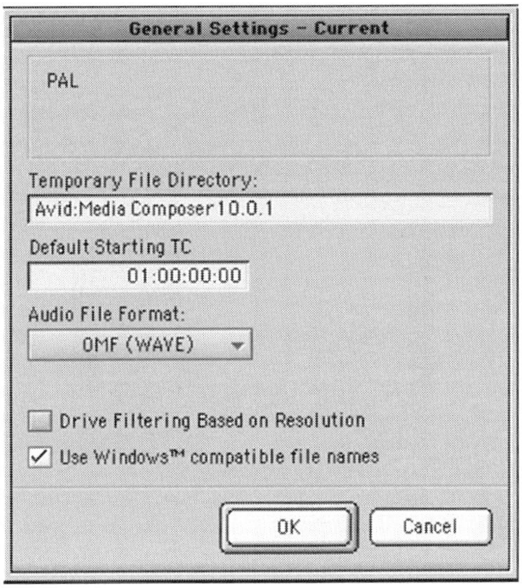

General Settings – Current

PAL

Temporary File Directory:
Avid:Media Composer 10.0.1

Default Starting TC
01:00:00:00

Audio File Format:
OMF (WAVE) ▾

☐ Drive Filtering Based on Resolution
☑ Use Windows™ compatible file names

OK   Cancel

Figure 3.2 General Settings

check the Avid documentation for details on drive and striping requirements. Some drive configurations will only play one stream of video at a particular resolution, others will play two streams, giving 'real-time' effects (see Chapters 10 and 11). To set the resolution in early versions, use the Video Input Tool (see later in this chapter).

In the General setting (Project window – Figure 3.2) is an option called 'Drive Filtering Based on Resolution'. This is designed to prevent users digitizing footage on to drives that cannot play them back. Normally, leave this selected. If you use non-Avid drives, however, deselect Drive Filtering, or you will not be able to select your media drives in the Digitize Tool.

If you click the small disk icon on the left of the digitize window it will change to show two disk icons (Figure 3.3), allowing the user to target different media volumes with the audio and video. Leave this set to a single volume unless you are sending the audio to a different physical drive (not just a different partition). This can be useful in terms of media management or on older systems where playback at high resolutions can be improved by targeting different drives. Also, if you are using uncompressed video, Avid recommend sending audio to a drive other than the striped set used for the video.

Figure 3.3 One/Two disk toggle

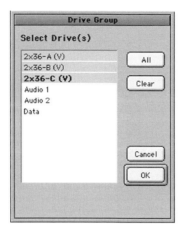

Figure 3.4 Choosing a drive group

Click in the pop-up box to choose your target volume. The window marked 'disk' shows an estimate of storage available on the chosen volume. Some systems limit the largest file that may be digitized, thus there may be more space available than you can fill with a single media file. To digitize long clips, choose 'Change group' in the pop-up and a window appears (Figure 3.4). Now you can select media volumes (click and shift-click) to form a group for digitizing. The clips will be

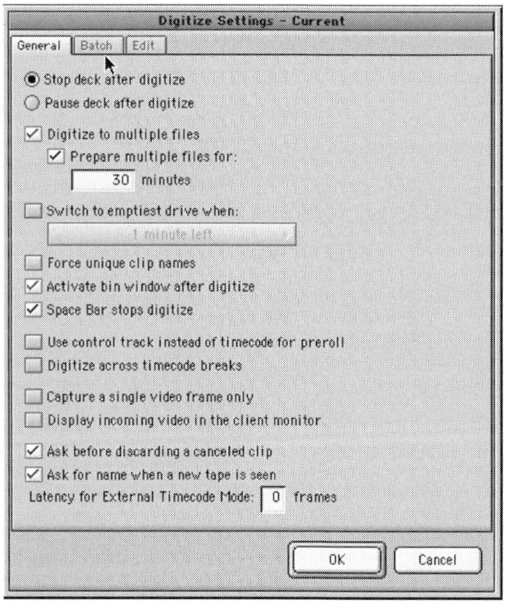

Figure 3.5 Digitize Settings – General

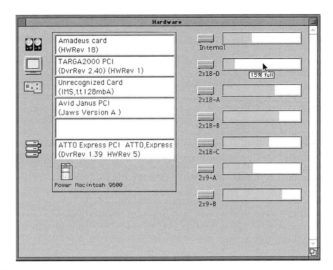

Figure 3.6 Hardware tool

linked to one or more media files. If you don't set these options, and you are digitizing on the fly, then the system will stop with an error message when the file size limit is reached but give you the option of keeping the media. On the other hand, if you are batch digitizing, you lose the media and you'll need to adjust the clip lengths or drive group and try again.

To adjust the maximum clip length, open the Digitize settings (Project window) and make sure that the 'Digitize to multiple files' options are set appropriately (Figure 3.5). The system will now allocate as much space as is needed (up to the limit you set), always assuming there is enough space on your drives.

Do not fill your drives or partitions completely – leave a couple of hundred megabytes of free space otherwise problems may arise. Either double-click on each drive on the desktop and note the free space, or select the Hardware tool (Tools menu) and check the percentage of free space before using the Digitize tool (Figure 3.6).

Tape numbering

When you insert a tape, you are normally prompted for the tape name. There is a bug in some Meridien systems prior to Media Composer v10, Symphony v3 and Xpress v4 in that the system forgets to prompt for a tape name if the Avid has previously been used for output to tape (Digital Cut). Things revert to normal after a relaunch. Tape naming or numbering is a vital consideration, particularly if the job is to be conformed in a tape suite (see Chapter 16). It is safest to use numbers only for tape identification; start each project with new tape numbers starting at 001; the leading zeros mean that that tape names will be listed numerically when the 'Select Tape?' window appears. Avoid spaces in tape names as this can cause problems on NT systems. Even if you plan to finish the job on the Avid, try to use numbers in case the job ends up in a tape suite at some point in the future.

Don't use tape names like Graphics-1 and Music-1 if you plan to conform on tape. If the edit controller can only cope with numbers and not letters in tape names, the EDL manager (which converts your edited sequence to an EDL) may strip out the letters and assign a name based on the numbers it finds in the original name. If it finds the same number in one or more tape names, they will be renumbered to avoid a conflict. If you need to use numbers and letters together in a tape name, try to restrict the length to six characters, with numbers leading, i.e.: 123TUE, not TUE123. Something like MINIDVTAPE97 will be truncated and renamed, whatever EDL format is used.

If library numbers have to be used, what happens to tapes 100111 and 200111? Some EDL formats can only deal with three-digit numbers. In these cases EDL manager will detect a supposed duplicate and reassign a number. You may need to temporarily renumber a tape for a particular job; the same applies if you 'borrow' a tape from another programme. If the job is definitely not going to a tape suite, more flexibility is available; tapes from other projects can be indicated in the tape name – EP6Tape014, perhaps.

Video line-up

Select the Video Input Tool (from the icon in the Digitize Tool or from the Tools menu) and select the video input format from the 'Input' pop-up, if this hasn't already been done (Figure 3.7). Click the small waveform and vector icons in the window to open the waveform monitor and vectorscope. Before digitizing, cue up the tape on the colour bars (if you can find any) and make sure that the TBC

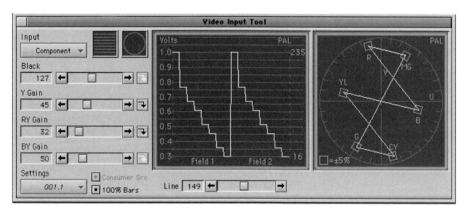

Figure 3.7 Video Input Tool (PAL)

Figure 3.8 Full field bars

controls on your VTR are at 'Preset'. However well you line up, bear in mind that the shots on the tape may or may not stay within the limits indicated by the bars.

Note that the Avid Video Input Tool will only read one scan line at a time and will only respond in real time when the tape is playing, not when digitizing and not when playing back from disk. The following adjustments assume that you are inputting analogue component video (no adjustments are available when using the SDI input).

PAL

When working in PAL, you will commonly have 75 per cent EBU colour bars at the head of your tape. As PAL bars are normally full-field (Figure 3.8), set the line selector somewhere in the middle of the slider range. Play the tape and adjust the black level slider so that the bottom of the waveform is sitting on the 0.3v line. Now adjust the Y gain (luminance) until the top of the waveform display sits no higher than the 1.0v line. Next take a look at the vectorscope. Adjust the B-Y and R-Y sliders until the corners of the vector display hit the targets as nearly as possible (Figure 3.7).

On ABVB systems, note that the vectorscope is only useful for assessing bars of 75 per cent chrominance, and can't be adjusted (see note below on dealing with 100 per cent bars).

NTSC

The SMPTE colour bars found on NTSC tapes are not full field (Figure 3.9) so the line adjuster needs to be set appropriately. To read luminance, set the slider to somewhere between line 203 and line 262. Play the tape and adjust the black level slider so that the black level in the waveform monitor is sitting on the 7.5 IRE line (Figure 3.10). Now adjust the Y gain (luminance) until the white level sits no higher

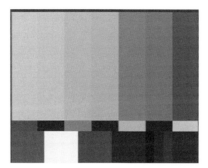

Figure 3.9 SMPTE bars

than the 100 IRE. Before adjusting chrominance, move the line adjuster somewhere into the region between line 21 and line 182. Looking at the vectorscope, adjust the B-Y and R-Y sliders until the corners of the vector display hit the targets as nearly as possible (right-hand display in Figure 3.7).

Saving settings

Once you have adjusted the input levels, you may save the settings by clicking in the box at the bottom of the Video Tool. The setting name offered will match the tape name – accept this and the Video Tool will return to this setting next time that tape is used. This only makes sense if you use the same VTR and that the deck's TBC controls are on preset. An alternative method at the finishing stage is to leave the input tool set to default (click on all the down-pointing arrows so they turn green) and use the TBC controls on the deck to adjust levels. An external waveform monitor should be used for finishing.

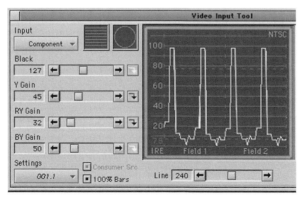

Figure 3.10 SMPTE bars in WFM

The Video Input Tool in each new project defaults to Composite. To change this, switch to the input of your choice (say Component), and save it with the name 'Default'. Now drag this setting from the Project window into the Site Setting window (see Chapter 8). The Video Input Tool will now be set to Component for each new project created.

100 per cent bars

If your tape has 100 per cent bars, and you are using an ABVB system, then the white and black levels can be set using the waveform monitor but do not attempt to adjust the chrominance. On a Meridien system, click the '100%' button and the vectorscope will read these bars correctly.

Problem sources

The Meridien video system is sensitive to the quality of the video signals being input – it is not very happy with signals from (say) VHS decks without a timebase corrector. If you have a problem with unstable pictures, try clicking the 'Consumer Source' button in the Video Input Tool. This may help (at the expense of softening the image) but will not work with all sources. The ABVB systems are less sensitive and do not have this button. If you have problems on a Meridien setup, you may need to use a timebase corrector between the video deck and the Avid.

Manual TBC adjustment may be necessary if inputting material from Mini-DV cameras, many of which seem to over-record luminance. The Avid luminance slider may not offer enough correction.

Audio preparation

Set the audio sample rate appropriate to your project in the Audio Project setting (Project window); the choices are 44.1 or 48kHz (Figure 3.11). This applies to lower end systems with the Digidesign Audiomedia card and also the latest eight channel Pro-Tools systems. On a system with a four-channel Pro-Tools board (442), set the switch on the front panel. In MC v7, Symphony 1 and Xpress 2, use the Audio setting. Note that prior to Media Composer v10, Symphony 3 and Xpress 4, mixed audio sample rates would not play in the same sequence, so it was vital to stick to one sample rate. In the current versions, Avid will attempt to convert clips with incorrect sample rates on the fly but if some of your clips are at the wrong setting, they will need to be converted before putting your programme to tape.

The General Settings (Project window – Figure 3.2) offers a choice of format for the audio media files; depending on the system, the options are Sound Designer II, AIFF-C or WAV. This is important if your sound is to be exported or moved to another system for sound mixing. Check first!

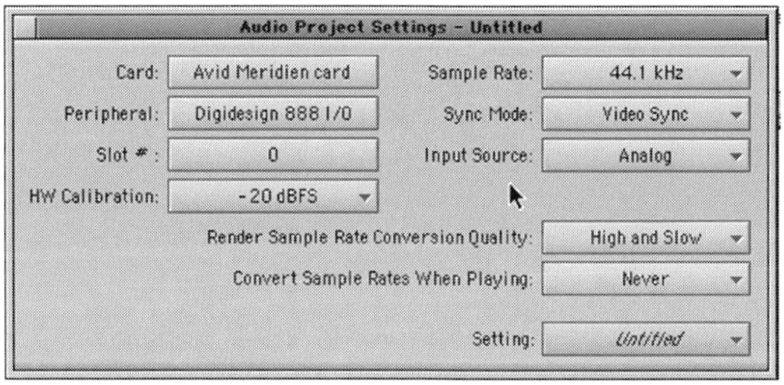

Audio Project Settings - Untitled
Card:
Avid Meridien card
Peripheral:
Digidesign 888 I/O
Slot #:
0
HW Calibration:
-20 dBFS
Sample Rate:
44.1 kHz
Sync Mode:
Video Sync
Input Source:
Analog
Render Sample Rate Conversion Quality:
High and Slow
Convert Sample Rates When Playing:
Never
Setting:
Untitled

Figure 3.11 Audio Project Settings

Now cue the tape to the line up tone (if any). The tape box may tell you what the tone level is supposed to be but many do not. Open the Audio Tool (Figure 3.12), from the icon in the Digitize Tool or from the Tools menu. If you know the LU tone

Audio Tool
RP
PH
0
0
1
2
+0
-4
-8
-14
-20
-26
-30
-35
-40
-65
-90
+20
+16
+12
+6
0 VU
-6
-10
-15
-20
-45
-70

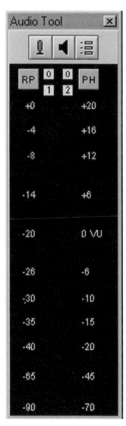

Figure 3.12 Audio Tool (two-channel)

level, then play the tape and adjust the output from the VTR so that the tone registers the appropriate level. –18dB on the left-hand (digital) scale in the Audio Tool is equivalent to 4 on a normal UK PPM meter. The right-hand scale is an analogue scale that can be calibrated relative to the digital scale if required. Run down into the programme material and check that peak levels don't exceed –10dB digital; do not let levels approach the 0dB mark or you will get distortion. If there is no line up tone or it is of unknown level, this is all you can do. The Audio Tool will display either two, four or eight bar graphs, depending on the number of channels on your audio hardware.

If your Avid has the Pro Tools hardware, then there is no way of setting input levels on the computer and you will have to rely on the output pots on the deck or go through a mixer (a good idea). On Xpress systems and Media Composers with the Digidesign Audiomedia card, it is possible to click on the little microphone icon in the Audio Tool and adjust the input level globally on the slider that appears. This cannot be saved as a setting.

Beginning to digitize

Digitizing on the fly

You can start digitizing simply by clicking on the big red button on the Digitize Tool. The deck will begin to play and digitizing commences (you may miss a few frames at the beginning of the clip). Click the button again, or press the 'Esc' key on the keyboard to stop. In Media Composer v10.0, Symphony v3.0 and Xpress v4.0, an error message will appear if the Escape key is pressed. Ignore this and click the 'keep media' box. On ABVB systems, the 'B' key on the keyboard will start digitizing. On Meridien systems, press f4. A new Master Clip appears in your bin, and one or more media files are created on your media drive(s). The default name of the clip is the bin name with a number appended, such as 'Interviews.09'. A clip name may be typed during digitizing; press 'Tab' and you can type a comment. This will appear in a comment column in a bin in Text view, or appear in the comment box in Script view. Prior to Media Composer v10, Symphony v4, the input focus always switches to the bin after each clip is digitized so that the clip can be immediately named. In later versions, there is an option to do this in the Digitize settings (Project window) (Figure 3.5).

A more controlled way is to mark the In and Out points and then click the red button. The deck will pre-roll and then capture the clip. You can adjust the deck pre-roll in the Deck settings, accessed via the Deck Configuration settings (Project window) in all versions (Figure 3.13). In recent versions it is possible to make a temporary adjustment in the Digitize Tool (Custom Pre-roll). If you are conforming in a tape suite, then keep the pre-roll set to at least 5 seconds – this will give you

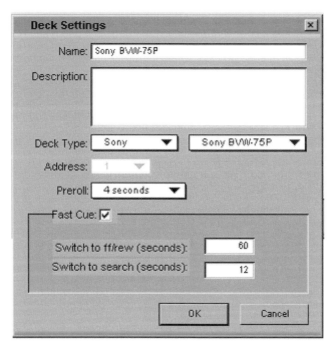

Figure 3.13 Deck Settings

a warning if there is a timecode problem. If you plan to finish on the Avid then this figure can be reduced. This, and the previous method, are fine for the odd clip but for a large number of clips the best course is to log first, then Batch Digitize.

Logging clips

If you are lucky a log may have been prepared – there is a useful Avid program called Medialog which can be used on a Mac or PC and lets you drive a VTR and log clips into a bin. You don't even need Medialog to do some useful preparation. Avid provide (in the Input and Output guide or Avid Log Exchange manual) a format for a simple text file that can be imported into a bin. With the Mac able to read DOS and Windows disks, some kind of list can be extracted from most PCs or laptops. See the section 'Importing a Shot Log' in Chapter 4 for an example of a text file prior to importing into a bin.

To log on the Avid, click the button marked 'Dig' (top centre of the Digitize Tool, Figure 3.14) and the tool switches to logging mode. The media drive selectors vanish and the red Record button now toggles between 'Mark In' (Figure 3.15) and 'Mark Out and log' (Figure 3.16). Now shuttle up and down the tape, pressing the button once to set the In timecode and a second time to set

Figure 3.14 Digitize/Log toggle

Figure 3.15 Log – Mark In

Figure 3.16 Mark Out and log to bin

the Out timecode and log the clip to the bin. The clip can be named at this stage
or later. On ABVB systems, the 'B' key on the keyboard will log the clip; on
Meridien systems, press f4.

You can use the keyboard Mark In and Mark Out buttons to set the timecodes,
too. In this case, once both marks are set, the main button shows a pencil icon
(Figure 3.17). Click this or press 'B' or f4 to log the clip.

The Medialog logging tool resembles the Digitize Tool in log mode very closely.
Medialog is like the editing applications in that projects and bins are created as
described earlier. Bins created in Medialog can be simply copied on to the editing
system before digitizing gets under way.

To avoid problems with batch digitizing, be careful how you mark your Ins and
Outs. Watch the little green light next to the timecode display on the digitize
window – it indicates good timecode. Avid will roll the deck across a momentary
break but if the light goes out for longer, there is a timecode break that will cause

Figure 3.17 Log to bin

Figure 3.18 Batch Digitize Settings

an error during digitizing. There is an option in the Batch Digitize settings (Figure 3.18) to 'Log errors to the console and continue' (not Xpress). The Console (Tools menu) is a window showing information about the system. It is well worth selecting this as the usual errors encountered are breaks in timecode and failure to find the pre-roll point. You can set the deck pre-roll to a low figure but this might lead to problems in the online. If in doubt, and the job is to be conformed in a tape suite, speak to the online editor (always a good idea). If you don't turn 'Log errors . . .' on, then the batch digitize will halt at the first error, and you'll come back from lunch and find the job unfinished. To see a list of errors during the digitize session, open the Console window (Tools menu).

If your chosen in point is immediately after a timecode break, there is an option in the Digitize settings (Figure 3.5) called 'Use control track instead of timecode for pre-roll'. Again, if the job is going to a tape suite, make a note to tell the online editor that you have done this. Only use this option when you need to, as deck cueing takes longer and the start point will not be set as accurately as under normal circumstances.

The option 'Digitize across timecode breaks' is not quite what it seems. If this is chosen and you attempt to digitize a long section from a tape with breaks in timecode, the system will carry on until the first break, then stop and create a clip consisting of footage up to that point. The VTR will then play on over the TC break and the system may take a few seconds to recognize continuous TC. It will then begin the pre-roll. This means that several seconds are lost after each break in timecode. It may be better to log carefully or digitize on the fly to get the footage immediately after the TC break.

Modifying clip information

You can alter information about a logged master clip – after logging but prior to digitizing, most clip information can be changed. Select the clip in the bin and go to 'Modify' in the Clip menu on Media Composer and Symphony or the Bin menu on Xpress (Figure 3.19). Here you can alter the tracks logged, the timecode in and out (including Increment and Decrement, which could be used to add handles to a bunch of clips) and the source. This is very useful if you inadvertently chose an incorrect tape name but take care – the clip's source goes with it through to the EDL and the online or redigitize.

In and out timecodes can be altered directly in the bin display (text view), by clicking on the timecode, entering a new value and pressing 'Enter' (numeric keypad). Note that if a new In timecode is given, the Out timecode alters to match and the clip's duration remains the same. If you wish to lengthen or shorten the duration, you must alter the Out timecode too. It is important to set the tracks correctly as once you start batch digitizing, the logged tracks are what you get, even if you deselect 'Digitize the tracks logged' in the Digitize settings. This only lets you deselect tracks already logged, not add in tracks that have not been logged.

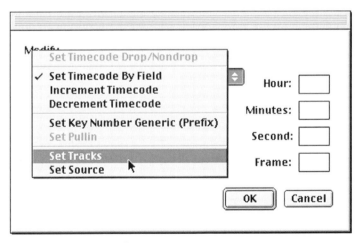

Figure 3.19 Modify options in the Clip menu

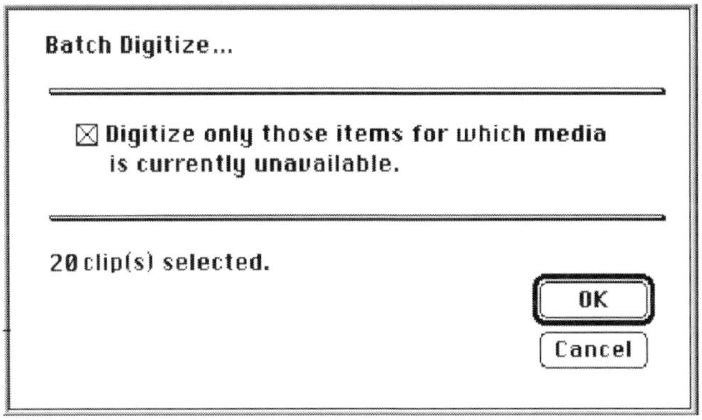

Figure 3.20 Batch Digitize dialogue

Batch Digitizing

To Batch Digitize your clips, select them in the bin (Click then Shift+click or ⌘+A for all) [Click then Ctrl+click or Ctrl+A for all]. If some clips in the bin have already been digitized, the option 'Select Offline Clips' in the Bin menu will highlight only the clips without media (in this case Offline means clips without media). To find out the total duration of your selected clips, choose 'Get Bin Info' from the File menu. The Console window will automatically open displaying the information.

Now choose 'Batch Digitize' from the Clip menu (Media Composer and Symphony) or the Bin menu (Xpress). When you do this, an option appears asking if you wish to only digitize those clips for which media is unavailable (Figure 3.20). Normally leave this checkbox selected, as this will avoid redigitizing material you already have. If you have some master clips digitized at the wrong resolution or the wrong video or audio level, then deselect the box and the system will redigitize your clips and delete the original media. The system doesn't discriminate in terms of resolution – any media file associated with a clip is detected.

Capturing sources without timecode

To digitize from sources without timecode, and which you cannot control using the Digitize tool, click on the 'Toggle Source' button (it looks like a VTR) and it will change to show a large red oval and bar (Figure 3.21). In Media Composer v10, Symphony v3 and Xpress v4 only, a second click will switch to external timecode mode – click again to get back to normal. When in 'No Timecode' mode, video and audio can be digitized from a CD, microphone or a VHS tape for example. It is still

Figure 3.21 Digitize without timecode

necessary to select a source (click the Tape Name pop-up, choose 'New' and call your source 'Mic' or 'CD123' or whatever). Now start your source playing and click the red digitize button. Avid will apply timecode to the new clip based on time-of-day from the computer's internal clock. Bear in mind that this timecode is not associated with the original material so that batch digitizing or redigitizing cannot be done in future, nor can an EDL be made.

If you are digitizing from a deck that you can control from the Digitize Tool as normal, but don't wish to take the timecode, simply deselect the TC button next to the track selection buttons in the Digitize Tool. Time-of-day timecode will be applied to the clip. Make sure TC is reselected before working normally again!

Digitizing to the Timeline

It is possible to have the clips that you digitize edited straight into the Timeline. Once you have become familiar with the editing process, you might try this feature. In Media Composer v10, Symphony v3 and Xpress v4, click in the Edit tab of the Digitize settings (Project window) and select 'Enable Edit to Timeline'. Splice-In and Overwrite buttons will now appear in the Digitize Tool (Figure 3.22). In previous versions, these buttons were always visible. Some versions of Xpress will not have this feature.

To digitize to the Timeline, place the position indicator where you'd like the new clip to appear in your sequence (or mark In and Out) and select either Splice-In and Overwrite in the Digitize Tool (see Chapter 5 for basic editing techniques). It is possible to set handles (extra frames before and after the logged section) in the Digitize settings (Edit tab). Now, the clips that you digitize will be edited

Figure 3.22 Digitize to Timeline buttons

Figure 3.23 Check Decks

automatically into the Timeline, speeding up the basic assembly. In Media Composer v10, Symphony v3 and Xpress v4, it is possible to patch your new material to chosen tracks in the Timeline by clicking and holding on the track selectors in the Digitize tool; earlier versions could only send V1 and A1 to V1 and A1 in the sequence, and so on.

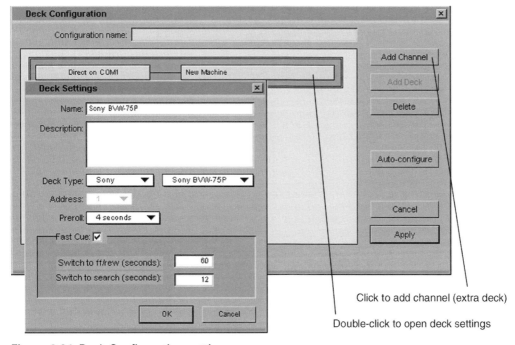

Figure 3.24 Deck Configuration settings

Deck communication problems

The Avid communicates with the VTR by a cable connected to one of the serial ports on the computer. If a message such as 'No Deck' or 'I/O Error' appears in the Digitize Tool, click on the deck pop-up (Figure 3.23) and choose 'Check Decks'. This sends a wake-up call to the VTR and control should be restored. If a new deck is connected, choose 'Auto-configure' to have Avid work out what kind of deck you have. By using the Deck Configuration settings (Figure 3.24), it is possible to gain control of more than one VTR (choose 'Add Channel') and to manually configure the deck settings.

4 Working with bins

The information about the clips in your bins can be displayed in several different ways, making it easy to quickly find the clips you need.

In Text view, you can make or modify your own views by clicking on column names and deleting them, or adding new columns (Bin menu/Headings – Figure 4.1). Save the bin view (click the box at the bottom of the bin) and the bin view can be used on any other bin in any project you edit (Figure 4.2). Early versions of Xpress lack this feature. When adding and removing columns in the headings window on NT systems prior to Media Composer v10, Symphony v3 or Xpress v4, hold down the Ctrl key as you click or all other columns are deselected.

You can go further by creating your own custom columns in text view. Either choose 'Custom' from the box at the bottom of the window, or start with a view you

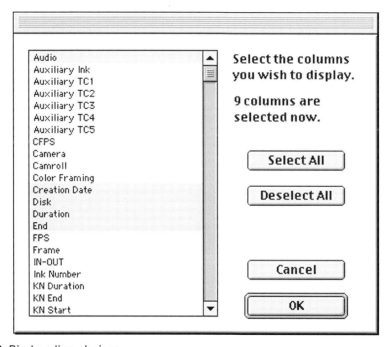

Figure 4.1 Bin heading choices

Custom column name

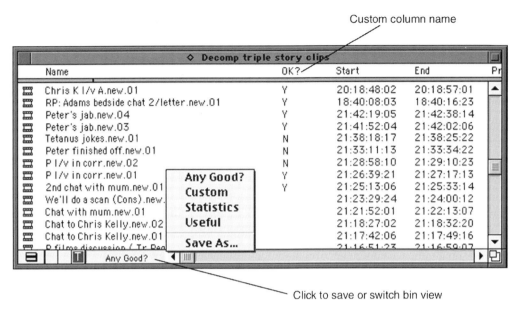

Figure 4.2 Custom bin view

already have. Now click in the white area between the title bar of the bin and the grey divider. A text cursor appears – type in your custom column name. Now click below the name in the main bin window and you can enter information. For instance, if your column is called 'Lens' then you can enter '20mm', 28mm', '75mm' and so on. Save the bin view by clicking on the current view name at the bottom of the bin – this may well read 'Statistics' (a standard view) or 'Custom' until a view is saved. All bin views are part of your User settings. Saved bin views are not available in Xpress v2 and v2.5.

If you have many clips in the bin, you don't need to type the entry in the custom column cell every time. Simply click on an empty cell in the custom column with the option [Alt] key held down and a menu of previous entries appears. Release the mouse on the chosen item. To edit a custom column name, Option [Alt]+click on it and it can be modified.

In Frame view, the frames can be enlarged or reduced from the options in the Edit menu; the keyboard shortcuts ⌘+L and ⌘+K [Ctrl+L, Ctrl+K] will also enlarge or reduce the frames. The bin background colour may be changed; look in the Edit menu. The Bin menu has options to make the frames neatly fill the window and to display the frames in the order the clips were sorted in text view. The frames can also be dragged into any position in the bin. This can be used prior to a 'Storyboard edit' (see Chapter 9). The system reads the clips from top left to bottom right when making a sequence from a storyboard.

If the bin is in Frame view, and is dragged on to the Edit (normally the right) monitor on a Mac Media Composer, a frame can be played in the bin (and on the video monitor) simply by selecting (clicking) the frame and pressing Play on the keyboard. The L and J keys allow forward and reverse play – In and Out marks can be set on the fly from the keyboard (although not when stopped). The frame that is displayed is known as the Representative Frame – you can choose any frame simply by playing through the clip in the bin and stopping on the chosen frame (or by using the Step buttons; see Chapter 5). This is the frame that will always be displayed in frame view. On NT systems, frames will play in the bin on either monitor.

In Media Composer v10, Symphony v3 and Xpress v4, if a number of clips are selected in a bin, they can be played in succession in the Source monitor or Xpress pop-up using the Loop Selected Clips option in the Bin menu.

Clips can be renamed at any time by clicking on the clip name in the bin so that the text is highlighted. Clips can be moved at any time from bin to bin, even if they have been previously used in a sequence, making it easy to organize your material. If a clip is Option [Alt]/dragged to another bin, an identical clip appears in the new bin. If one clip is renamed or otherwise altered, the copy is altered too. This makes it easy to digitize into bins based on tape names (say 'Tapes 1–5') and then move copies of the clips into working bins (say 'Interviews').

In Media Composer v8 (Mac), v9 (NT), Symphony v2 and Xpress v3 and later, the Clip Color can be set for selected clips. Highlight the clips and choose Clip Color from the Edit menu – useful for classifying different sorts of clips in a visual way. The Timeline can be set to display the clip colour (see Chapter 8). A coloured column is one of the choices in the Bin headings menu.

It is possible to delete clips (and their associated media files) from bins – see Chapter 14. To prevent inadvertent deletion, clips may be locked in the bin – select a number of clips and choose 'Lock Clips' from the Clip menu. Locking a clip locks the associated media files, too.

To Sort clips in a bin, click on a column name and choose 'Sort' from the Bin menu or the fast menu. All clips in the bin will be sorted; sorting by name or by timecode or tape is useful. All new items added to a bin appear at the top of the list in Text view – sorting can be used to re-order the clips. Hold down option [Alt] while choosing Sort and a Reverse Sort is carried out.

To search for something in a bin, go to the Bin menu (or the fast menu on the bin) and choose Custom Sift (Figure 4.3). Type in a text string in a box on the left, then choose a column to search in from the pop-ups (Figure 4.4). The bin window will now only display those items found during the sift; the other clips are hidden.

You could search for things such as parts of the clip names, tape numbers or video resolutions. A bit of thought when naming clips and making bin views will pay off later when you need to find something. The sifted items can be moved to

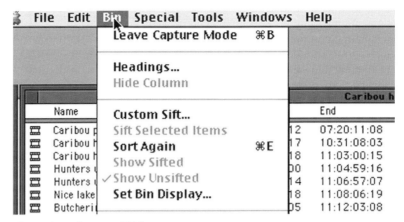

Figure 4.3 Choosing 'Custom Sift'

Show clips that:

✓ contain	Caribou	in the
begin with		in the
match exactly		in the
contain		in the

✓
Name
Tracks
Duration
Start
End
Tape
Disk
Video
Start to End Range
Any

column
column
column
column
column
column

Also show clips that:

contain		in the	column
contain		in the	column
contain		in the	column

Clear   OK   Cancel

Figure 4.4 Custom Sift dialogue

◇ Caribou hunt (sifted)

Name	Tracks	Start	End	Duration	Ta
Dead Caribou pans	V1 A1-2	11:14:48:15	11:15:19:08	30:18	
Butchering Caribou	V1 A1-2	11:08:16:05	11:12:03:08	3:47:03	
Caribou hunt B	V1 A1-2	11:00:33:18	11:03:00:15	2:26:22	
Caribou hunt A (boat etc)	V1 A1-2	10:27:42:17	10:31:08:03	3:25:11	
Caribou pan	V1	07:19:59:12	07:20:11:08	11:21	

Media

Figure 4.5 Bin sifted on word 'Caribou' in the Name column

a different bin, deleted or copied, as desired (Figure 4.5). To leave the sifted items where they are and move the remaining clips, select all the clips in the sifted view, then choose 'Show Unsifted' from the Bin menu to see all the clips. Now choose 'Reverse Selection' and the highlighted clips are deselected and the remainder are highlighted in their place.

Importing a shot log

To import a shot log (for example from a logging program or a text file you have created), insert the floppy disk, select the bin into which the logged clips will go, and choose 'Import' from the file menu.

The Mac and NT import dialogue boxes differ: on the Mac (Figure 4.6), choose 'Shot Log' as the file type (bottom left corner – the default is Graphic/Audio). Navigate to the desktop and double-click on the floppy icon. Select the log or log files on the disk and click 'Add'. The files are added to a list on the right-hand side of the window. Click 'Done' and the bin fills with the logged clips.

On NT (Figure 4.7), select a bin, choose 'Import' from the file menu and navigate to the floppy drive. Now click and Ctrl+click on the files you wish to import, then click 'Open'.

Figure 4.8 shows how to lay out shot log information in a text file prior to import.

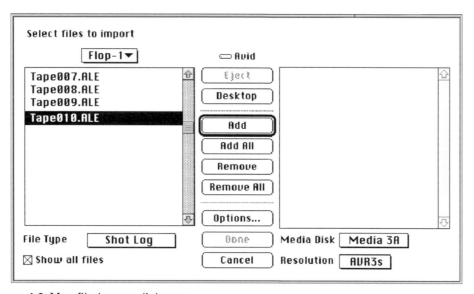

Figure 4.6 Mac file import dialogue

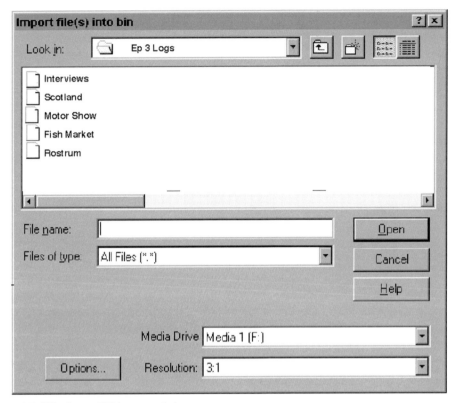

Figure 4.7 Windows NT import dialogue

```
Heading
FIELD_DELIM      TABS
VIDEO_FORMAT          PAL
AUDIO_FORMAT          44 kHz
TAPE     004
FPS      25

Column
Name                  Tracks   Start              End

Data
Audrey & Ivor wait    VA1      10:00:00:00        10:00:59:00
Pan back to Ivor      VA1      10:01:01:00        10:02:09:00
Choir finishing       VA1      10:02:10:00        10:02:33:00
Ivor lays wreath      VA1      10:02:34:00        10:04:09:00
Dragon+clouds         VA1      10:04:11:00        10:05:00:00
CU dragon             VA1      10:05:01:00        10:05:14:00
```

Figure 4.8 Text log prior to import to bin

Saving Bins

Bins are saved at timed intervals – the default is every 15 minutes; see the Bin Setting (Project window). As far as the computer is concerned, a bin is just a file, so everything in it is saved together. A bin that has not been saved recently has a diamond (Mac) or asterisk [NT] next to the bin name in the top bar (Figure 4.5). Bins can be saved manually by selecting them and choosing 'Save Bin' from the File menu or using ⌘+S [Ctrl+S]. For more details on saving your work, see Chapter 13 'Files and Media'.

5 Basic editing part 1

- Composer window and settings
- Loading, playing and marking clips
- Mouse Jog and Shuttle and Digital Audio Scrub
- Starting to edit
- The Track panel and sync locks
- Moving along the sequence
- Removing material
- Magnifying the Timeline view

The Composer window

Media Composer and Symphony

Before we start, let's take a look at the Composer window and some of the associated settings. The Composer window (Figure 5.1) is the upper of the two

Figure 5.1 Composer window – Media Composer

windows (the lower is the Timeline) on the Edit monitor (normally the right hand of the two computer monitors on a Media Composer or Symphony). On the left side is the Source monitor, on the right is the Record monitor. The workflow is to load clips into the Source monitor, mark a section, and edit the marked section into the sequence that is in the Record monitor. The sequence is also displayed in a graphical way in the Timeline; this is where much of the fine-tuning of the sequence takes place.

The default Composer window gives you large monitors, one row of buttons on each side (for common editing commands) and one row of information above the monitors (such as clip name and T/c readers).

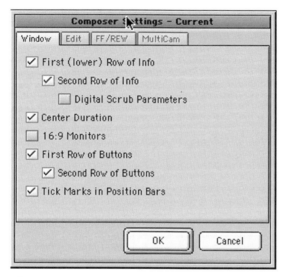

Figure 5.2 Composer Settings

To change the display, click on 'Settings' in the Project window and double-click on the word Composer. Here we can choose more or fewer buttons, more or less information, and can control other things, such as how the FF and REW buttons work. Figure 5.2 shows the Window tabs in the Composer setting on Media Composer v10 and Symphony v3; earlier versions had all the choices in one large window. For those starting out on Avid, it is worth selecting both rows of buttons, and the option 'Center Duration'. This displays the offset between the In and Out marks as you work.

Xpress

Avid Xpress uses a single Composer window to save space on the computer monitor (Figure 5.3). This window shows the edited footage as it is assembled. The

Figure 5.3 Xpress Composer window

workflow on an Xpress is to load a clip into a pop-up monitor (a smaller version of the Composer window), mark a section (Figure 5.4), and edit the marked section into the sequence. The Composer window display cannot be changed on Xpress.

Figure 5.4 Xpress pop-up monitor

Loading, playing and marking clips

From this point on, 'Source Monitor' should be taken to mean the left-hand (Source) monitor on Media Composer or Symphony, or a source pop-up on Xpress. 'Record Monitor' should be taken to mean the right-hand (Record) monitor on Media Composer or Symphony, or the Composer window on Xpress.

Choose a clip from an open bin, and either drag it across to the Source monitor (or an open pop-up on Xpress) or double-click on it. When in frame view, drag or double-click on the frame; when in text view, drag or double-click on the small icon to the left of the clip name. Double-clicking a clip in Media Composer, Symphony or Xpress v4 automatically loads it into the Source monitor. In earlier versions of Xpress, a new pop-up is opened for each new clip unless the option [Alt] key is held down while double-clicking. The double-click action can be reversed in the Bin settings (Project window) in Media Composer, Symphony and Xpress v4 (Figure 5.5).

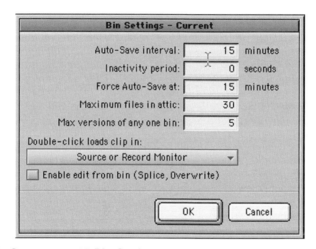

Figure 5.5 Media Composer v10 Bin Settings

Under the Source monitor, click the Play button. Press the space bar or click Play again to stop. To move frame by frame, use the Step 1 frame or Step 10 frames buttons (forward or back) (Figure 5.6).

Before making the first edit, we need to mark a section of our clip, and also choose which tracks to include. To mark part of the clip, press Mark In on the first frame you wish to use, and Mark Out on the last frame (Figure 5.6). The In mark always sits on the 'upstream' side of the frame, and the Out mark always sits on the 'downstream' side, thus if you mark In and Out on the same frame without moving, you will mark one frame. If you set an In mark on one frame and advance ten frames, and set an Out mark, you will have marked 11 frames (the one you started

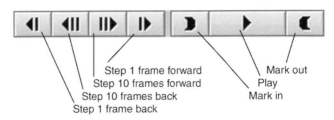

Figure 5.6 Step, Play and Mark buttons

on plus the ten you advanced). You can set marks on the fly using the keyboard. There can only ever be one In and one Out per clip, so resetting a mark simply moves it. Option [Alt]/dragging a mark will move it (not Media Composer v7, v8 NT nor Xpress before v3). Keys to Clear In and Clear Out are on the standard button sets and on the keyboard (Figure 5.7). When a clip is in the Source monitor, a small panel with purple buttons appears at the left-hand end of the Timeline (Figure 5.8). This is the Track Panel; click on the track lights to select source tracks for editing. Active tracks are purple.

To move more rapidly through a clip, use the J, K and L keys on the keyboard; J plays backwards, L plays forwards and K pauses play. Pressing J or L for a second or third time increases the speed of play. Sound will follow up to three times sync speed. Hold down the K key while pressing J or L and the clip plays at a quarter sync speed and plays the sound – useful for cueing. Holding K and tapping J or L moves one frame and scrubs the sound, but you may not find this to be the easiest way to find a cue.

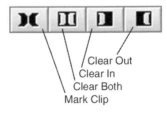

Figure 5.7 Clear In and Clear Out

Figure 5.8 Source Track Panel

Finding audio cues

Mouse Jog and Shuttle

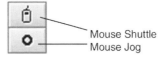

Figure 5.9 Mouse Jog and Shuttle

Another way to cue audio is to use Jog or Shuttle (Figure 5.9; not Xpress v3 and earlier). To engage Mouse Jog on Media Composer or Symphony, press the N key on the keyboard; on Xpress, you'll need to program a keyboard key or a Fast menu button before using Mouse Jog or Shuttle (see 'The Command Palette' in Chapter 8). With Jog enabled any movement of the mouse jogs slowly through the clip, playing the sound; the further the mouse is moved, the further you jog down the clip. Use the keyboard to set marks and press the space bar to get back to normal play. Shuttle is on the semi-colon key on Media Composer or Symphony; this time a mouse movement results in a speed increase or decrease (the speed and direction is shown in the pop-up or Composer window). Again, press space to quit. Holding down the mouse button in either mode switches to the other mode.

Digital Audio Scrub

Digital Audio Scrub lets you move through a clip and cue the audio while listening to a frame or frames at the correct pitch – it plays with a distinctive stuttering sound compared to the smooth scrub of the other methods. The default is to play one incoming frame (i.e., the frame ahead of the position bar). To enable scrubbing, hold down the shift key (temporary) or press Caps Lock (latches on). Now use the step buttons to move though the clip – you'll hear the audio one frame at a time. It can be quite difficult to hear where you are, so it is possible to change the scrub settings to play more than one frame. Open the Audio Settings (Project window) to do this. Scrubbing two incoming frames is a good starting point, any more and you'll find it difficult to identify your cue. The scrub settings control how many frames are played, not how far the position indicator moves. Note that the windows are labelled wrongly in Media Composer v7–v9, Xpress v2–v3 and Symphony v1–v2 – the right-hand window should be labelled 'incoming' and vice versa (see illustration in Chapter 9).

Although up to eight audio tracks can be played when going forward at normal speed, not all tracks are played when scrubbing, using J, K and L or jogging and shuttling. Look at the small speaker icons next to each track light (Figure 5.8).

Depending on the system, the scrub track(s) will be indicated by a small hollow speaker, or a green or gold speaker outline (solid black speakers play but don't scrub). Option [Alt]+clicking on a speaker enables it for scrubbing. Media Composer v7 and v8 (NT), Xpress v2 and Symphony v1 can only scrub one track at a time. Media Composer v8 (Mac) and v9 (NT), Xpress v3 and Symphony v2 can scrub one or two tracks. Media Composer v10, Xpress v4 and Symphony v3 always scrub a minimum of two tracks and can scrub more, depending on the hardware. To isolate, or solo, one track for both forward and reverse play, ⌘[Ctrl]+click on the speaker of the track you wish to hear – the entire button turns green.

Starting to edit

On Media Composer and Symphony, the two main editing buttons are in the centre of the Composer window, below the Source and Record monitors (Figure 5.10), and on the keyboard (V and B). On Xpress, the keyboard keys are usually used but mouse users can find the two buttons in the pop-up or Composer fast menus. The yellow one is called 'Splice in' and the red one is called 'Overwrite'. When editing within a sequence, Splice-In will break the sequence and insert new material; Overwrite will overwrite a marked duration with new material – for the first edit either will do. Having marked your source clip (see earlier), click one of these two buttons and your marked section is edited across to the Record monitor as the first part of your new sequence.

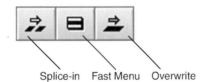

Splice-in   Fast Menu   Overwrite

Figure 5.10 Editing buttons

   A sequence is a kind of clip and needs to be stored in a bin, just like the master clips you digitized. If there is only one bin open when you begin to edit, a sequence clip called 'Untitled Sequence.01' (Figure 5.11) appears in your bin. If more than one bin is open, a dialogue box invites you to choose a destination bin for the sequence; select a bin and click 'OK'. Click on the sequence name in the bin and type in a sensible name. It is worth making a bin for your sequences in order to separate them from the master clips as this simplifies things later, particularly when it comes to backing up your work. Note that if you mix up sequences and master clips in a bin in frame view, you cannot distinguish them, whereas in text view you can tell them apart by the icons.

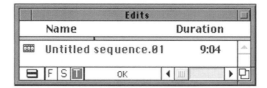

Figure 5.11 Bin after first edit

The blue position indicators in the Record monitor and the Timeline move to the end of the clip you have edited, ready for the next clip (Figure 5.12). Keep assembling material until you have enough to view. Note how the Timeline shows the assembly you have made. As you are adding each new shot to the end of the sequence, it doesn't matter which editing button you use. Media Composer and Symphony automatically create tracks in the sequence to accommodate the active tracks from the source clip (see next section). Xpress automatically creates a sequence with two video tracks and four audio tracks, regardless of the tracks chosen for the first edit.

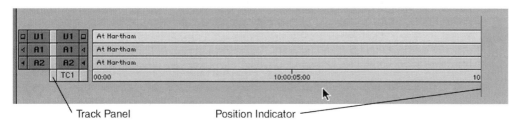

Figure 5.12 Timeline after first edit

Xpress users can click in the pop-up and drag a clip into the Timeline; an outline of the clip can be dragged along and will snap to existing cuts. The clip will be spliced into the sequence unless the shift key is held down – in this case the clip will overwrite existing material.

The Track Panel

When you load a clip into the Source monitor, or there is a sequence in the Record monitor, a small panel with purple buttons appears at the left-hand end of the Timeline (Figure 5.13) . This is the Track Panel and it determines which tracks get edited. The left-hand set of buttons belongs to the Source monitor or pop-up; the

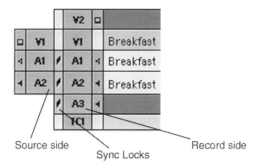

Source side   Sync Locks   Record side

Figure 5.13 Track Panel

right-hand set belongs to the sequence. To turn tracks on and off, click on the track lights (V1, A1, etc.) with the mouse; to overwrite only video (say) make sure that the video track lights are selected on both source and record sides, and make the edit. The key to avoiding mistakes is to check the track lights on the record side. Only those selected (purple) will be edited or modified. If you have an audio-only clip in the Source monitor (say) and you have all the track lights selected on the record side, filler (black) will be edited on to the video track. If you splice into just the video track on the record side, you will put the sequence out of sync, unless the sync locks are on. The sync locks are enabled by clicking in the small boxes between the source and record track lights (Figure 5.13). With sync locks on, all material downstream from the edit point is kept in sync – Avid will cut sections or add filler to unselected tracks to maintain sync. To enable sync locks for all tracks, click the box next to the TC1 button. As you edit, extra tracks can be added to your sequence by using the clip menu. The track panel is also used for selecting clips and tracks for deletion, rendering effects and other things. Keyboard buttons can also be used for selecting tracks. To toggle between source and record sides with the keyboard, use the Escape key.

Moving along the sequence

When editing within your sequence, you may wish to park exactly on an existing cut (although you don't need to, of course). If you can always move exactly to the position you wish, then you'll avoid flash frames and black holes.

Using buttons

On Media Composer and Symphony the FF and REW buttons (Figure 5.14) will move you the next cut in the sequence, depending on the track lights. For instance,

REW/FF (Media Composer and Symphony)
Go to next edit (Xpress)

Figure 5.14 Moving to the next cut

if V1 and A1 are turned on, and you press FF, then the position indicator will move to the next cut or transition where both tracks cut. In a complicated sequence, with many tracks and split edits, you may find the position indicator shoots straight to the start or end of the sequence, these being the only points where all the tracks cut together (Figure 5.15). On Xpress, the 'Go to next edit' buttons (Figure 5.14) have this function. Buttons with the same icons exist on Media Composer and Symphony, too, but here they are called 'Go to transition' and work differently. 'Go to transition' moves to the next cut, or transition (again depending on the track lights) and enters Trim mode (see Chapter 6) at the cut.

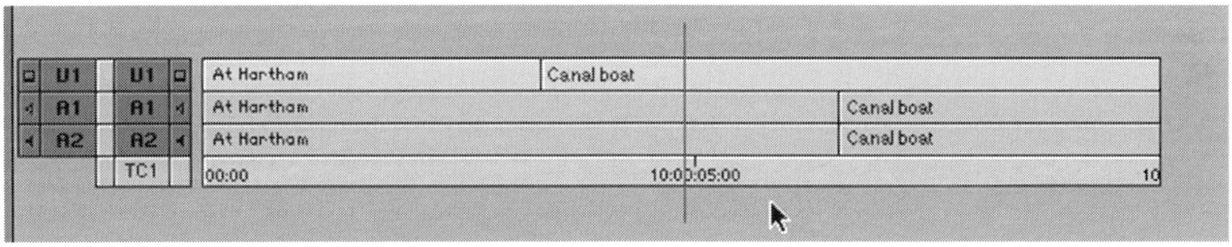

V1	V1	At Hartham	Canal boat	
A1	A1	At Hartham		Canal boat
A2	A2	At Hartham		Canal boat
	TC1	00:00	10:00:05:00	10

Figure 5.15 Timeline showing split edit

This track light dependence can be turned off by holding down the option [Alt] key while using FF, REW and the 'Go To' buttons. Alternatively, there is an option in the Composer settings to do this (Media Composer and Symphony only). By default, the position indicator parks on the first (head) frame of the incoming clip. This is fine if you wish to set an In mark, but if you want to set an Out mark at the cut, you need to step back one frame so that the Out mark is on the downstream side of the last frame of the outgoing clip. This, too, can be changed in the Composer settings (not Xpress).

The FF and REW keys on Xpress are used to go to the next Locator (see Chapter 8). The FF and REW keys on Media Composer and Symphony can be modified to do this, too, in the Composer settings.

Using the mouse

A simpler way of moving to any cut, regardless of track lights, on any system, is to hold down the command (🍎) [Ctrl] key while clicking or dragging the position

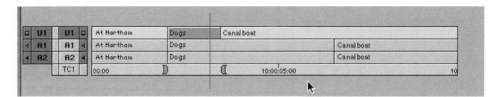

Figure 5.16 Marked clip in Timeline

indicator along the Timeline. The indicator will snap to the head frames of every cut regardless of track lights. To get to a tail frame, hold down ⌘+option [Ctrl+Alt] as you drag or click. This is helpful if you wish to mark an Out on the last frame of a clip (an In is always set on the upstream, and an Out on the downstream side of a frame).

To mark an entire clip, park on the clip and press the 'Mark Clip' button (Figure 5.7). This, too, is dependent on the track lights, unless you hold the option [Alt] key down, in which case an In is set on the nearest upstream cut, and an Out on the nearest downstream cut, on any track, regardless of track lights. In Figure 5.16, the clip 'Dogs' (video only) is selected.

Moving by numbers

To move a number of frames along a clip, use the numeric keypad – type plus or minus followed by a number (1–99 frames), then 'Enter'. A figure greater than 99 is treated as seconds and frames (i.e., 1:11), unless followed by a lower case 'f' (no quotes). To mark an exact duration (say 2 seconds), set the In mark, then type in a figure one frame less than you need (in this case +1:24 PAL or 1:29 NTSC) as the frame you first mark will be included in the total.

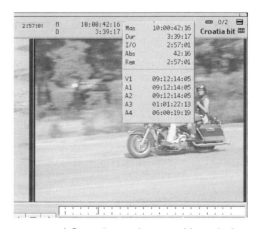

Figure 5.17 Media Composer and Symphony time tracking choices

It is also possible to move to an absolute timecode; for this to work, ensure that the upper (not Xpress) of the two TC displays above the Source or Record monitor shows the TC you are interested in – click on the current display to show a pop-up window of timecodes then move the mouse to the timecode of your choice (Figure 5.17). Now simply type in the timecode on the numeric keypad and press 'Enter'. If the TC exists in the clip, the position indicator will move to that frame. Timecode choices include Master, Duration and V1, A1, etc. (clip source timecodes). Xpress monitors only display one row of tracking information but a second reader can be displayed on all systems in the form of the Timecode Window (Tools menu). Xpress models can display one row of information in the Timecode Window; Media Composer and Symphony can display either 8 or 48 rows.

Undo/Redo

Any editing operation can be reversed by choosing Undo from the Edit menu (+Z) [Ctrl+Z]. It is also possible to redo the operation (+R) [Ctrl+R]. There are 32 levels of Undo/Redo. Also in the Edit menu is the Undo/Redo list. By clicking in the list it is possible to move back several editing decisions (all the operations up to that point are undone; you can't just choose one from the list!).

Actions such as deleting a track from a sequence can be undone, but deleting clips from bins cannot. It is possible to restore an earlier version of a bin from the Attic folder, however; see Chapter 13, 'Files and Media'. If a new sequence is loaded into the Record monitor, the Undo list is cleared. In Media Composer v10 and Symphony v3, it is possible to have the Undo/Redo list only count record-side events; set this in the Edit tab of the Composer settings (Project window).

Removing material

Extract and Lift

To remove clips or parts of clips from your sequence (all versions), use Mark In and Mark Out to mark the section you wish to remove, and turn on the track lights for the tracks from which you wish to remove material. Now use either 'Lift' or 'Extract' to remove your clips (Figure 5.18). These buttons are on the keyboard (Z and X; all versions) and on the standard record-side button set on Media Composer and Symphony. Xpress users can find them in the Composer fast menu. Lift will lift out the material, leaving filler (black) in the sequence. The In and Out marks remain, so that new material can be edited in. Extract removes the material and closes the gap in the sequence. Using Lift will not

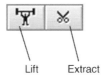

Lift   Extract

Figure 5.18 Lift and Extract

break sync, while Extract will put you out of sync if you (for example) extract material from the video track but not from the matching audio track (Figure 5.16). Using the Sync Locks (see earlier) will prevent this by cutting the same amount of material from all the tracks.

Top and Tail

In Media Composer v10, Symphony v3 and Xpress v4, two extra buttons are provided for rapidly extracting material: 'Top' and 'Tail' (Figure 5.19). To remove material from the head of a clip, park on the frame you'd like to be the new in frame and press Top. To remove material from the tail of a clip, park on the first frame you'd like to remove and press Tail; the remainder of the clip will be extracted. The normal rules of track light dependency apply – if working on clips with split edits, and all track lights are on, all material is extracted back to the point where all selected tracks cut (Figure 5.20). Top and Tail are part of the standard keyboard settings on Xpress v4 ('Y' and 'U'). Media Composer and Symphony users will need to program keys or buttons of their choice (see Chapter 8).

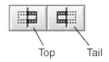

Top   Tail

Figure 5.19 Top and Tail

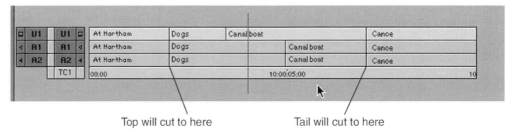

Top will cut to here   Tail will cut to here

Figure 5.20 Using Top and Tail

Focus   Magnification slider

Figure 5.21 Timeline magnification

Magnifying the Timeline

As the sequence gets longer, it can be difficult to see individual clips; to magnify
the Timeline horizontally, either drag the zoom slider (Figure 5.21). or click the
Focus button (not Xpress). The Focus button applies a fixed magnification that
toggles back to the previous magnification when the button is clicked again. When
the Timeline is zoomed in, a lighter section in the time track under the Record
monitor shows how much of the entire sequence is currently visible in the Timeline
window. There is more information on working in the Timeline in Chapter 7.

6 Basic editing part 2

- Trim mode
- Extend
- Slipping and Sliding
- Segment editing

Trim mode

After making a rough assembly, you will probably need to do some fine-tuning. Up to this point we have looked only at Source/Record mode. In the centre of the Composer window, on Media Composer and Symphony, below the editing buttons are three other buttons; from left to right they are: Source/Record mode, Trim mode and Effect mode (Figure 6.1). Trim mode allows us to adjust the cut or transition between two clips in our sequence. The Trim mode button is also on the keyboard; it is the 'Y' key on a Media Composer or Symphony keyboard. On Xpress, it is the '[' key. It is not on the standard Xpress Composer button set but is in the fast menu.

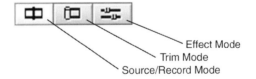

Figure 6.1 Source/Record mode, Trim mode and Effect mode buttons

To trim, park close to a cut and make sure the required track lights are turned on. Click the Trim mode button and you will enter Trim mode at the transition. Alternatively, click and drag a lasso starting in the area of the Timeline outside the tracks around the cut or cuts (one per track) that you wish to trim. This has the effect of making the track selection for you – quite a time saver. To lasso a cut inside a stack of tracks, hold down the Control key while you lasso on a Mac system; on NT, hold down Alt.

Last frame of outgoing clip   First frame of incoming clip

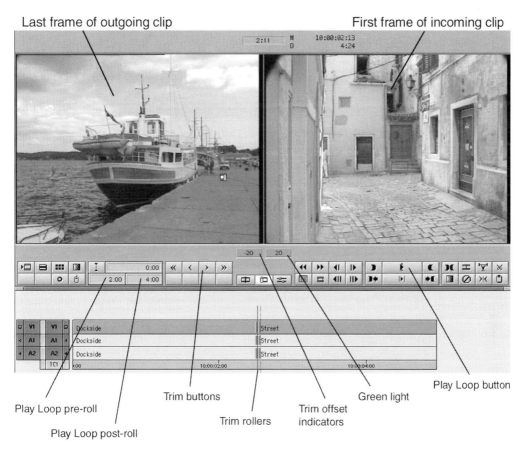

Play Loop pre-roll

Play Loop post-roll

Trim buttons

Trim rollers

Trim offset
indicators

Green light

Play Loop button

Figure 6.2 Trim display (Media Composer and Symphony)

As you enter Trim mode, the Composer display changes to show the last frame
of the outgoing clip, and the first frame of the incoming clip. Media Composer and
Symphony use the full width of the monitor – 'Big' Trim mode (Figure 6.2). In
Xpress trimming takes place in the smaller Composer window (Figure 6.3). Media
Composer and Symphony users can switch to 'Small' trim mode (all trimming in
the Record monitor) by clicking the Trim mode button for a second time. The
default trim display can also be adjusted in the Trim settings (Project window).

Trimming lets you add frames to, or remove frames from, the outgoing (A side)
clip, the incoming (B side) clip, or both together. When Trim mode is first entered,
the default is to trim both incoming and outgoing together, as this is unlikely to put
the sequence out of sync. You may trim by dragging in the Timeline, by using the
trim buttons either in the window or on the keyboard, by using mouse jog or shuttle
(not Xpress before v4) or by using the J, K and L keys (not Xpress before v4).
Figures 6.4a–c show the different trim roller displays in the Timeline.

Figure 6.3 Xpress Trim display

Figure 6.4 a, Trim outgoing clip;   **b**, Trim both clips;   **c**, Trim incoming clip

Trimming with the mouse

To trim (extend or shorten) the outgoing (A side) clip, click with the mouse over the left-hand (outgoing) frame in the Composer window. A pink trim roller is now visible only on the outgoing side, and a purple box appears only under the outgoing frame. If you now move your pointer on to the roller in the Timeline and drag right, you will come out of the shot later. Drag left and you come out earlier. To trim the

Figure 6.5 Trim icons in the Timeline

incoming shot (B side), click on the right-hand (incoming) frame and make the adjustment. Be sure to click and drag as soon as the mouse pointer turns into the trim icon as you approach the rollers in the timeline (Figure 6.5). If you overshoot and click, you may end up trimming a single track on the wrong side.

To trim both sides together, click on the bar between the two frames and trim rollers will appear on each side of the cut. Now, dragging the rollers will extend one shot and shorten the other. Note that if you are trimming both sides, you will only see an A side or B side icon at the mouse position, depending on the side from which you approach the transition. Trimming both sides is most often used for creating a split edit. In drama, for example, it is usually quickest to edit using straight cuts on audio and video to get the pacing right, then to trim on video only to create a split edit, i.e., to come to the video cut earlier or later than the audio cut. By trimming on both sides, the incoming audio remains in sync, as an equal number of frames is added to, or removed from each side of the cut.

Trimming with buttons

A set of Trim buttons (Figure 6.6) is part of the usual trim window display and is on the standard keyboard on all systems. These act like the normal Step buttons except that they trim one frame or ten frames in each direction. Pressing the Step buttons will exit Trim mode.

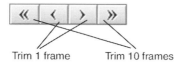

Figure 6.6 Trim buttons

Trimming by numbers

The numeric keypad can also be used for trimming – type a plus or minus followed by a number (see previous chapter), then press 'Enter'. On a dual-roller trim, plus moves the cut down the Timeline. When trimming the outgoing it will extend the clip, again moving the cut to the right; when trimming the incoming, the clip will be entered later and frames removed from the head. Entering a minus figure has the opposite effect.

If the end of the clip is reached using any trim method, a corner frame appears in the monitor and you are prevented from trimming further. Likewise, if you trim the shot away completely (i.e., you hit the next cut), trimming will stop. If you release the mouse and continue, you will trim into the next shot.

Monitoring a trim

To monitor the audio when trimming, use Digital Audio Scrub or mouse Jog or Shuttle (not Xpress prior to v4). An intuitive way of extending or shortening a clip is to use the J or L key (all systems except Xpress prior to v4). This moves the cut point while playing the clip and makes it easy to judge the pace of the shot. Trimming will stop at either the end of the digitized media for the clip being trimmed, or one frame before the next cut in the sequence. This way a shot is not completely trimmed away by accident.

When trimming both sides of the audio on a cut, it is important to decide which audio you monitor, the incoming or the outgoing. Do this by moving the green light (under the purple boxes below the monitors) to the incoming or outgoing side. Simply float the mouse pointer, without clicking, from one monitor to the other. If you trim one side only, you always monitor the correct sound. The green light also sets which side of the cut is seen on the video monitor when trimming both sides.

It is possible to trim a split edit – in this case you will need to decide whether to monitor at the video or the audio cut. Set up the trim by either lassoing a video and adjacent audio cut, or by selecting one cut and shift-clicking on the other cuts you wish to trim. Now carefully click with the mouse on the roller at the cut you wish to monitor so that the blue position indicator is set there (Figure 6.7). It is important to get this right, particularly if you are attempting to trim a small split edit that

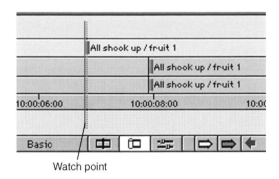

Figure 6.7 Trimming a split edit

Pre- and Post-roll   Play Loop

Figure 6.8 Trim button display

appears to be a straight cut in the Timeline – in this case, magnify the Timeline until you can see what is going on. The choice of monitoring position is called the Watch Point.

To review a trim, press the Play Loop button (Figure 6.8) that appears in place of Play when Trim mode is entered (the Play keys on the keyboard also switch to Play Loop when trimming with the exception of 'L'). The system backs up to a couple of seconds before the cut, and plays on a couple of seconds after the cut. The pre-roll and post-roll can be changed by typing new values in the two small boxes in the Trim mode window (Figure 6.8), or in the Trim settings (see later).

Analysing the audio at the cut

Sometimes there is an audio glitch at the cut but it isn't clear if it is at the end of the outgoing or at the start of the incoming clip. To make the play loop play only up to the cut, press 'Q' (Go to In) while in Loop play. To play from the cut onwards, press 'W' (Go to Out) while in loop play. The play loop button icon changes to show the looping mode.

Trimming on the fly

When in Loop play, it is possible to 'Trim on the fly'. While playing, press any Mark key on the keyboard (Mark In or Mark Out). The cut will jump to that point. This is good for double-sided trims or for shortening a clip. To extend a clip in a single-sided trim, drag out the clip beyond the desired point, then adjust using 'Trim on the fly', as it is difficult to judge the cut point when not seeing or hearing the extra frames from the clip.

When trimming on the fly, the cut can also be adjusted by pressing the trim buttons on the keyboard, for fine tuning. Trimming on the fly is probably the most intuitive way to trim on Xpress v3 and earlier (which lack JKL trimming).

Staying in sync

If there are many audio or video tracks in the sequence, it is important to keep the material downstream of the trim point in sync. If the sync locks are turned on, sync will not be lost but this may not be helpful in all cases (sometimes sync locks prevent you from trimming at all, or split clips in two and insert filler). There are several things that can be done to enable trimming to take place without sync being lost. Small arrows at the end of the Timeline point to cuts off screen that have been inadvertently selected. Figures 6.9 and 6.10 show this problem.

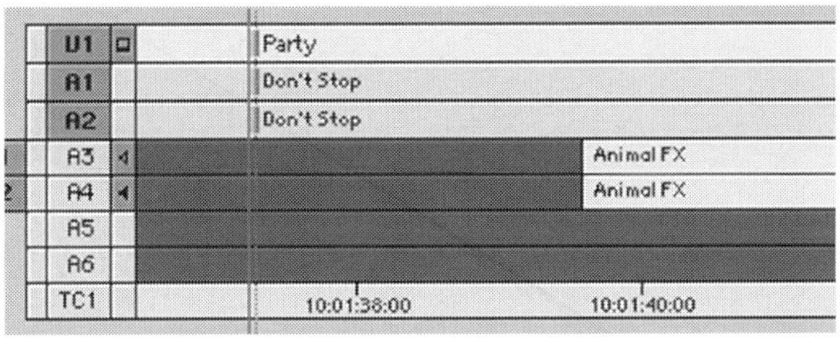

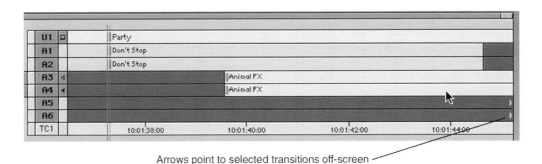

Figure 6.9 Problem: how to trim incoming frames on V1, A1 and A2 but keep all tracks in sync

Arrows point to selected transitions off-screen

Figure 6.10 Arrows indicate inadvertently selected cuts off screen

1 If there are clips beyond the point being trimmed that are on tracks that are not selected, then the Add Edit button (Figure 6.11 – more details in Chapter 8) can be used to place cuts in the filler on these tracks and the trim can then include these cuts (frames in filler act like frames in a clip, and can be trimmed). This can be done quickly by holding down the option [Alt] key and clicking Add Edit while in Trim mode. Add Edits will be automatically placed on any filler tracks at the trim point so that all tracks are trimmed together (these tracks don't need to be selected – Figure 6.12). This button is on the default Xpress keyboard and on the default Media Composer and Symphony Composer button set.

Figure 6.11 Add Edit

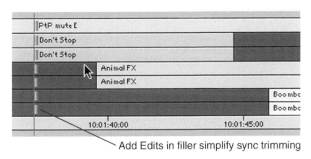

Figure 6.12 Add Edits automatically placed on filler tracks

2 As an alternative, shift-click on additional cuts on tracks in the sequence to ensure that one cut per track is included in the trim, as when selecting cuts for trimming a split edit. Simply turning on additional track lights may not be the answer, as you may remove material in inappropriate positions. In the example, if the bottom four audio tracks had simply been selected, the trim would have removed frames from the head of 'Animal FX' and 'Boombangabang'. In a situation like this it is possible to trim in two directions simultaneously (known as an asymmetric trim); as long as the same number of frames is removed from each track, sync will be maintained. In the example, outgoing filler frames will be trimmed off tracks A3–A6 while incoming material is removed on V1, A1 and A2, but sync is not broken (Figure 6.13).

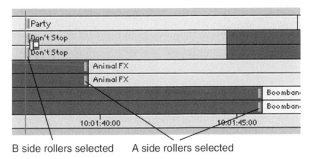

Figure 6.13 Asymmetric trim

3 Occasionally, there is a need to remove material from one side of a cut only, on one track, without breaking sync. This can be done on Mac systems by holding down the Control key while trimming – black (filler) replaces the clip as it is trimmed away. On NT systems, use the Alt key. Keep the modifier key held down until trimming is completed (Figure 6.14).

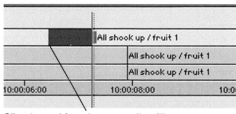

Clip trimmed from here revealing filler

Figure 6.14 Filler replaces clip to avoid breaking sync

Leaving Trim mode

To leave Trim mode on Media Composer or Symphony, either click the Source/
Record button, click on the TC track in the Timeline, click any Step button (1 frame
or 10 frames) or press the Escape key. Xpress users should click the Trim mode
button for a second time, click the TC track or press one of the Step buttons.

Trim Settings

You may wish to take a quick look at the Trim Settings. Two useful features can be
found: the possibility of adding an 'Intermission' between cycles of the play loop,
and the ability to enable 'Render on-the-Fly' in Trim mode. Render on-the-Fly (see
Chapter 10) previews real-time and unrendered effects and is normally off in Trim
mode as it slows down response when trimming transition effects. It can usefully be
turned on when trimming clips to which segment effects have been added (Figure
6.15). The Xpress Trim settings have far fewer options.

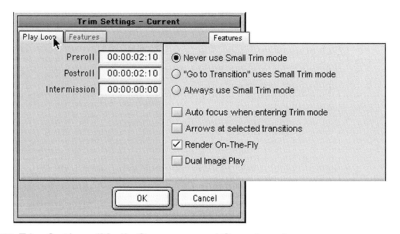

Figure 6.15 Trim Settings (Media Composer and Symphony)

Extend

The Extend function (Figure 6.16) offers a quick way to do the equivalent of a 'double-roller' trim on one or more tracks. Think of it as resetting the In or Out point of a clip. To extend the tail of a clip, put a mark Out further down the Timeline and press Extend. If there is enough material, the clip is extended and the following clip shortened, as in a double-roller trim (Figure 6.17). To extend the head of a clip back to an earlier point in the sequence, put a mark In further up the Timeline and press Extend. If there is enough material, the clip is extended back and the preceding clip shortened, as in a double-roller trim (Figure 6.18). Extend is available on all systems except Xpress prior to v4.

Figure 6.16 Extend button

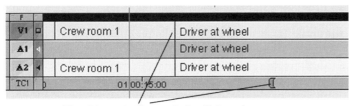

The video cut will move to the Out mark

Figure 6.17 Extend to Out

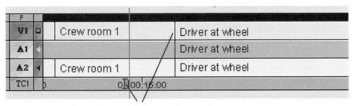

The video cut will move to the In mark

Figure 6.18 Extend to In

Slipping

Slipping is a form of trimming – in effect it trims both ends of a clip at once. If you have edited a clip into your sequence and are happy with the position, but not with the part of the clip you have used, slipping lets you access earlier and later material in the clip. Slip and Slide (next section) are not available on Xpress before v3.

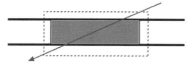

Figure 6.19 Lasso R–L to enter Slip mode

In the Timeline, drag a lasso from right to left across the cuts at the start and end of your clip (Figure 6.19) and the Composer window (Media Composer and Symphony) changes to show four frames. From left to right, these are the last frame of the preceding clip, the head and tail frames of the clip being slipped, and the head frame of the following clip (Figure 6.20). Xpress systems display only two frames, the head and tail frames of the clip being slipped. If you now use any of the trimming methods described in the last section, it is possible to come into and leave the clip earlier or later. Slipping left reveals earlier frames and slipping right shows later frames. If you reach the end of the clip, trimming stops. An alternative way to select a clip for slipping, if a cut at one end is already being trimmed, is to double-click on the clip in the Timeline. Holding Shift and double-clicking on extra segments will include them in the Slip.

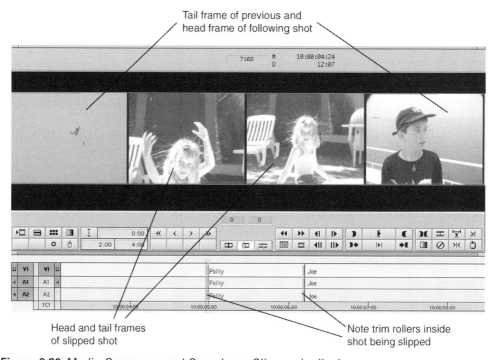

Figure 6.20 Media Composer and Symphony Slip mode display

Sliding

Sliding a shot is very similar to slipping, and again is a form of trimming. To slide a shot, drag from right to left around both ends of the clip but this time with the option [Shift+Alt] key(s) pressed. Alternatively, if one end of the clip is already selected for trimming, option [Alt]+double-click on the clip to select it for sliding. The selected shot can be moved along the sequence unchanged, trimming the adjacent shots as it goes. A similar four or two-frame display appears when sliding. If the shot is slid up to a cut in either of the surrounding shots, it will stop.

If trimming on the fly when Slipping or Sliding, press Mark In to set the head frame of the clip and Mark Out to set the tail frame. Make sure the blue position indicator is set at either the head or tail of the clip as appropriate when sliding to monitor the correct part of the audio on the tracks beneath.

Segment editing

Segment editing allows the editor to move clips (segments) in the Timeline to a different position in the sequence. One or more segments may be selected. The two segment editing buttons are coloured red and yellow and are found at the bottom of the Timeline window on all systems (Figure 6.21). These buttons are standard on the Xpress keyboard (colon and quote keys) and can be programmed to the keyboard (Media Composer and Symphony). They share some features with the yellow Splice-in button and red Overwrite button.

Extract/Splice-in   Lift/Overwrite

Figure 6.21 Segment editing buttons

To select a segment, either draw a lasso around one or more clips from left to right (Figure 6.22), or click on one of the segment editing buttons to activate it and then click on a segment. Shift-clicking will add more segments to the selection.

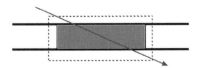

Figure 6.22 Lasso L–R to enter Segment mode

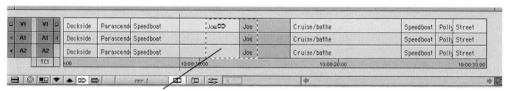

Outline of moving segment

Figure 6.23 Timeline during segment editing

When a segment is dragged using the red Lift/Overwrite button, it will overwrite material when the mouse button is released, and the space where the segment started will then contain filler. Using the yellow Extract/Splice-in button, material will be spliced into the sequence after it has been moved, and the spot from where it was extracted will close up, as with the Extract button (Figure 6.23). This is a quick way to swap two shots in the Timeline. Note that segment editing normally overrides the sync locks and that it is easy to break sync with Extract/Splice-in. It is best to 'unsplit' any split edits before using Extract/Splice-in. Some versions offer a 'Segment mode Sync Lock' feature in the Timeline settings (Chapter 7). For this to work, the track panel sync locks must be on, too.

Xpress systems automatically snap the head of a moving segment to an existing cut, the position indicator (which remains stationary while a segment button is active), or an In or Out mark. To snap the head of a moving segment to a cut on Media Composer and Symphony, hold down the [Ctrl] key as you approach the desired position. To snap the tail of a segment to a cut (all systems) when using Lift/Overwrite, hold down +option [Ctrl+Alt]. To move a segment vertically, but to stop it slipping left or right, hold down Ctrl [Shift+Ctrl]. To move two segments vertically together (say A1 and A2), there must be two clear tracks above or below for the segments to land on. It is not possible to move non-contiguous segments. If you wish to move two segments separated by filler, select the filler as well. Xpress users who need to move a segment to a position not at an existing cut, should move the position bar to the destination first – the segment will snap to the bar.

During Segment editing, the Composer window (Media Composer and Symphony) shows a four-frame display similar to that seen during Slipping and Sliding (Figure 6.24). The central two frames are the head and tail frames of the moving segment(s), and the two outside frames will be the ones immediately before and after the segment when the edit is finished. If you are mostly moving segments to align with other cuts in the sequence, you may not wish to have the four-frame display visible each time you move a segment. This particularly applies if you are manipulating a number of segments with unrendered video effects. To turn off the display, open the Timeline settings in the Project window and deselect the 'Show Four-Frame Display' option. Now your segments will move rapidly into place. In

Head and tail frames of moving segment

Figure 6.24 Media Composer and Symphony four-frame segment display

early versions this option is labelled 'Show Segment Drag Quads'. Xpress does not display the moving frames.

The segment buttons can be used to quickly delete complete clips from a sequence. Simply select some clips in segment mode and press the Delete key (Backspace/delete, not the small key marked 'Del' on a Mac). In this case clips need not be contiguous. Lift/Overwrite is best for this, as Extract/Splice-in will easily break sync. Note that if any clip has an effect placed on it (such as a video segment effect), then this will be deleted and a further press of the Delete key is needed to remove the clip. The same applies to audio data; if a clip's level has been adjusted (see Chapter 9) this audio data is deleted.

7 Timeline and settings

- Showing more detail
- Enlarging and reducing track size
- Timeline fast menu
- Saving Timeline views
- Adding and deleting tracks
- The Timeline setting

The default Timeline display shows tracks and background in shades of grey, and the name of each clip displayed as text. The Timeline can give us far more information than this; we can change the display, choose colours, change track widths, show audio information and much more. On all versions except Xpress prior to v4, Timeline views can be saved as part of the User settings and used in other projects.

The Timeline normally displays the sequence in the Record monitor but Media Composer and Symphony users can toggle the Timeline to show the contents of the Source monitor (Figure 7.1). This is very useful if a sequence or very long clip is loaded into the Source monitor. The Toggle button and position indicator turn green to remind the user of the change.

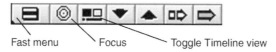

Figure 7.1 Timeline buttons

Showing more detail

Drag the slider on the Scale bar below the Timeline to expand and contract your view. If you are looking at a small section, use the Scroll bar to the right to view a different part of the Timeline. The Focus button (Media Composer and Symphony only) toggles to a fixed magnification and back again (Figure 7.1). This can be set

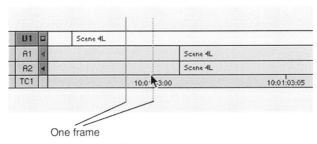

Figure 7.2 Timeline at extreme magnification

to happen automatically when entering Trim mode (see Trim Settings). On an Xpress, the keyboard up and down cursor keys magnify and reduce the Timeline horizontal magnification. If the scale is magnified greatly, the position bar appears split into two, with the left-hand (solid) bar indicating the upstream side of the frame being viewed, and the right-hand (dotted) bar indicating the downstream side of the frame (Figure 7.2). See the fast menu options (below) for other ways of magnifying the Timeline.

Track height

Track height can be changed in two ways; either select the tracks you wish to adjust (make sure any tracks you don't want to change are deselected on both source and record sides of the Track Panel) and choose 'Enlarge track' (⌘+L) [Ctrl+L] or 'Reduce track' (⌘+K) [Ctrl+K] from the Edit menu. The alternative for Media Composer and Symphony (which offers more flexibility) is to hold down the option key [Ctrl on NT] and click and drag on the black dividing line between two tracks in the Track Panel. On Xpress, this feature works without the use of the modifier key (Figure 7.3).

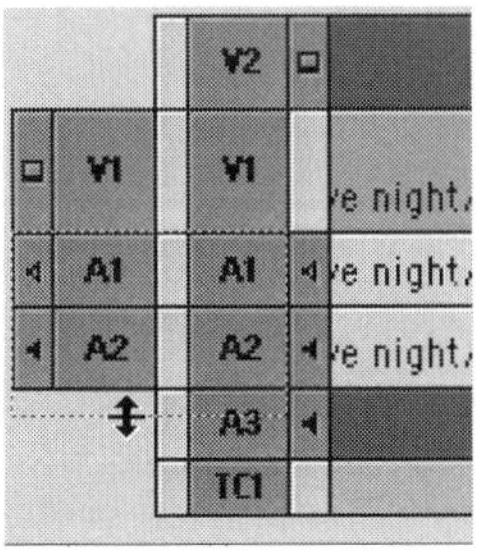

Figure 7.3 Dragging to change track height

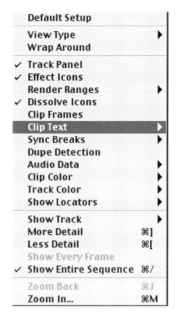

Figure 7.4 Timeline Fast Menu main choices

Timeline fast menu

The fast menu, the small icon that looks like a hamburger at bottom left of the Timeline (Figure 7.4) offers a number of choices (not all choices are available on all systems and versions). The most useful features are as follows.

Zoom In

This option (not Xpress) changes the mouse pointer to a small rectangle with arrows; click and drag to magnify one specific area of interest. Use 'Zoom back' to return to the previous magnification. For speed, the keyboard shortcuts ⌘+M [Ctrl+M] and ⌘+J [Ctrl+J] are worth remembering, as are the shortcuts for 'More Detail', 'Less Detail' and 'Show Entire Sequence', also in this menu.

Track Color

It is possible to change the track colour; this makes it easier to distinguish between the contents of various tracks (you may decide to have one colour for narration and a different one for music, for instance). Select the track or tracks in the Track Panel (record side only required) and then click on the Timeline fast menu and choose Track Color. Pick a colour from the palette, or for more choice, hold down the option [Alt] key and a colour picker appears, giving more variety.

Show Track

This option (not Xpress) allows some tracks to be hidden in the Timeline (without deleting them from the sequence). This can be convenient but also may lead to confusion as some clips may appear to be out of sync with an invisible track. This option also allows a film track to be displayed. The option 'Clip Frames' is similar but shows one representative frame at the head of each clip. A film track is always displayed on Xpress but may be reduced so that the frames aren't visible.

Dupe Detection

Dupe Detection indicates any frames that have been used more than once in the sequence – they are highlighted with a band of colour. It is possible to flag 'duped' frames at differing distances from one another, useful for film projects; set this in the Timeline setting (Project window).

Clip Text

There are several useful variations on the default text (the clip name); look for these in the Clip Text sub-menu (Figure 7.5) on Media Composer and Symphony (Xpress users will see some of these choices in the main menu):

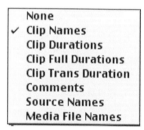

None
✓ Clip Names
Clip Durations
Clip Full Durations
Clip Trans Duration
Comments
Source Names
Media File Names

Figure 7.5 Timeline Clip text choices

Clip Durations shows the clip length from cut to cut.
Clip Full Durations displays the full length of each clip used, including overlaps for transition effects (see Chapter 10).
Clip Transition Durations displays the duration of any effect at the head or tail of the clip, and the duration of the remainder of the clip not part of the effect.
Comments can be added from the monitor menu (hidden under the current clip name in the Composer window) after highlighting a clip with a segment editing button. These comments can be added to an EDL. If the Clip Text Comments option is selected, the comment will display in the Timeline.

Audio data

It is possible to display waveforms (most useful with the Show marked waveforms option in the Timeline settings), or volume information (Figure 7.6). Xpress users have fewer choices. Figure 7.7 shows a waveform display on an Xpress system.

Figure 7.6 Timeline Audio choices

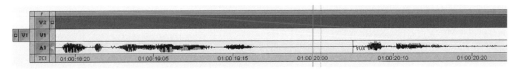

Figure 7.7 Timeline waveform display

Use the 'Clip Gain' and 'Auto Gain' displays with a wide track width to display audio levels within a clip. Prior to Media Composer v10, Symphony v3 and Xpress v4, this choice is simply 'Volume' (see Chapter 9 for details on working with audio).

Show Locators

A choice of locator colours (not Xpress) can be displayed in the Timeline from this sub-menu (see Chapter 8 for information on locators). This option is only available in Media Composer v10 and Symphony v3 and later.

Clip Color

Colours assigned to clips (see Chapter 5) can be displayed in the Timeline using the choices in this sub-menu. This is not available in Media Composer v7, Xpress v2 or Symphony v1. In the sub-menu, 'Source' refers to the colour assigned to source clips in bins. 'Local' colour can be assigned to a segment in the Timeline; select a segment and choose Clip Color from the Edit menu. This only works if 'Local' is selected in the Clip Color sub-menu (Figure 7.8).

Figure 7.8 Timeline Clip Color choices

Render Ranges

Unrendered or partially rendered Effect clips can be highlighted in the Timeline with this option in recent versions only (Figure 7.9).

Most other options in the fast menu are self-explanatory. If the track width is sufficiently wide, several items of information can be displayed per clip. At the top of the fast menu is an option to return the Timeline display to its default.

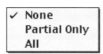

Figure 7.9 Timeline Render Range choices

Saving Timeline views

Once you have customized the Timeline, you can save it as a setting (not Xpress prior to v4). Click on the box at the bottom of the Timeline (it will show the name of the current view or the word 'Untitled'). Click on 'Save As' and name your view (Figure 7.10). Your views are listed in the Project window when Settings are displayed. You may have a number of different views – some dealing with audio (see later), one showing dupes, one showing transition durations and so on. Get into the habit of saving views and switching as required – it will speed up your work rate.

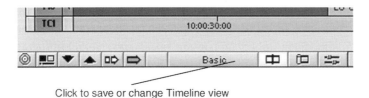

Click to save or change Timeline view

Figure 7.10 Timeline views

Adding and deleting tracks

As you work, you will need to add extra video and audio tracks. Add a new track to your sequence from the Clip menu. A useful keyboard combination to remember is option+&+U [Alt+Ctrl+U], which offers a choice of video or audio track and the choice of track number. Normally the next unused track is automatically added.

When clips are edited, they are sent to the adjacent track in the record side of the track panel. To send your source audio or video to a different track of your choice, click on the source track light and drag to the desired destination track light (Figure 7.11). Alternatively, set Auto Patching (see the next section). Hidden in the Special menu (Media Composer and Symphony only) is an option to 'Restore Default Patch' – very useful when editing parts of one sequence into another.

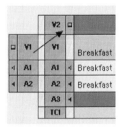

Figure 7.11 Patching tracks

To delete a track from your sequence, deselect all the other tracks and press the Delete key.

Timeline Settings

The Timeline Settings (Project window) work in conjunction with the current Timeline view. Figure 7.12 shows the two tabs for choices in Media Composer v10 and Symphony v3. Xpress and earlier versions of Media Composer and Symphony have fewer choices. Some of the more useful options are:

Show Marked Waveforms displays audio waveforms only between an In and an Out if one of the waveform options is selected in the Timeline fast menu.
Show Marked Region turns the purple highlight over a marked region on and off in the Timeline.
Scroll while Playing moves the Timeline past a stationary position indicator. This works more reliably on a Mac if the Timeline is moved to the Bin (left-hand) monitor during Digital Cut (output to tape).

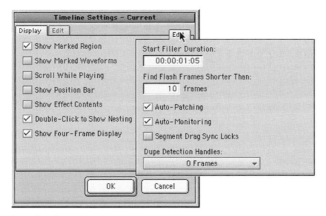

Figure 7.12 Timeline Settings

Show Four-Frame display (not Xpress) turns on and off the four-window display usually seen when segment editing. This can speed up the moving of segments when the user plans to snap the moving segment to a particular cut or mark – useful when working with unrendered effects as the system does not have to spend time previewing the frames. This is shown as 'Show Segment Drag Quads' in Media Composer v7.

If **Auto Patching** is selected, source side tracks automatically patch themselves to selected record side track lights in a logical way (tracks can still be patched manually).

Auto Monitoring forces the video monitor in the Timeline to move to the track being edited – this may not always be desirable when working with unrendered video effects so it can be disabled here.

By adjusting the **Dupe Detection Handles**, frames that are very close to other frames that have been included in the sequence will be flagged as being duplicated. This is valuable for film projects.

Segment Drag Sync Locks prevent sync being broken when moving segments with the Extract/Splice-in button. The Timeline sync locks need to be on, too, for this to be effective.

Start Filler Duration (Media Composer v10, Symphony v3 and Xpress v4 and later) sets the amount of filler added at the start of a sequence when using the 'Add Filler' command in the Clip menu. Earlier versions added a fixed duration.

Find Flash Frames is new for Media Composer v10, Symphony v3 and Xpress v4. Set this and then use the 'Find Flash Frames' command in the Clip menu.

8 Further editing techniques

- Command Palette
- Subclips
- Clipboard
- Duplicating sequences
- Workspaces
- More on settings
- Storyboard editing
- More useful buttons
- Editing with ganged pop-ups
- Multicamera editing

Once beyond the basic editing stages, there are many other useful techniques to be explored; a selection is detailed in this chapter.

Command Palette

Although many useful buttons are provided on the standard button sets in the Composer window and on the keyboard, there are further buttons available. It is also useful to be able to move and modify the existing buttons. All the buttons are available from the Command Palette in the Tools menu (all systems except Xpress v3 and earlier). Open the palette and you'll find a series of tabs under which the buttons are sorted into areas of use – Move, Edit, FX and so on. Figure 8.1 shows the Media Composer and Symphony 'Move' tab.

To modify a button on screen, make sure that 'button to button' reassignment is selected and simply drag the button from the palette to its destination, which can be any visible blank or assigned button in the Composer window (Media Composer and Symphony only) or the small Command Palette (under the fast menu in the Composer window). To programme the small Command Palette, open it before opening the main Command Palette (or make sure 'Active Palette' is selected in the full Command Palette) and drag it to a convenient position on the screen. To programme the keyboard, double-click on the Keyboard setting in the Project

Figure 8.1 Media Composer and Symphony Command Pallette – Move

window and a map of the keyboard is displayed. Although most keys can be changed, the main keys are probably best left alone (or the key caps will need to be moved). In Figures 8.2 and 8.3 the light coloured keys are the ones that may be changed. Hold down the shift key and the shifted keys can also be programmed. On a Mac system, function key f1 can be used, but on NT systems this is the standard Windows Help key and cannot be changed.

Figure 8.2 Media Composer NT default keyboard

Figure 8.3 Xpress NT v4 default keyboard

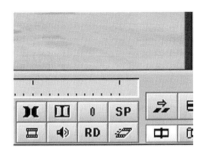

Figure 8.4 Custom buttons in Composer window

It is also possible to put menu items on to buttons – useful to rapidly access functions that are hidden away or have no keyboard shortcuts. To do this, select 'Menu to Button' reassignment in the Command Palette, click on the destination button or keyboard key, then go to the chosen menu and release the mouse on the menu function of your choice. A two-letter abbreviation of the function will appear on the key (Figure 8.4).

If you wish to use a button directly from the Command Palette, select 'Active Palette' (Figure 8.1) and press the button. Media Composer v7 and Symphony v1 don't have this option – on these versions deselect both 'Menu to Button' and 'Button to Button' and the palette can be used. Remember to close down the palette and the keyboard setting window when finished.

Subclips

It can be very useful to break down long master clips into shorter sections. This can be done by making subclips. A subclip acts in a similar way to a master clip in that it can be named, loaded, edited and trimmed and so on. Examples of where this could be useful are long interviews (subclips could be made of each question/

	Name	Tracks	Duration	Start
Renamed subclips	Roadworks	V1 A1-2	1:18	21:2
	Border crossing	V1 A1-2	4:06	21:2
Subclips based on 'Drive Alps'	Drive Alps.Sub.02	V1 A1-2	23:11	21:2
	Drive Alps.Sub.01	V1 A1-2	5:02	21:2
Master clip	Drive Alps	V1 A1-2	6:00:21	21:2

◇ Tape 013
F S T   Useful 1

Figure 8.5 Bin with subclips

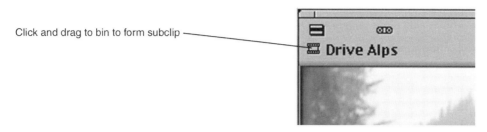

Click and drag to bin to form subclip

Figure 8.6 Making a subclip (Media Composer and Symphony)

answer) or entire tapes that have been digitized in one long clip. The digitized media is not cut or modified by making a subclip.

To make a subclip on any system, load a master clip into the Source monitor, mark an In and an Out, set the track lights, then option+click [Alt+click] on the centre of the monitor and drag back to a bin. The subclip is formed and is ready for naming (Figure 8.5). Media Composer and Symphony users can also click and drag the icon next to the clip name above the monitor back to a bin (Figure 8.6).

If your master clip is called 'red dog', the first subclip will be called 'red dog.sub.01' and so on. If the bin is in text view you will see the small subclip icon. Don't be too worried about making your subclips exactly the right length, as it is possible to trim beyond the end of a subclip into material from the original master clip.

Figure 8.7 Make subclip button

If you wish to make many subclips, there is a Make Subclip button in the Edit tab of the Command Palette (Figure 8.7) that can be mapped to a button (Media Composer and Symphony). This is a standard button in the Xpress pop-up and Composer fast menu. Using this method, the new subclip will arrive in the last bin selected. Holding down the option [Alt] key while using this button opens a dialogue box offering a choice of destination bins for the subclip. Subclips (or in this case subsequences) can also be made from parts of a sequence in the Record monitor – this is useful for saving part of a sequence prior to modifying it, or saving part of a sequence for use in another sequence altogether.

Subclips can also be used in conjunction with the Consolidate command (see Chapter 13) offering a simple way of clearing unwanted media from your drives.

Using the clipboard

Whenever part of a sequence is cut or lifted, it is not immediately lost, but is placed on Avid's clipboard. The section can then be retrieved and edited into a different position, or used as the basis of a new sequence. A marked section can also be copied to the clipboard (the 'C' key or a standard button under the Record monitor on Media Composer and Symphony – Figure 8.8). To see the clipboard contents, select Clipboard from the Tools menu (Media Composer and Symphony) and it will appear in the form of a pop-up monitor. There is a 'Show Clipboard' button in the Xpress Composer fast menu. All or part of the contents can be edited into a sequence. The button set under the Clipboard monitor always mimics that under the Source monitor on Media Composer and Symphony (Figure 8.9).

Figure 8.8 Copy to Clipboard button

Figure 8.9 Media Composer and Symphony Clipboard monitor

Select the pop-up then use the Timeline track panel to set the tracks. Now click back on the pop-up to select it and use the splice or overwrite keys on the keyboard to make the edit – if the buttons on the Composer window are used, the contents of the Source monitor will be used instead (Media Composer and Symphony).

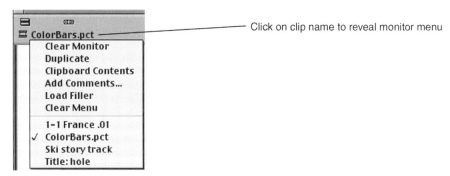

Click on clip name to reveal monitor menu

Figure 8.10 Media Composer and Symphony monitor menu

Alternatively, on Media Composer and Symphony, the clipboard contents can be loaded into the Source monitor by clicking on the current clip name and selecting Clipboard Contents from the monitor menu (this menu is revealed by clicking and holding on the clip name above the Source or Record monitor (Figure 8.10) – this is not the same as the fast menu). If you immediately wish to re-edit the material you remove or copy from your sequence, then hold down the option [Alt] key as you cut, lift or copy and the section will be automatically loaded into the Source monitor (Media Composer and Symphony only). The clipboard is a very quick way to move sections of your programme around, and is often more convenient than segment editing, particularly in a long sequence.

Duplicating sequences

A powerful feature of working on a computer-based system is the ability to have different versions of your edited sequences, at various stages. If you are asked to make major changes to a sequence, don't work on the existing sequence, make a duplicate. A sequence may be duplicated in a bin (select then +D [Ctrl+D]) or from the monitor menu in the Record monitor (if more than one bin is open, you'll see a dialogue box offering a choice). If this is done, the duplicated sequence is loaded into the Record monitor. Rename the duplicate in the bin to avoid confusion. It is good practice to store older versions of sequences in a bin separate from the current sequence. This way, when changes are made to the current sequence and the bin is saved, the system does not have to resave all the older sequences, too. The duplicated sequence uses the same media as the original sequence (media is not duplicated) but it may be re-edited as you wish.

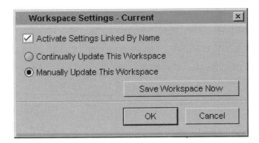

Figure 8.11 Workspace Settings

Workspaces

The idea of an Avid Workspace (not Xpress prior to v3) is to save a 'snapshot' of the windows on the monitors and allow the user to return to this setup later. For instance, when digitizing, the Digitize Tool, the Audio Tool and the Video Input Tool will be needed, and it is useful not to have the Project window obscured by the Digitize Tool. When editing normally, the user may want the Project window in one location on screen, with the Audio Tool, Audio Mix window, Timecode window and Effect Palette (Chapter 10) in particular places. Other configurations will come to mind.

To configure a Workspace, click Settings in the Project window and scroll to the bottom of the list. There will be one setting called Workspace. Duplicate this (click then Edit menu/Duplicate or &+D [Ctrl+D]). Now you have two Workspace settings. Name one of them 'Digitize' (click in the blank central area of the Project window next to the setting name and type). Make sure that the small tick (indicating the active setting) is next to the new Digitize Workspace setting. Now open and arrange the tools and windows you need for digitizing. That's it! Then, click next to the other Workspace setting and name it 'Edit' (or whatever) and rearrange the windows and tools as you'd like them for normal editing. You have made two workspaces (make more if you wish).

To swap workspaces, you can click next to a Workspace setting in the Project window, but it is faster to have buttons or keyboard keys programmed to do this. Open the Command Palette (not Xpress v3 and earlier) and in the Other tab are a number of workspace buttons (W1, W2, etc.). These can be mapped as desired. Note that in Xpress v3 and later, function keys f9–f12 are already mapped to give W1–W4. The workspace buttons automatically assign themselves to the workspaces you have created, in alphabetic or numeric order. Thus, if you have workspace settings named 'Audio', 'Digitize' and 'Normal', they would be activated by buttons W1, W2 and W3.

In Media Composer v7 and Symphony v1, your workspaces will change and update each time a tool or window is moved, opened or closed so be rigorous in switching workspaces rather than opening and closing tools as normal. In later versions (including Xpress v3 and later) it is possible to open a Workspace setting (double-click) and control how the workspace is updated (Figure 8.11). 'Manually Update' allows you to update the workspace only when you wish to. In the settings window is a further option: 'Activate Settings Linked by Name'. If (for example) you have a workspace named 'Effects', you could also have a Timeline view saved with the same name – this would be automatically activated when the Effects workspace was used – a powerful feature.

Active settings

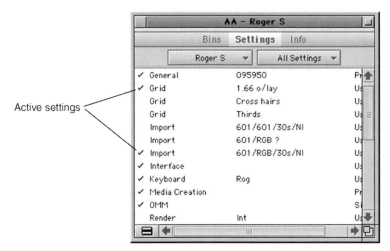

Figure 8.12 Custom settings

More on settings

Duplicating settings

It is possible to duplicate settings (click on one in the Project window to select it then Edit menu/Duplicate or &+D [Ctrl+D]. This is useful if there are two variations of a setting you'd like to use regularly. Simply modify one of the settings and name it (click in the centre of the Project window and name the setting). To switch settings, simply click to the left of the setting of choice and a tick appears (Figure 8.12).

Site settings

If you would like any of your custom settings to become the defaults for future new users and Projects, open the Site Setting window from the Special menu (Media

Composer and Symphony only) and drag settings from your Project window into the Site Setting window; close it when done. These will now over-ride the factory settings. To open and save Site Settings on Xpress, select Settings in the Project window, then choose 'Open Setting File' from the file menu. Navigate to Settings folder inside the Avid Xpress folder and open the Site Setting file. When you have moved your settings, close and save the settings file.

On NT versions of Xpress, take one more step. Minimize Xpress (do not quit) and navigate to the Site Setting file in Windows Explorer. Right-click on the file, choose 'Properties' and set the file to 'Read Only'. If you don't do this, Xpress will overwrite your customized settings with the factory defaults. When you quit from Xpress, you'll see an error message – ignore it. Next time you start, your Site settings will be active. You can now safely deselect 'Read Only' on the setting file.

Storyboard editing

Storyboard editing offers a quick way to make a rough cut from a number of clips in a bin. It is not suitable for every occasion but can be a real time saver. To prepare for a storyboard edit, move your chosen clips into a bin and put the bin into frame view. Now click and drag the clips around the bin until they are displayed in the order you'd like them to appear in the sequence (reading top left to bottom right in the bin). Unless you set in and out marks, the entire clip will be used. This means that if there are parts of long master clips that you'd like to use at different points in the sequence, you'll need to make subclips first.

Make a new sequence (Clip menu) and select all the clips in the bin. Now, with the option [Alt] key held down, click on one of the clips and drag them all into the Record monitor. Keep the option [Alt] key held down until after you release the mouse button. When done, your clips will have been edited into your sequence in the order you set in the bin. This technique can also be used to add one clip to an existing sequence by dragging from a bin. In this case, use option [Alt] to splice a clip and use shift to overwrite a clip. The clip is edited at the position indicator. On Xpress systems, no modifier key is needed when the clips are dragged into the Composer window, unless overwriting; in this case hold down the shift key.

More useful buttons

Match Frame

The basic use of Match Frame is to take the frame currently in the Record monitor and to load that frame into the Source monitor – this is useful if you need to make a Freeze Frame or Motion Effect, both of which can only be done from the Source monitor. Another use would be to get access to other tracks (say audio) associated with a clip where only one track (say video) had originally been edited.

The Match Frame button (Figure 8.13) is in the Composer fast menu, but it is well worth programming one of the Record monitor buttons or keyboard keys (not Xpress v3 and earlier) as this function is regularly needed. With the Record monitor active, press Match Frame and the frame on which the position indicator is parked will be seen in the Source monitor – the whole clip is loaded, giving access to adjacent frames (the highest track selected in the Timeline is matched). An In mark is placed on the matched frame and any Out mark cleared. If the option [Alt] key is held down while matching, any marks on the source clip remain unchanged – useful if making different motion effects from the same marked section.

Figure 8.13 Match Frame button

Users of Media Composer v10, Symphony v3 and Xpress v4 and later can quickly match a clip on any track without having to set the track lights. Mac users should ⌘+double-click on a track light in the track panel; Windows users should right-click on a track light and choose 'Match Frame Track' from the menu. The clip at the position indicator will be used for the match.

Match Frame can be used with the Source monitor active but has a modified function. Source side match frame lets you match a frame from a subclip, sequence, motion effect or freeze frame back to the matching frame on the original master clip. If a master clip is already in the Source monitor, a match cannot be made and an alert sound is heard.

A final variant is Reverse Match Frame (not Xpress); this checks the frame in the Source monitor (on the highest selected track) and searches the sequence in the Record monitor for a matching frame. To use Reverse Match Frame on a Mac, hold down Ctrl+Match Frame. On NT systems there is a specific Reverse Match Frame button in the Command Palette (Figure 8.14). It is not in the fast menu so it will need to be mapped to a button for regular use. This is available on both Mac and NT in Media Composer v10, although the Mac shortcut still works.

Figure 8.14 Reverse Match Frame button

Find Bin

Pressing Find Bin (Figure 8.15, not Xpress v3 and earlier) with the Source monitor active will open (or bring forward) the bin containing the current source clip, and highlight the clip in the bin. On the Record side, the sequence is highlighted in its bin. If the option [Alt] button is held down when pressing Find Bin on the Record side, the actual clip at the current position, on the highest active track, rather than the sequence, will be highlighted in its bin.

Figure 8.15 Find Bin button

Find Frame

Pressing this button (Command Palette, Media Composer and Symphony only, Figure 8.16), prompts the user to load the tape related to the current frame in the Source or Record monitor. Once loaded into the VTR, Avid will spool through the tape and cue up on the frame.

Figure 8.16 Find Frame button

Locators

The Add Locator button (on the standard button set or the Composer fast menu, Figure 8.17) adds a locator (or cue mark) to a master clip, subclip or sequence (all versions). The default locator appears as a reddish oval shape in the displayed frame in the Composer or pop-up. By clicking on the locator in the frame, a window appears in which text can be added, which is displayed at the bottom of the frame. This is very useful for quickly making notes about a clip or sequence. In Media Composer v10, Symphony v3 and Xpress v4, option [Alt]+clicking Add Locator automatically adds the locator and opens the text entry box and the Locator Tool (Figure 8.18).

Figure 8.17 Add Locator button

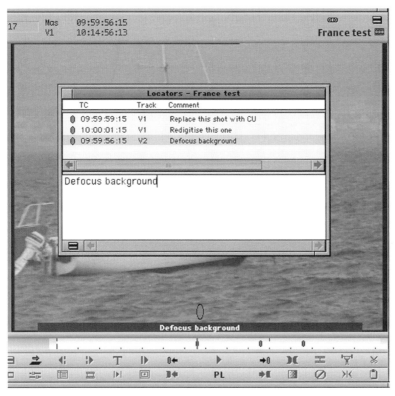

Figure 8.18 Locator Tool (Media Composer v10)

The Locator Tool in the Tools menu displays a window of all the locators associated with a clip or sequence. It is possible to edit and copy the text, colour code and sort the locators (from the fast menu) and to quickly move to a spot in the clip by double-clicking on the appropriate locator in the list. Locators are easily deleted from the Locator Tool window by selecting and pressing Delete. To delete a locator from the Composer window, move to the frame and press Delete with the appropriate track selected.

Figure 8.18 shows the Locator Tool in Media Composer v10, Xpress v4 and Symphony v3. In earlier versions the Locator Tool shows all the locators for a clip but does not automatically appear when adding a new locator or modifying an existing locator in the Composer window.

Locators can be added when digitizing single clips (all versions except Xpress) and when Batch digitizing (Media Composer v10 and Symphony v3). Press key f3 while digitizing and red locators will appear in the clip when digitizing is finished. Since f3 always does this when digitizing, it is a good idea to program that key with the locator button for use at other times, too. In Media Composer v8 (Mac), v9 (NT) and Symphony v2 and later, various coloured locators can also be added during digitizing using function keys f5–f12.

If the Add Locator button is mapped to the keyboard, locators can be added on the fly while editing. In recent versions, various coloured locators can be added by using the keys in the Command Palette ('More' tab). This feature is not available in Media Composer v7, Xpress v3 and earlier, and Symphony v1. Coloured locators of your choice can be displayed in the Timeline (see Chapter 7).

It is possible to set the FF and REW keys to stop at locators – do this in the Composer settings (all versions except Xpress). All Xpress models use FF and REW solely for this purpose. In Media Composer v10, Symphony v3 and Xpress v4 and later, there are specific buttons to go to locators; Figure 8.19 shows these buttons programmed to the Composer button set.

        Go to previous locator   Go to next locator

Figure 8.19 Go to Locator buttons

Add Edit

The Add Edit command (Figure 8.20) puts an artificial cut in a clip. It is useful to split an audio clip so that a change can be made in one part and not another and it can be used on video clips so that an effect can apply to one segment and not another. An Add Edit can be placed in filler on a track so that sync trimming can take place (see Chapter 6). Once these 'invisible' edits are in place, Avid refers to them as 'Match Frame Edits'. There is an option in the Clip menu to remove them (not Xpress v3 and earlier) – this works globally on selected tracks or between marks on selected tracks. Note that if audio or video changes have been made on one side of the Match Frame edit, 'Remove Match Frame Edits' will not work. In this case, either reset the offending clips to their default state or trim the edit to one end of a clip, when it will vanish. Match Frame Edits selected in Trim mode can be removed by pressing 'Delete'.

Figure 8.20 Add Edit button

Replace Edit

Replace (not Xpress v3 and earlier) is another editing command (Figure 8.21). The Replace key (in the Composer fast menu) allows you to replace a clip in the Timeline without setting any marks. It has the valuable property of synchronizing the position of the source position indicator with the record position indicator – great for synchronizing music beats or sound effects with action.

Figure 8.21 Replace Edit button

To use Replace, park on a clip in the Timeline (with the appropriate track lights on); load a clip into the Source monitor and park on the frame which you'd like to hit the record position indicator. Press Replace and the clip in the Timeline is replaced from cut to cut with the new clip. Replace also works with segments of differing lengths on different tracks (Figure 8.22). In this case, if all three track lights are on, all three segments will be replaced.

ns	Mini sidece	Beach		Breakfast			Breakfast	E
ns	Mini sidece	Beach			Breakfast	Breakfast		E
ns	Mini sidece	Beach			Breakfast	Breakfast		E

10:00:50:00   10:01:00:00

Figure 8.22 Replacing segments (1)

What if the synchronizing point is within one segment, but not within the others? Select all of the segments with either of the segment editing buttons and the marked segments will be replaced, synchronizing correctly (Figure 8.23). Replace can also be used to overwrite a marked section on the record side, instead of replacing an entire clip.

ns	Mini sidece	Beach	Breakfast			Breakfast	E
ns	Mini sidece	Beach		Breakfast	Breakfast		E
ns	Mini sidece	Beach		Breakfast	Breakfast		E

10:00:50:00   10:01:00:00

Figure 8.23 Replacing segments (2)

Sync Point Editing

Sync Point Editing (not Xpress) takes the idea of Replace a step further. With Sync Point Editing turned on (select the Composer window then look in the Special menu), it is possible to set marks on either the source or record sides, and synchronize the frames where the position indicators are set. A total of two marks is needed, either both on the source side, both on the record side or one mark on each side. When Sync Point Editing is active, the black box beneath the Overwrite button in the Composer window shows an orange indicator (Figure 8.24). Turn off Sync Point Editing when finished.

Orange light appears during Sync Point Editing

Figure 8.24 Overwrite (Sync Point Editing)

Editing with ganged pop-ups

If your footage has been shot with multiple cameras (perhaps a sitcom or a concert) there are ways to edit this material quickly and effectively on Media Composer and Symphony. Xpress does not offer any multicamera features but a workaround is described later. The simplest way to see all the camera angles on Media Composer or Symphony is to load one clip into the Source monitor and the other clips into pop-up monitors. To force a clip to load in a pop-up, hold down option [Alt] when double-clicking the clip in the bin. Note that the pop-ups will only play on the Edit monitor on a Mac system. On NT, they will play on either monitor.

To synchronize your clips, move to a common frame on each pop-up and the Source monitor. This can be done by timecode, by finding a slate or clapper, or simply by identifying a common point in all the clips. Now lock all the pop-ups, the Source monitor and the Record monitor together using the Gang button or icon (Figure 8.25). The gang button looks like two chainwheels linked together and the icon can be seen above the Source and Record monitor if two rows of information are displayed (see Composer settings). If it isn't visible there it will be on the second row of buttons under each monitor or in the fast menu. Simply click the gang button on the record side and the Source monitor will be ganged; then click the gang icon on each pop-up and all are locked together.

Figure 8.25 Gang button

As you edit, only one monitor will play in real time but all ganged monitors will catch up when play stops; thus, after each edit, all monitors will be in step and the next shot can quickly be chosen. Edit from the pop-ups as described in the section on the Clipboard.

Multicam and Group clips

An alternative method (not Xpress and not all models of Media Composer) is to use Group clips. A Group clip contains multiple master clips but can be edited as one clip. When loaded into the Source monitor, up to four (prior to Media Composer v10) or nine (Media Composer v10 and Symphony v3) sources can be viewed simultaneously (Figure 8.26). Clips can be grouped based on In or Out marks, or on timecode. To group clips with common timecode, move the clips into one bin and select them. Now choose 'Multigroup' (if available) from the Bin menu. This command will automatically group and synchronize the clips and a Group clip will appear in the Bin (Figure 8.27).

If your clips do not have common timecode, load each one into the Source monitor and set either an In or Out mark at some convenient sync point such as a visual cue or clapper board. Now select all the clips in the bin as before and choose 'Group Clips' from the Bin menu; choose the appropriate sync method

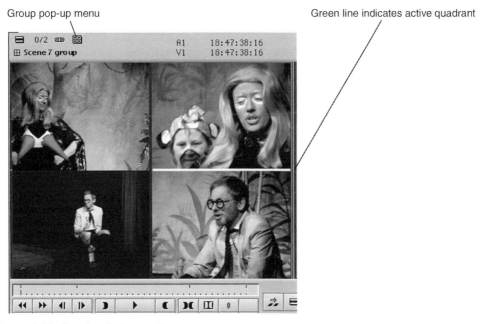

Group pop-up menu   Green line indicates active quadrant

Figure 8.26 Quad split in monitor

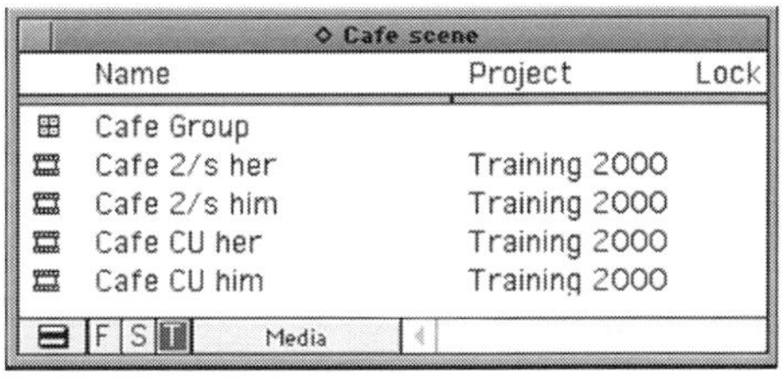

◇ Cafe scene		
Name	Project	Lock
⊞ Cafe Group		
▱ Cafe 2/s her	Training 2000	
▱ Cafe 2/s him	Training 2000	
▱ Cafe CU her	Training 2000	
▱ Cafe CU him	Training 2000	
▤ F S T Media ◁		

Figure 8.27 Group clip in bin

from the dialogue box that appears. Click OK and your new group clip appears in the bin.

Group clips and multicamera editing are most effective if Avid's real-time multicam playback is available. This was not available in Media Composer v8 and v9 and Symphony v1 and v2. In Media Composer v7, if the system had the Hardware Multicam option, and the clips were digitized at one of the 'm' (multicam) resolutions, then up to four 'quads' could be played in real time. Multicam resolutions returned in Media Composer v10 (an option) and Symphony v3 as standard. If your system does not have this option, most of the multicam routine can still be used.

Load a group clip into the Source monitor and only one camera angle initially appears. Pressing the up and down cursor keys on the keyboard will toggle through the camera angles in the monitor (these two keys are programmed with the 'Next in Group' and 'Previous in Group' functions, by default (Figure 8.28). From the Composer fast menu, choose Quad or Nine-way split (Figure 8.29) and four or nine (depending on the system) camera angles appear (Figure 8.26). The current active angle is indicated with a green line. If you have more sources in your group than can be displayed, hold down the control key and click on one segment; a pop-up menu showing all the angles will appear from which an alternative can be selected. If the clip is played, only the active angle is seen, unless the multicam options (described above) are available. Note that although mixed resolutions work within the 'm' family, and they will play as a cut in the Record monitor, they won't play as a multi-way split.

Figure 8.28 Next in Group and Previous in Group buttons

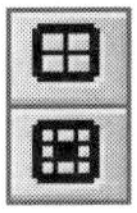

Figure 8.29 Quad and Nine-way Split buttons

Figure 8.30 Group icon menu

If the group clip is edited across to the Record monitor, it will be possible to change the camera angles on the fly, from the keyboard. If you'd like the audio to cut with the video, choose 'Audio Follow Video' from the menu that appears when you click on the Group icon above the Source monitor (Figure 8.30). Once the group clip is edited into the Record monitor, choose Multicam mode from the Special menu; the Composer window changes (the source side buttons are hidden – Figure 8.31).

Figure 8.31 Multicam mode

On the standard keyboard setting in Media Composer v7, function keys f9–f12 are programmed as Q1–Q4 (quads). In Media Composer v10 and Symphony v3, function keys f9–f12 are programmed as M1–M4 (multicam) and shift+f9–shift+f12 give M5–M8. As the sequence is played these buttons can be pressed to edit on the fly. Nothing appears to happen in the Timeline until play stops, at which point all the cuts can be seen. Parking on a segment in the Timeline and using 'Next in Group' or 'Previous in Group' changes the segment to a different angle. An alternative approach is to play through the Group clip on the Record side, pressing Add Edit at each chosen cut point. When done, go back and change the angles as described above.

Note that on ABVB systems with a 3D board, no effects, rendered or real-time, will play with the 'm' resolutions. To see effects that you add to the sequence on a 3D system, disable the 3D board when launching Media Composer. This is done by holding down the 'f' and 'x' keys on the keyboard when launching. A message appears asking whether to enable or disable the 3D board. Choose 'Disable'. The 3D board will be back on next time the program is launched normally.

Multicam editing on Xpress

There are no specific multicam editing tools on Xpress systems, but a useful workaround can be applied. If you have four cameras, make a new sequence with four video tracks. Now carefully edit camera one's footage on to track one, camera two's to track two and so on, synchronizing by timecode or clapper. Now, by moving the video monitor in the track panel from track to track each angle can be viewed. Use Add Edit to break up the clips then use Segment editing (Lift/Overwrite) to move clips down to V1. As a refinement, consider breaking up each clip and lifting out the NG sections before editing.

9 Working with audio

- Audio Settings
- The Audio Tool
- The Audio Mix Tool
- Using audio keyframes
- Audio gain automation
- Audio Punch-in
- The Equalization Tool
- AudioSuite plug-ins
- Audio Mixdown
- Importing CD tracks

Audio can be dealt with in many ways on Avid systems. All the audio can be balanced, mixed and equalized on the computer and output to tape as the final mix or, when offline editing, little audio work may be done and the mix completed in a dubbing suite. In between are other options, such as outputting tracks via a mixer and balancing the sound on the fly, or outputting multiple tracks directly to a suitable tape machine for further work elsewhere. If you plan to finish on the Avid, the edit suite really needs a good amplifier and loudspeakers and appropriate sound deadening and isolation. The typical setup with the disk drives and computer whirring and whistling next to the editor does not make for a good audio environment!

Audio Settings

The Audio Settings (Project window) offer a choice of pan as the clips play back (the default is 'L/R', i.e., tracks 1, 3, 5, etc., play left and tracks 2, 4, 6, etc., play right). The alternative is 'All tracks centered'. Note that clips can be changed individually later, during editing. This is also the place to set the scrub parameters (Figure 9.1, described in Chapter 5). In Media Composer v7, v8 NT, Symphony v1, and Xpress v2, the features of the Audio Project setting (Chapter 3) are combined with the Audio settings.

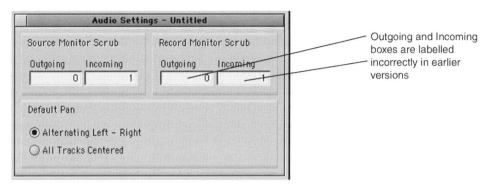

Figure 9.1 Audio Settings (Media Composer v10)

The Audio Tool

The Audio Tool (Tools menu) (⌘+1) [Ctrl+1] is used for checking levels when digitizing but it is also needed while editing (Figure 9.2). Clicking on the small speaker icon opens a slider for master output level. Don't be tempted to use this for changing your monitoring level as your output levels will be changed, too. Systems

Figure 9.2 Audio Tool (Xpress)

with a Digidesign Audiomedia card also have a microphone icon in the Audio Tool. Clicking on this reveals a slider for globally adjusting input levels (see Chapter 3, p. 30).

Clicking on the rightmost icon (Figure 9.3) reveals the output options. Default output is a stereo mix to channels 1 and 2 and this can be changed in the pop-ups, depending on the total number of hardware output channels on the system. Figure 9.4 shows options for eight-channel systems. Mono output is available, or the stereo output can be routed to a different pair of channels. It is also possible to map Timeline tracks to particular output channels when using Direct Out. The number of channels available (which is not the same as the maximum number of tracks in a sequence, usually 24) will be either two, four or eight, depending on the hardware. All systems covered will monitor up to eight tracks, regardless of the hardware.

Figure 9.3 Audio Tool options button

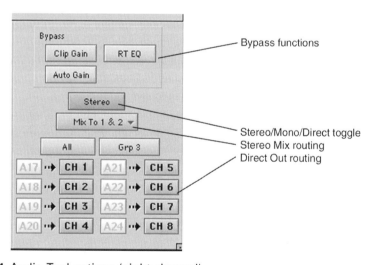

Figure 9.4 Audio Tool options (eight channel)

The output options include the ability to bypass or override EQ, Clip Gain and Automation Gain – see later. A further menu is hidden under the 'PH' (Peak Hold) button (Figure 9.5). Here are choices to recalibrate the meters and to create and play back line-up tone (see later).

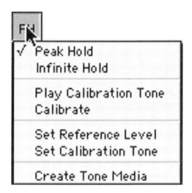

Figure 9.5 Audio Tool Peak Hold menu

Audio Mix Tool

There are two main ways to adjust audio levels in a sequence. The first is by the use of the Audio Mix Tool (Tools menu – Figure 9.6). This allows the adjustment of level and pan on a clip-by-clip basis. It also allows the adjustment of the audio of a source clip, if the Source monitor is active when using the Audio Mix tool. This is particularly useful if a clip that will be edited several times is too loud or too quiet – setting the level in the Source monitor means it only has to be done once. From Media Composer v10, Symphony v3 and Xpress v4, it is possible to display only four of the eight tracks available in the Audio Mix Tool, thus saving desktop space. Earlier versions always show the maximum number of tracks.

To enable a track for adjustment, make sure that there is a speaker icon next to the track in the Track Panel, or choose a track from the pop-ups in the Audio Mix Tool. Unusually, the track lights do not need to be set when using Audio Mix. Now it is possible to change the level of the clip at the position indicator by adjusting the slider. The level can also be adjusted in small increments by using the keyboard cursor keys; values can also be typed in using the numeric keypad. These levels are not absolute, they all relate to the 0 dB point on the slider, which is the level at which the clip was digitized.

Pan can be adjusted by clicking in the box below the channel and dragging the slider (Figure 9.7). To quickly set the pan to the mid-point, option [Alt]-click on the slider (option [Alt]-clicking on the level slider sets the level back to 0 dB). To adjust more than one channel at once, click on the gang buttons on each channel (they turn green) and the chosen channels will be locked together. Channels don't need to be at the same level for ganging to work – once ganged, any offset between them is maintained.

Note that only the clip (or clips) at the position indicator will be adjusted. To adjust all the clips on a track, first make the adjustment on one clip. Now (on versions up to Media Composer v8, Symphony v1 and Xpress v2) click on the gang

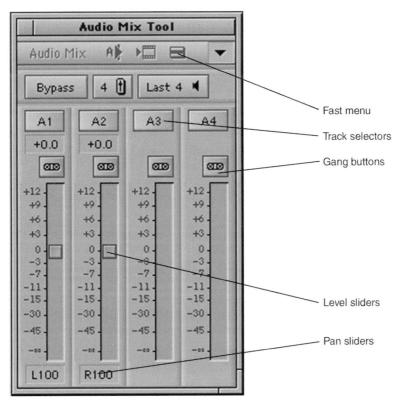

Figure 9.6 Audio Mix Tool

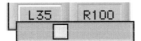

Figure 9.7 Pop-up Pan slider

button on the appropriate channel or channels. Next click on the Audio Mix fast menu and use the options for setting the level or mix globally, i.e., for the whole track (Figure 9.8). On later versions the fast menu is only operational if the track selectors (the boxes indicating the track number in the Audio Mix window) are clicked. When selected, they turn purple.

To adjust a number of clips, but not the whole track, set an In mark somewhere in the first clip, and an Out in the last clip (the marks don't need to be set exactly at the beginning or end of the clips, entire clips are adjusted) and the options in the fast menu change to 'Set . . . In/Out'. Another choice is 'Adjust . . .', which will display a dialogue box allowing overall adjustments of volume and pan.

Figure 9.8 Audio Mix fast menu choices

To see a display in the Timeline of the audio level you have set, choose Clip Gain in the Timeline fast menu (see Chapter 7). In versions earlier than Media Composer v10, Xpress v4 and Symphony v3, choose Volume.

If you are using Media Composer and Symphony and have many source clips that need the pan centring (perhaps narration recorded on only one track), this can be done quickly by selecting them in a bin and choosing 'Center Pan' from the Clip menu. Think before you do this as, in versions prior to Media Composer v10 and Symphony v3, there is no way of reversing the operation other than loading each clip into the Source monitor in turn and adjusting the pan with the Audio Mix Tool. In current versions, selected clips can have the default pan restored (Clip menu).

Using audio keyframes

Audio keyframes allow different audio levels to be set within a clip. This can be done manually (described next) or by riding the levels on the fly, using either the mouse or an external mixer connected via a MIDI interface to the computer (much easier).

To add audio keyframes manually, first prepare a Timeline view with one or more wide audio tracks with the audio Volume (earlier versions) or Auto Gain (later versions) displayed (see Chapter 7). If the track is sufficiently wide, dB levels will be shown. Each keyframe that is added acts as an anchor point – the audio can ramp up or down as it approaches the next keyframe (Figure 9.9). Select the appropriate track (or tracks) and press the Add Keyframe button (on the keyboard – Figure 9.10) and a keyframe will appear in the clip. If no keyframe appears, try widening the track a little; keyframes don't appear in very narrow tracks.

The audio level at the keyframe is the default unless the level of the whole clip has been changed using Audio Mix. In this case, in versions prior to Media Composer v10, Xpress v4 and Symphony v3, the keyframe takes the adjusted clip level (−4 dB, +7 dB or whatever). In fact, if the clip level has been changed, even if no keyframes are added, a black line indicates the level in these versions. This will not display in

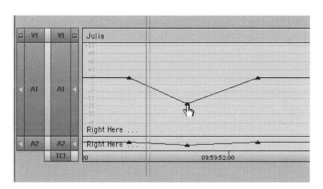

Figure 9.9 Audio keyframes in Timeline

Figure 9.10 Add Keyframe

Media Composer v10, Xpress v4 and Symphony v3 unless Clip Gain is selected in the Timeline fast menu instead of or in addition to Auto Gain.

By moving the mouse pointer over the keyframe and clicking and dragging, the level can be changed – the level is shown in a small window at the bottom of the Timeline.

By adding more keyframes, the level can be changed from point to point. If a keyframe exists at the same point on selected tracks, all the keyframes will be adjusted together – an exception is if some of the tracks are so narrow that the keyframes will not display. To move a keyframe along to left or right, option [Alt]+click+drag. To delete a keyframe, float the mouse pointer over the keyframe (on a selected track), wait until the pointer turns into a hand, and press Delete. To adjust the level of multiple keyframes, place an In mark upstream and an Out mark downstream; all keyframes will move together when one is dragged (Figure 9.11).

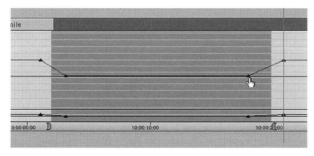

Figure 9.11 Adjusting multiple audio keyframes

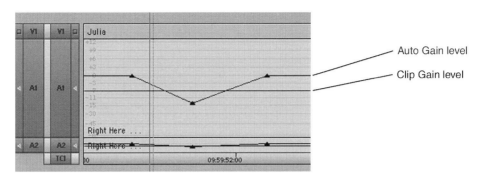

Figure 9.12 Clip Gain and Auto Gain in the Timeline

In Media Composer v10, Xpress v4 and Symphony v3, Auto Gain is independent of Clip Gain and either can be adjusted at any time. Auto Gain still takes the Clip Gain level (set by the Audio Mix Tool) as a baseline, but this is displayed as 0 dB. Any adjustment above or below this is an offset from the Clip Gain level. In these versions and later, an overall level change can be made by going back and making an adjustment in the Audio Mix Tool. Figure 9.12 shows both Clip Gain and Auto Gain displayed in the Timeline.

In earlier versions, if Auto Gain has been applied, the Audio Mix Tool displays the word 'Auto' under the track number and Audio Mix cannot be used again until all Auto Gain has been removed. Likewise, if a level has been set using Audio Mix, then if the Auto Gain window is in use (see next section), the word 'Clip' is visible under the track number, indicating that the level has been set using Audio Mix. In both cases, the track fader is removed. In the latter case, however, keyframes can be added in the Timeline and adjustments made. The track fader will then appear in the Auto Gain window.

Audio Gain Automation

To change levels on the fly, open the Automation Gain tool (Tools Menu). Levels can be adjusted and keyframes automatically added by dragging with the mouse on the faders or by means of an external JL Cooper or Yamaha mixer connected to the computer via a MIDI interface.

First mark a section (mark I/O) in your sequence. Select the tracks in the Timeline and set the gang buttons for the tracks you wish to adjust in the Automation Gain tool (Figure 9.13). Set a pre-roll and post-roll and you are ready to go (the pre-roll lets you listen to the levels as you approach the point where adjustment will begin). Click the Record button – as you reach the Mark In in the sequence, click and drag on one of the activated faders to set the level – you'll hear

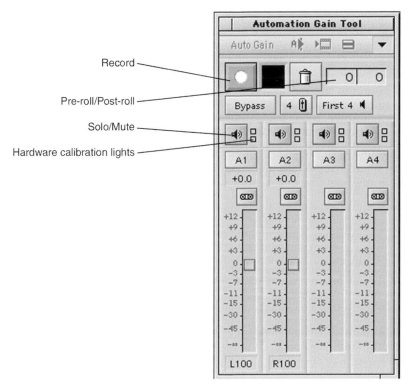

Figure 9.13 Automation Gain Tool

the change. If you are using the mouse, let go of the button as soon as you are happy or you will add too many keyframes. Also, in versions prior to Media Composer v10, Xpress v4 and Symphony v3, the position indicator doesn't update while the mouse button is pressed. When you've finished, you'll see a number of new

Figure 9.14 Auto Gain fast menu choices

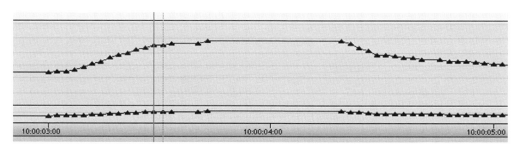

Figure 9.15 Audio keyframes before filtering

keyframes in the Timeline and you can play back the section. If things go wrong, click the trash icon in the window.

At this stage it is advisable to cut down on the number of keyframes (this will increase the chances of the ramping playing successfully in conjunction with other real-time effects). Go to the fast menu in the Automation Gain tool (Figure 9.14) and choose 'Filter Automation Gain'. Make sure that the gang buttons are still lit on your tracks (early versions) or the channel selectors are on (later versions). This will remove around 10 per cent of the keyframes; repeat the process until the number of key frames is reduced so far as to keep the ramping without too many frames. In early versions, masses of keyframes are visible in the Timeline after using Automation Gain. In later versions, fewer keyframes are displayed unless the Timeline magnification is increased but this filtering still needs to be done (Figure 9.15). In recent versions, small pink keyframes appear in the Timeline on audio clips where Automation Gain has been used, even if the audio levels are not part of the Timeline display.

As mentioned, in earlier versions the Audio Mix tool cannot be used on a clip containing keyframes – remove them by either selecting the clip with a segment editing button and pressing Delete (all audio modifications will be removed), or using 'Remove Automation Gain Global' in the Automation Gain tool fast menu.

Figure 9.16 Audio Tool selector pop-up

It is possible to switch between Audio Mix, Automation Gain, Audio Equalization and AudioSuite Plug-ins by clicking on the name of the current tool at the top left of the window (Figure 9.16). Like the Audio Mix tool, The Automation Gain tool can be set to display either four or eight tracks in current versions.

Audio Punch-in

Audio Punch-in is a facility to allow recording to the Timeline while the sequence is playing back – useful for quickly laying narration to picture (Figure 9.17). The Punch-in Tool (Tools menu) offers the choice of recording to an existing audio track or adding a new track (click on the track pop-ups). The microphone or mixer will need to be connected to one of the inputs on the audio interface or audio card. The usual default offered is the highest pair of channels available (i.e., three and four on a four-channel Avid or seven and eight on an eight-channel Avid). To change the channel, option [Alt]+click on the channel pop-ups in the window. The two pop-ups at the bottom of the window allow a choice of bin in which to store the new clip and a media drive to store the media.

Like the Automation Gain tool, you can set a pre-roll and post-roll before pressing the red record button. The trash icon will abort the recording. You may wish to solo one or more existing tracks in the Timeline before recording; +click

Figure 9.17 Audio Punch-in Tool

[Ctrl+click] on one or more audio monitors (current systems) to solo those track(s). Not all versions allow you to solo more than one track. When recording is finished, clips will appear in the designated bin and in the Timeline.

With a bit of clever audio patching, the Avid output can be routed to a piece of outboard audio hardware such as a compressor, and the modified sound recorded back into the Timeline.

Audio equalization

All Avid systems described here offer clip-based audio EQ; the EQ Tool is in the Tools menu (Figure 9.18). Audio equalization means that we can boost or cut particular frequencies, rather than the entire audio spectrum. This can help clean up the sound or make selected clips stand out from the background music or effects. The Avid has what is known as a 'parametric' equalizer. This means that the editor can pick a frequency that may need to be boosted or cut, and then define a narrow or wide range (bandwidth or 'Q' as an audio engineer would put it) around that frequency to adjust.

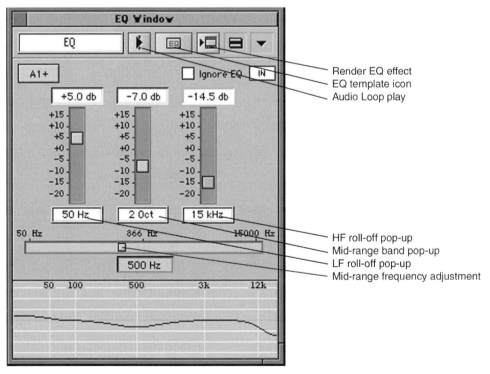

Figure 9.18 Audio EQ Tool

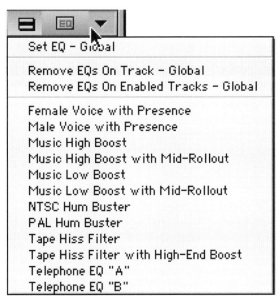

Figure 9.19 EQ Tool preset effects

To apply EQ to a clip or clips, park the position indicator on the selected clip in the Timeline and turn on the appropriate track lights (more than one track can be adjusted at one time) and open the EQ Tool. There are three faders: low, mid-range and high. Beneath the low and high faders are pop-up boxes offering a choice of frequency to start the boost or roll-off. The main frequency dealt with by the mid-range fader is set by the position of the horizontal slider and the bandwidth addressed by this fader is set from the pop-up (a wide two-octave bandwidth or narrow quarter-octave band). Simply dragging one of the faders will apply an EQ effect to the clip in the Timeline. As with the Audio Mix window, there are choices in the fast menu to apply the EQ to a selection of marked clips.

As you adjust the EQ, you can use the Audio Loop Play button in the EQ window to repeatedly play a marked section. Keep the section fairly short – the change you make will be played the next loop around. If no marks are set, the system loops the duration of the shortest audio segment at the position indicator.

Once you are happy with the equalization, you can save the parameters as a template. Simply click on the EQ icon (top centre in the window) and drag it back to a bin, where it can be renamed. The template may be applied to a clip by simply dragging from the bin to the Timeline or (after selecting multiple segments) by double-clicking. Several useful preset EQ templates are available from the fast menu (Figure 9.19). These are stored in a Site EQs Bin, inside the Site Effects folder in the Avid application folder. If this bin is opened, your own templates can be added to the list.

Figure 9.20 AudioSuite plug-in choices

AudioSuite plug-ins

A more comprehensive array of software audio tools is available in the form of the AudioSuite plug-ins (Tools menu). Like the EQ tool, the AudioSuite effects are clip-based and are applied in a similar way. Park on the clip you wish to modify and open the AudioSuite window and check that the correct tracks are set in the pop-up on the left of the window (hold down the shift key to add extra tracks to the active track). Now click on the plug-in selection window (it will display 'None' at the start) and pick a plug-in. Figure 9.20 shows the standard plug-ins available in Media Composer v10 (other versions and systems may have different plug-ins). More plug-ins (either from Digidesign or other manufacturers) may be installed (Mac) in the Plug-ins folder, in the DAE folder in the System Folder, and (Windows) in C:\Program Files\Digidesign\DAE\Plug-Ins. Included in the range of effects are Invert (which inverts the phase of a clip), Reverse (which reverses the playback of a clip), Time Compression Expansion (which is a bit like a motion effect for sound) and Pitch Shift (great to make your interviewees sound like Pinky and Perky).

Once an effect has been chosen, press the large Plug-in icon and a control window specific to the effect will open. Several buttons at the top of this window are common to all effects: Preview (which doesn't work on all effects), Render (all effects need to be rendered before playing back the entire clip), Bypass, Cancel and

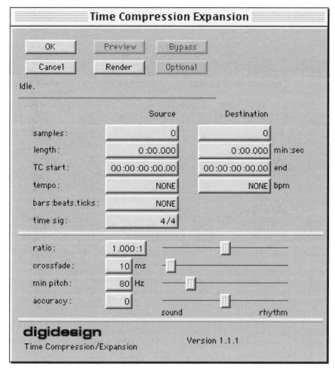

Figure 9.21 Time Compression/Expansion plug-in parameters

OK. Preview will play back a short section of the clip; a pop-up for choosing the destination media drive for the rendered effect is below the plug-in selection pop-up. Figure 9.21 shows the controls for the Digidesign Time Compression/Expansion plug-in.

All versions allow AudioSuite plug-ins to be applied to segments in the Timeline (Figure 9.22) but Media Composer v9, Symphony v2 and Xpress v2.5 and later also have the ability to create new master clips. This is especially useful with effects such as Time Compression Expansion, which will create a clip that differs in length to the original. To make new master clips, simply drag and drop

Figure 9.22 Plug-in in Timeline

Figure 9.23 AudioSuite window showing Master Clip options

an existing master clip or clips on to the AudioSuite window and the window expands (Figure 9.23) with extra controls and parameters. These options allow choice of source clip, loading the clip from the Source monitor into the window, loading the new clip back into the Source monitor and choice of bin to save the new clip. When the new master clip is saved, an AudioSuite template is also saved to the bin. This may be dragged back into the AudioSuite window and be applied to other clips.

Audio Mixdown

If your audio is complex and has many tracks, you may wish to do a premix on some or all of the audio tracks. To do this, set a Mark In and a Mark Out (or set no marks and do the entire sequence). Now choose Audio Mixdown from the Special menu (Media Composer and Symphony) or the Clip Menu (Xpress). It is possible to mix down to a mono track or to a stereo pair (Figure 9.24). If the default destination tracks offered are not what you want, choose a new destination track or tracks from the pop-up box. Choose a bin for the mixdown clip to be stored in and a media drive for the new media file(s) that will be created. Check that the selected section of your sequence is the piece you intended (look at the timecode boxes on the right) and press OK. A copy of the sequence prior to the mixdown will be saved if 'Save Premix Sequence' is selected.

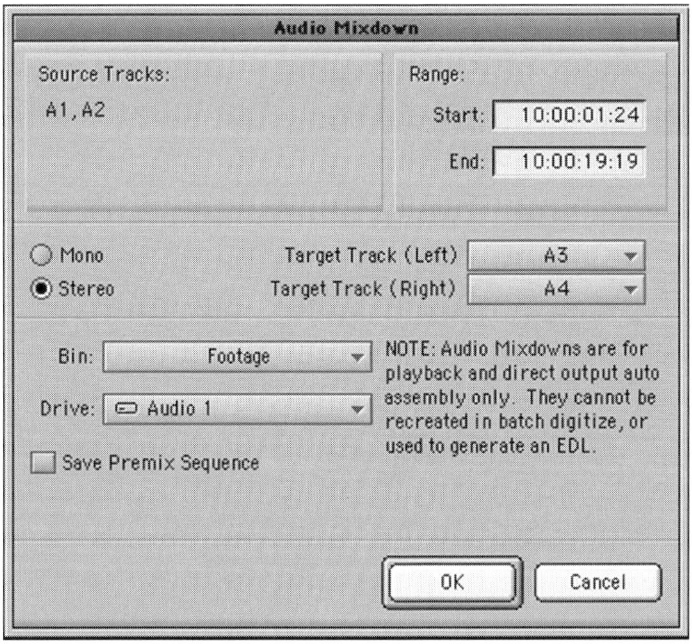

Figure 9.24 Audio Mixdown window

Note the warning at the right-hand side of the window – audio mixdowns contain no timecode and no way of matching back to the original clips. Audio Mixdown is a good way to simplify your audio prior to exporting a Quicktime file.

Importing CD tracks

Media Composer v10, Symphony v3 and Xpress v4 allow direct import of tracks from audio CDs in the computer's CD-ROM drive. Insert a CD, choose a bin and choose 'Import' from the file menu. Navigate to the CD and choose your track(s). See Figures 4.6 and 4.7 for illustrations of the Mac and Windows Import dialogue boxes.

Users of earlier versions cannot import audio directly. See Appendix B for methods of importing audio on earlier systems.

10 2D video effects

Video effects on Avid can mean many things. At one extreme is the simple transition effect (a dissolve or wipe from one clip to another) while at the other, a clip may be colour-corrected, be resized and moved, played at a different speed and be keyed over a different background. Most of the controls are fairly straightforward and logical and the skilled editor can bring various effects together to construct complex composites.

Most current Avid systems will play two video streams, in real time, providing that the right combination of drives or drive striping for the chosen video compression is used. Any more, and some rendering has to be done (rendering an effect creates a new media file to play the effect). Some earlier systems had no real time effects at all and, amongst the current systems, Xpress DV has no real-time effects (i.e., everything must be rendered). Another exception would be a current system with the single-stream uncompressed video option; here all effects involving more than one stream of video would need to be rendered. Some effects on Xpress Plus and Xpress Deluxe will have to be rendered where they would play in real time on other systems.

Effects may be divided into horizontal (transition or segment effects on one video track) and vertical (effects on multiple video tracks). A transition effect makes a change from one clip to the next – examples would be dissolves and wipes. Segment effects modify the appearance of a segment – examples would be a mask or a resize. Effects involving multiple tracks include superimpositions, titles and imported graphics with alpha channels. This chapter will not be a tedious listing of every Avid effect – once the techniques have been learned on a typical transition or segment, they can be applied to others.

In addition to the video streams, Avid has a third uncompressed real-time graphics and title stream – the Downstream Keyer (DSK). On some Xpress models and versions, titles and graphics are not real-time. See Chapter 12 for more details.

Effects can be added to a sequence in Source/Record mode or in Effect mode. Transition effects can also be added in Trim mode. The Effect Editor gives control over all effect parameters (such as image position, scale, colour, border, background and so on). Motion Effects and Freeze Frames are created in a different way to the other effects; we'll start with those.

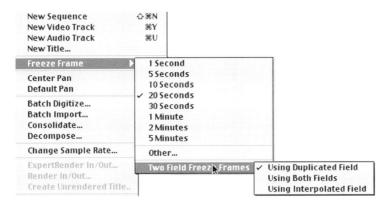

Figure 10.1 Freeze Frame dialogue

Freeze Frames

Avid deals with Freeze Frames by making a new clip that must then be edited into a sequence. If the shot you wish to freeze has already been used, use Match Frame to get the original master clip into the Source monitor (Freeze Frames cannot be made directly from a sequence). Now choose Freeze Frame from the Clip menu (Figure 10.1). If you are working with a single-field resolution, simply choose a duration (or choose 'Other' and enter a duration). You will be prompted for a media drive on which to store the new media file, and for a bin in which to store the effect clip. When done, the effect clip will be loaded into the Source monitor, ready to be edited into the sequence.

Using two-field resolutions

If you are working with a two-field video resolution, check the options at the bottom of the Freeze Frame dialogue box. The default is 'Duplicated Field'. This uses field one twice and reduces the resolution of the image. If the frame you are freezing has no movement, use 'Both Fields'. However, if there is motion in the shot then the moving object will be in a slightly different position in each field (as field 1 was recorded before field 2). Making a Freeze Frame using 'Both Fields' will now look terrible as the differences between field 1 and field 2 are repeated – field 1, field 2, field 1, field 2 and so on as the clip is played (the image flickers badly). Try 'Interpolated Field' – this improves the appearance of the effect by taking field 1 and building a new field 2 by combining scan lines from the first field. Results are good but some softening may be seen on some clips. The menu needs to be accessed twice – once to set the option, and again to choose the Freeze Frame duration.

Recreating Freeze Frames

If you are offlining with a single-field video resolution, then it is possible to recreate the freeze frames with a two-field option after redigitizing only on versions before Media Composer v10, Symphony v3 and Xpress v4. See 'Re-rendering Motion Effects', below. In current versions, Freeze Frames will always be recreated the way they were originally made, so consider using 20:1 or 10:1 as the offline resolution if you have a large number of freeze frames in your sequence.

To remake an effect, remember that you can only make a Freeze Frame from a master clip, so use Match Frame in the Source monitor to step back to the original clip.

Motion Effects

Motion Effects (slomos and other speed changes) are made by creating a new clip and media from an existing Master clip. The new Effect clip will then need to be edited into the sequence. If the section in question has already been edited, use Match Frame to get the original Master clip into the Source monitor. The Motion Effect button (Figure 10.2) is in the Composer fast menu (Media Composer and Symphony) and under the source pop-up on Xpress. A new clip will be created that can be either faster or slower, reversed, or have a strobe effect.

Figure 10.2 Motion Effect button

Single-field Motion Effects

Figure 10.3 shows the Motion Effect dialogue box for Media Composer v10, Symphony v3 and Xpress v4 and later; earlier versions differ slightly. The speed change can either be entered as a percentage (normal speed = 100 per cent), a new frame rate or as a new duration. Changing one parameter updates the other two. Choose sensible speed variations (i.e., 200 per cent, 50 per cent, 20 per cent), or an uneven numbers of frames may be dropped or added giving a jerky result. To make a reverse motion clip, enter a figure preceded by a minus sign.

The 'Fit to Fill' option lets the user set an In and an Out in both the Source and Record monitors, and have the system calculate the speed change needed to make the marked source footage fit the marked duration in the sequence. This may come up with bizarre speed changes (you can see the proposed change before making the

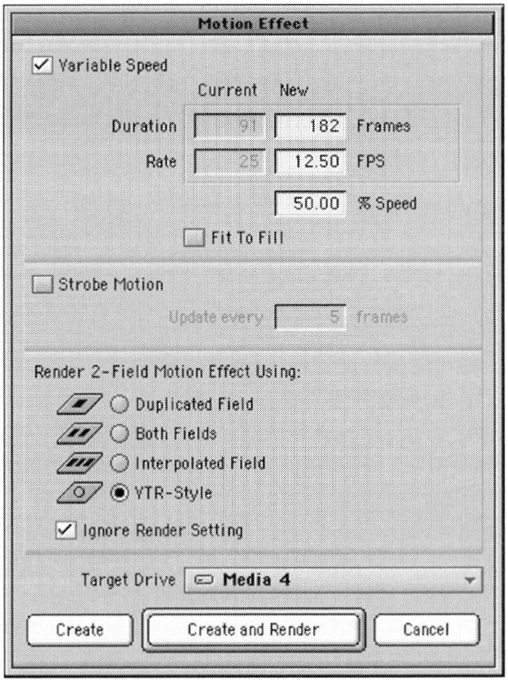

Figure 10.3 Motion Effect dialogue

clip) so it may be worth rounding the speed up or down to a sensible figure and adjusting the sequence. Some motion effects are real-time but others will need to be rendered. If the 'Create' button is black, the effect will play but some two-field effects (see below) will not play correctly until rendered.

Two-field Motion Effects

When working with two-field video resolutions, a set of choices similar to those for freeze frames is available, with the addition of 'VTR Style' in Media Composer v10, Symphony v3 and Xpress v4. The default when rendering two-field media is 'Duplicated Field', as with Freeze Frames. Again, 'Both Fields' is usable for clips other than those with much motion across the frame; with movement, a flickering effect may be visible as (with a slomo) the frames are being seen more than once in order to slow down the action. In a 50 per cent slomo, the effect is forced to show Frame 1, field 1, Frame 1, field 2, Frame 1, field 1, Frame 1, field 2 and so on – a kind of 'two steps forward, one step back' effect. 'Interpolated Field' improves the appearance of the effect by taking field 1 and building a new field 2 from scan lines in field 1. Results are good but rendering time is much increased and some softening may be seen. VTR Style (where available) uses one original field but

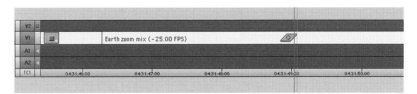

Figure 10.4 VTR-style Motion Effect icon in Timeline

creates a new second field by shifting an existing field by one scan line. This, too, is slow to render but offers sharper results than interpolated.

As you create the effect, you will be prompted for a bin in which to store the clip and a media volume on which to store the new media. Once created, the motion effect will need to be edited into the sequence. In current versions, an icon is displayed on the clip in the Timeline, indicating the class of effect; earlier versions did not display an icon (Figure 10.4). If a rendered motion effect is lengthened by trimming, it will need to be re-rendered before it will play correctly (see below).

Re-rendering Motion Effects

If a motion effect has to be re-rendered (for instance, if the sequence has been redigitized at a different resolution) the render method needs to be set, as the method originally used is not automatically recognized. In Media Composer Mac v8, NT v9 and later, Symphony v2 and later and Xpress v2.5 and later, open the Render Setting (Project window) and choose a preference (Figure 10.5). Note that choosing a render setting in this way will also override the choices made when making a new Motion Effect. Prior to v10, the only way round this was to change the render setting. In Media Composer v10, Symphony v3 and Xpress v4 and later, the render choice can be disabled in the Motion Effect dialogue box when making a new effect.

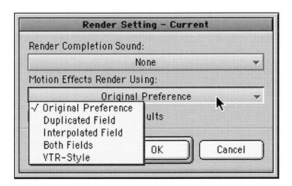

Figure 10.5 Render Settings (Media Composer v10)

To set the re-render method in Media Composer v7, Symphony v1 and Xpress v2, open the Console (Tools menu). In the command line at the bottom of the window, type *motionfxrendertype* followed by a number, then press Return:

motionfxrendertype 0 renders with duplicated fields
motionfxrendertype 1 renders with interpolated fields
motionfxrendertype 2 renders with both fields
motionfxrendertype 3 (–1 on Symphony v1) clears and resets the render type (this must be done before the options in the Motion Effect dialogue box can be applied to a new effect, as they are overridden by the console command). When a command is entered, the window shows the setting. These commands have no effect in current versions.

Note that motion effects nested inside other effects will not re-render correctly if the entire nest is rendered in some versions (see later). Step into the nest and re-render the motion effect individually if the effect appears wrong.

Prior to Media Composer v10, Symphony v3 and Xpress v4, the render settings worked with freeze frames, too. In current versions freeze frames always re-render the way they were originally made.

Horizontal Effects

Transition effects

Add Dissolve

The simplest Transition effect is the dissolve – use the Add Dissolve button – on the standard Composer window (Figure 10.6) or on the keyboard (this doesn't work on some early NT keyboards). Park on or close to a cut in the Timeline, select the tracks, press 'Add Dissolve' and the dialogue box appears. Figure 10.7 shows the Add Dissolve dialogue for all versions prior to Media Composer v10, Symphony v3 and Xpress v4. In later versions, the Add Dissolve button brings up a much improved 'Quick Dissolve' dialogue box (Figure 10.8).

When adding a transition effect to a cut, there must be sufficient media on the outgoing clip after the transition and enough media on the incoming clip prior to the transition (known as the 'handles') for the overlap to work. The default position for

Figure 10.6 Add Dissolve button

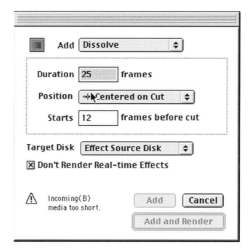

Figure 10.7 Add Dissolve dialogue (old version)

a transition effect is 'Centred on Cut' and the duration is 1 second (25 frames in PAL; 30 frames in NTSC). As a frame cannot be split in half, a 25-frame effect actually starts 12 frames before the cut and ends 13 frames after. To change the duration in the earlier versions, enter a new figure in frames; to change the position, use the pop-up. Alternative choices are 'Starting at Cut', Ending at Cut' and 'Custom Start'. To put a fade up at the start of a sequence, use 'Starting at'; to fade out at the end, use 'Ending at'. It is still possible to enter numbers in the current dialogue box but it is simpler to drag the effect duration slider to set position, and drag the ends of the slider to set duration (Figure 10.9a, b). The number of frames available is displayed in the window.

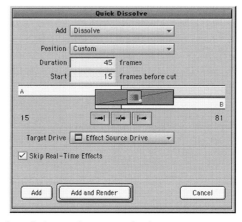

Figure 10.8 Quick Dissolve dialogue (new version)

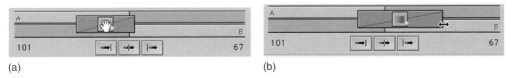

(a)   (b)

Figure 10.9 a, Adjust dissolve position; **b**, Adjust dissolve duration

A warning for insufficient source material will appear in the earlier Add Dissolve box if there is a problem (Figure 10.7, bottom left of window). The outgoing clip is the A side and the incoming clip is the B side. In the current versions, the effect will adjust to whatever media is available and adjustments can be quickly made.

Some similar transition effects ('Dip to Color', 'Fade to Color' and so on) are available from the pop-up at the top of the Add Dissolve window (Figure 10.10). If an In and Out mark are set in the sequence, an option appears to apply the effect to all transitions between the marks (Figure 10.11).

Figure 10.10 Quick Dissolve choices

Figure 10.11 Apply from In to Out

Although a video dissolve normally plays in real time, an audio dissolve needs to be rendered. The 'Skip Real-time Effects' button will render audio but not video, when a mixture of audio and video effects need to be added together – in this case press 'Add and Render'. If you wish to render effects later, just press 'Add'. Effects do not need to be rendered to appear in an EDL. See the section 'Real-time effects and rendering' for more information.

Other transition effects

Other effects (wipes, spins, etc.) can be dragged from the Effect Palette (Figure 10.12) in the Tools menu (⌘+8) [Ctrl+8] to the transition in Source/Record mode or applied by double-clicking the effect icon in the palette while a transition is selected in Trim or Effect mode. Choose a main category of effect from the left-hand column of the Effect Palette and then choose the actual effect from the right-hand column. An effect applied in this way is the default duration (1 second) and at the default position (centred on cut). If you have problems with insufficient media, use 'Add Dissolve' first as it lets you set position and duration in one operation – you can always change the effect for another after it is applied – the duration and position will not be altered.

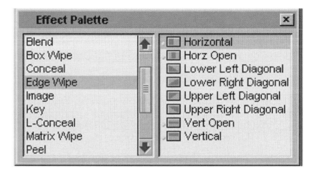

Figure 10.12 Effect Palette (Edge Wipe)

Once a effect has been applied, an effect icon will appear on the transition in the Timeline (Figure 10.13). The duration and position are indicated by a dotted line. The duration and relative position of an effect can be adjusted in Trim or Effect mode (Figure 10.14). If you extend a transition effect with an odd number of frames (25 frames, say), all the extra duration appears on the downstream side. Change a symmetrical effect (30 frames, say) and it is extended equally in both directions.

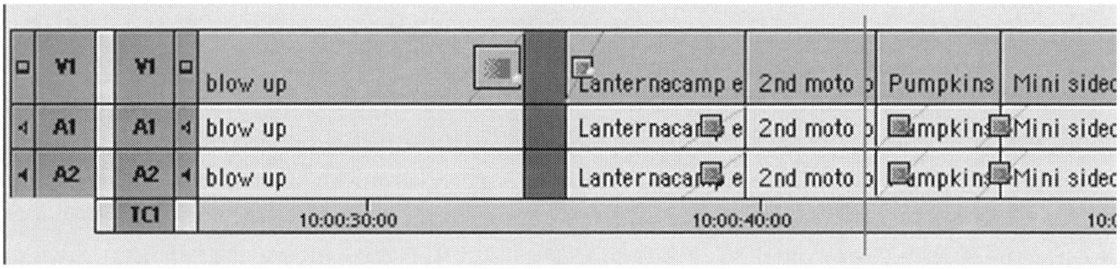

Figure 10.13 Dissolve icons in Timeline

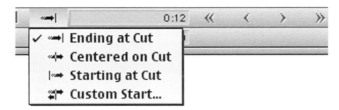

Figure 10.14 Adjusting position and duration in Trim mode

In Trim or Effect mode the problem of insufficient media is shown graphically (Figure 10.15 shows the warning in current versions). The 'Size to Fit' option attempts to keep the effect in place by adjusting duration or position. It is possible to inadvertently end up with an effect of zero duration (an effect icon will still be visible in the Timeline). Typing a figure in the duration box in Trim or Effect mode and pressing Enter applies the default effect (dissolve) at the default position. It is not possible to set the position before setting the duration if creating a dissolve this way.

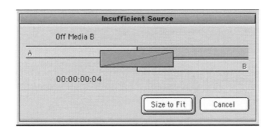

Figure 10.15 Insufficient media alert

What plays well as a cut may not work well as a transition effect (there may be a stray slate board or shot change on a source clip that can only be seen after the effect is added). The Transition Corner Display button in Trim mode (Figure 10.16 – not Xpress) changes the display to show frames from the outgoing (top) and incoming (bottom) clip at the start, centre and end of the effect (Figure 10.17). Click and drag the rollers in the Timeline to adjust the duration (normal trimming by dragging is disabled when Transition Corner Display is active). Option [Alt]+clicking the trim buttons will also adjust the duration.

Figure 10.16 Transition Corner Display button

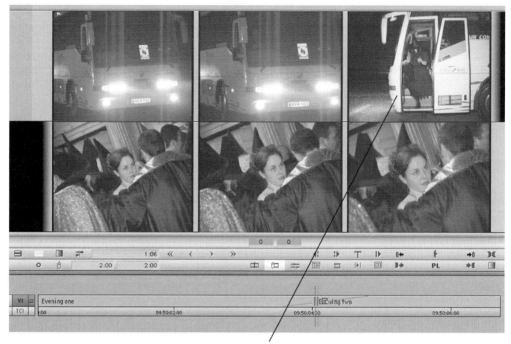

Note the rogue frame from the outgoing clip at the end of the mix

Figure 10.17 Transition Corner Display

You can remove an effect by clicking the 'Remove Effect' button (Figure 10.18) in Source/Record mode or by pressing Delete while an effect is selected in Trim or Effect mode.

Figure 10.18 Remove Effect button

Segment effects

Segment effects (Mask, Resize, Flip, Flop, Color Effect, etc.) can be applied in Source/Record mode by clicking and dragging from the Effect Palette or by double-clicking after selecting a segment or segments in Effect or Source/Record mode (see below). Flip and Flop have no parameters; common controls for other segment effects are described later.

Working in Effect mode

To enter Effect mode, click the Effect mode button (to the right of the Trim mode button in the Composer window in Media Composer and Symphony – Figure 10.19). Effect mode is a standard key on the Xpress keyboard (]) and can also be found in the Composer window fast menu. The Composer display now changes slightly to show a time track under the Record monitor, with keyframes (see later), for the effect being worked on. A slider at the left-hand end allows magnification of the track. If the edit monitor is set to a resolution of at least 1024 × 768 in Media Composer and Symphony, a second click of the Effect mode button will switch to Big Effect mode. Here, one pixel on the monitor equals one pixel of the image (Figure 10.20). Xpress users can drag to resize the window. The Media Composer

Effect Mode button

Figure 10.19 Effect mode button

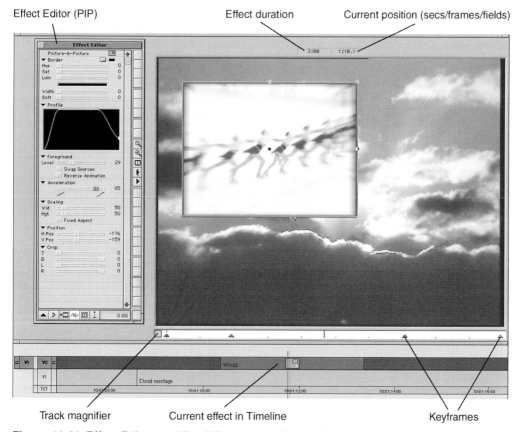

Figure 10.20 Effect Editor and Big Effect mode (Media Composer)

and Symphony button set changes to include a selection of effects buttons; the Xpress button set is unchanged.

In Media Composer and Symphony it is possible to select multiple transitions in the Timeline in Effect mode by lassoing from R to L (with nothing previously selected). Typing a number of frames duration in the Effect Duration box followed by Enter will add a dissolve to all the selected transitions; double-clicking on a suitable effect in the Effect Palette will add the chosen effect at a duration of 1 second to all the selected transitions. To select multiple segments in Media Composer and Symphony lasso from L to R (with nothing previously selected). Multiple effects can then be added by double-clicking.

Xpress users will find that it is not possible to work in Effect mode unless an effect is applied and selected. To add several effects simultaneously in Xpress, add one effect, select it in Effect mode, then lasso or shift-click to add more transitions to the selection. If any effect is selected already on any system, lassoing (either way) selects more of the same (segment or transition).

Real-time effects and rendering

Rendering creates new media to play effects that will not play in real time. Not all effects are classed the same way on all systems. Effects that normally play in real time have an orange dot (in the Effect Palette and in the Timeline). Effects that never play in real time (such as the matrix transitions) have no dot in the palette and a blue dot in the Timeline. These effects must be rendered before they can be played, although they can be previewed (see 'Render on the Fly' in the section 'Efficiency tips', below). Real time effects that are placed adjacent to other real time effects (for instance a dissolve between two flops) may display a green (conditional) dot indicating that they need to be rendered. The result of playing unrendered green dot effects may be unexpected – in the example given, the flops will play until the dissolve is reached. At this point the dissolve will play but the flops will vanish, to re-appear after the dissolve has ended.

A green dot will also appear on what would normally be a real-time effect on a system with a single-stream uncompressed (1:1) video option, or certain effects on Xpress that are classed as 'Fast Render' effects. These are faster to render than blue-dot (non-real-time) effects. On ABVB 2D systems (Media Composer v7 and Xpress v2) there is an Effect Setting, giving the option of real time wipes or real time keys. The unselected option displays a green dot in the Effect Palette. An ABVB 3D system or a Meridien 2D or 3D system will play both classes of effect in real time.

In Source/Record mode, effects may be rendered by a) pressing the 'Render Effect' button in the fast menu, b) choosing 'Render at Position', 'Render In/ Out' or 'ExpertRender' (where available) in the Clip menu or c) choosing 'Add and Render' in the Add Dissolve dialogue box. In Trim or Effect modes, the

'Render Effect' button is displayed (Figure 10.21). 'Render In/Out' does not allow selective rendering of either transitions or segments – all unrendered effects between the marks will be included. Using the Render Effect button offers more flexibility – you can choose to render one or more transition effects or one or more segment effects, but not both together. In Media Composer Mac v8, NT v9 and later, Symphony v2 and Xpress v2.5 and later, there is an additional option in the Clip menu: ExpertRender. This is designed to determine which effects need to be rendered and which don't when many effects are adjacent in the Timeline. Sometimes an experienced editor can work out a more efficient selection of effects to render than the ExpertRender feature (more on this later).

Figure 10.21 Render Effect button

When choosing a disk to store the rendered effect, the 'Effect Source Disk' option, which sometimes appears in the render dialogue box, is the media volume containing the media file for the selected segment or the outgoing (A side) clip in the case of a transition. Using the Effect Source disk is a good choice in many cases as the system doesn't have to jump to a different partition to play the effect and the possibility of someone removing the drive with your rendered effects is reduced. It is also possible to choose a specific drive for the rendered media. Holding down the Option [Alt] key when pressing the Render button sends the media to the last selected volume without asking.

If you have a real-time effect between two segment effects that you plan to render, add the transition effect before rendering and the 'handles' (overlapping media) will be rendered too.

On ABVB systems, the Color Effect (see later) is classed with all the other effects and normal rendering rules apply. On Meridien systems, it is possible to have two streams of video with real-time colour effects in addition to a real-time video effect such as a dissolve or wipe, or mask.

To see an estimate of how long a render will take, press 'T' while rendering; to see a percentage, press 'P'. To see the progress of the render on the video monitor, open the Render settings and select 'Show Intermediate Results'; if the result is not what you expected, the render can be stopped (see 'Partial Render' below).

The Downstream Keyer (DSK) will play titles and graphics with alpha channels in real time over the two video streams under most circumstances on most systems (see Chapter 12). Some models of Xpress earlier than v3 do not have the DSK and all titles and graphics must be treated as normal effects and be rendered when appropriate.

Partial render

In early versions, if rendering was stopped for any reason (intervention by the editor or some other reason), all the media was lost and the entire process had to be started again. From Media Composer v9.1, Symphony v2.1 and Xpress v3.1, if rendering is stopped, it is possible to keep the partially rendered media and resume later. The Timeline can display partially rendered clips (see Chapter 7). To stop a render, press ⌘+. (full stop) [Ctrl+.].

Render setting (ABVB systems)

When rendering (or when importing a graphic) on a Mac ABVB system, a message may appear indicating that the Frame Size Limit has been exceeded. Each AVR (video resolution on ABVB systems) has a frame size limit in KB (take a look at the console window when digitizing for an idea about frame sizes). To avoid playback problems, a warning appears if this limit is exceeded. The choices offered are 'Soften', which adds more compression, degrades the image and takes longer to render or 'Don't Soften'. Choosing 'Don't Soften' may lead to video underruns (an underrun occurs when the system can't play back the required video or audio from the drives). Softening the effect will guarantee playback. If the message isn't answered within 15 seconds or so, softening is applied.

One rendered effect over the limit may play by itself but may not play in conjunction with other real-time effects such as titles. The Render settings (Project window) on ABVB systems allow some control (Figure 10.22).

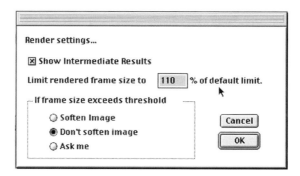

Figure 10.22 ABVB Render settings

If you have drives that allow two-stream real-time effects, then it is possible to set the limit above 100 per cent (up to around 120 per cent – experiment), although you may experience some underruns. Don't exceed 100 per cent on systems offering only single stream playback.

The Effect Editor

When an effect is selected in Effect mode, the Effect Editor appears with a number of Parameter Panes that are used to modify and adjust various aspects of the effect (Figure 10.23 shows parameters for a horizontal wipe). Not every effect has all the adjustments; some common parameters are horizontal and vertical position, scaling (size), crop and border; some effects on Xpress will have fewer parameters than the same effect on Media Composer and Symphony. Closed parameter panes can be opened by clicking on the right-pointing arrow next to the pane. Panes can also be opened by double-clicking the top centre of a pane. In addition, option [Alt]-clicking an arrow on an open pane closes all open panes; option [Alt]-clicking an

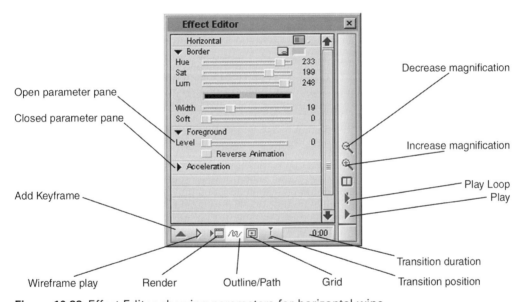

Figure 10.23 Effect Editor showing parameters for horizontal wipe

arrow on a closed pane opens all panes; option [Alt]-double-clicking in the middle of a pane opens or closes all panes.

Effect Editor buttons

Around the outside of the Effect Editor are a number of useful buttons; anti-clockwise from bottom left:

Add Keyframe.

Wireframe play shows a wireframe preview of certain non-real-time transition effects.

Render.

Outline/Path displays a wireframe on the monitor, showing the scaling and the path of the image. Scaling and position can be adjusted by dragging the wireframe (see later).

The **Grid** button will overlay a safe title/safe action grid on the monitor. Using the Grid settings in the Project window (not Xpress), the grid can be modified in many ways.

Transition Effect position and duration have been covered earlier – these are the same as in Trim mode.

Promote to 3D – on 3D systems, this button will promote the effect to 3D, translating the 2D parameters.

Play.

Play Loop (similar to Trim mode – plays the effect repeatedly).

The **Split Screen** button (not Xpress) enables a split 'Before/After' monitor, useful for several effects.

Magnify and Reduce: It is possible to magnify and reduce the image in the monitor. ⌘+L and ⌘+K [Ctrl+L, Ctrl+K] also work (but make sure that the Composer is the active window). This is not an effect – it is a monitoring device.

Adjusting the parameters

The Effect parameter sliders can be adjusted by click and drag, selecting (clicking) and typing in values in the numeric keypad (press Enter) or using the left and right arrow keys on the keyboard after selecting a slider (shift+arrow moves ten units). The Tab key moves the focus forward from slider to slider (and in recent versions Shift+Tab moves back). Most of the effect parameters can be changed over time using keyframes (see next section).

The result of using the Level control (Foreground parameter pane) varies depending on the effect. In a dissolve or other transition effect, such as a wipe, level is the amount of the incoming shot visible at any keyframe – in a dissolve, level will be 0 at the first keyframe and 100 at the last keyframe, for instance. In a multi-layer effect such as a picture-in-picture or a title (see later), level is the opacity of the top (foreground element). The Reverse animation button reverses the direction of the effect. Reverse changes the priority of background and foreground for some effects. In some early versions, there is one Reverse button, which covers both functions.

Acceleration (which is on or off for all keyframes) gives a gradual speeding up and slowing down of movement as keyframes are departed and approached. To speed up or slow down the entire effect, change the duration.

The Profile window (not Xpress) shows a graphical display of Level and Acceleration (See Figure 10.29).

Working with keyframes

Keyframes may be added using the button on the Effect Editor, or on the keyboard (as for audio keyframes). Keyframes may be added on the fly from the keyboard when using normal play. It is possible to set many parameters such as position, scale, level and so on, and have them change from keyframe to keyframe as Avid interpolates the changes over time. For instance, a picture-in-picture can start at one position and move to another. A selected keyframe is pink; an unselected keyframe is grey. Delete selected keyframes by using keyboard Delete; the first and last keyframes cannot be deleted.

Keyframe parameters may be copied and pasted from one to another using &+C [Ctrl+C] (copy) and &+V [Ctrl+V] (paste). To move a selected keyframe, Option [Alt]+drag or use the trim buttons on the keyboard. The first and last keyframes can't be deleted. You can select several keyframes by shift+clicking [Ctrl+click] or all by &+click or &+A [Ctrl+A]. Note that if you shift+click two keyframes on an NT system, all keyframes between the two will be selected.

The FF and REW keys jump from keyframe to keyframe on Media Composer and Symphony (Xpress users use 'Goto Transition'). Shift [Ctrl]+FF or REW adds keyframes to the selection as you go.

Keyframe parameters may be adjusted by selecting a keyframe and using the Effect Editor sliders, as described, or by working in the monitor with the wireframe display. This is not always available but is very useful on such effects as Picture-in-picture, Resize and Mask. Click the Outline/Path button to see the wireframe and

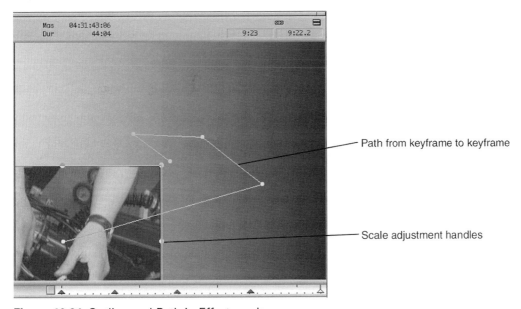

Figure 10.24 Outline and Path in Effect mode

adjustment handles (Figure 10.24). If the position indicator is not on an active keyframe when working by dragging the wireframe outline, the system will automatically add keyframes for you, as follows: if the position indicator is between two selected keyframes, any adjustment will change both the keyframes but if the indicator is between one selected and one unselected keyframe, any adjustment will automatically add a keyframe to record the change. If working this way, avoid clicking and dragging on the white dot in the centre of the frame. These dots represent keyframes – if you have four keyframes and no positional change has been made, and you plan to work on the last keyframe, clicking on the dot in the centre will activate the first keyframe instead (imagine a pile of pennies where the top penny represents the first keyframe). The trick is to click and drag anywhere else in the frame. As you drag the frame away from the default position, you will see 'your' white dot move with it.

If you are adjusting parameters using the sliders in the Effect Editor, make sure you are monitoring at the position of your selected keyframe – if not, you won't see the results of your adjustments correctly.

Efficiency tips

Sometimes, when working with a number of unrendered effects, the system slows down as it attempts to preview the composite. A feature called 'Render on the Fly' previews real-time and unrendered non-real-time effects. It can be turned on and off in the Special menu (Clip menu on Xpress). Render on the Fly is normally on in Source/ Record mode (but can be turned off), is normally off in Trim mode (but can be turned on in the Trim settings). To see the result of trimming a clip with an effect, Render on the Fly needs to be on. Render on the Fly is always on in Effect mode – the only variation being that if Render on the Fly is off in the menu, the monitor image won't update when dragging the Effect Editor sliders until the mouse is released. Note that Render on the Fly needs to be on to see a real-time effect (an unrendered title, for instance, will play, but become invisible when stopped, with Render on the Fly off).

Other ways of working more quickly with unrendered effects include monitoring the lowest track only or disabling monitoring altogether. Track soloing (+click [Ctrl+click] on the video monitor icon) allows real-time play of an unrendered effect over a black background. When segment editing, consider disabling the four-frame display in the Timeline settings (not Xpress) if dragging a segment to align with a cut or mark.

To avoid having to re-render a long segment effect just for a small change, use Add Edit to split the effect and make the change in one new segment and re-render. To avoid a jump, don't alter the new end keyframe of the first segment or new start keyframe of the second segment. Try to split the effect on an existing keyframe but, if there is movement in the clip, particularly if acceleration has been used, a jump may be unavoidable.

Saving effect templates

Clicking on the effect icon (top right of the Effect Editor, Figure 10.25) and dragging back to a bin saves a template of the effect (the template can be renamed – Figure 10.26). This template acts as a custom effect and can be used as normal. An open bin containing templates appears at the bottom left of the Effect Palette, with the templates (and other effect clips such as titles) listed in the right-hand window (Figure 10.27). To apply just one parameter (say colour) from your template, drag the template back to an open parameter pane in the Effect Editor on an existing effect. The values as set at first keyframe of the template are applied to

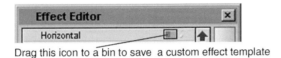

Drag this icon to a bin to save a custom effect template

Figure 10.25 Effect icon

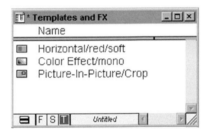

Figure 10.26 Effect templates in bin

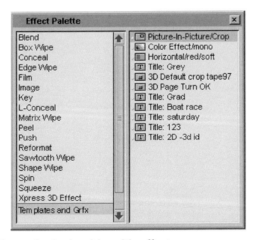

Figure 10.27 Effect Palette displaying bin with effects

the selected keyframes in the destination effect. Parameters such as border width, colour, position and scale can be applied in this way. Option [Alt]+dragging an effect icon to a bin takes the source material as well (not on a transition effect). The resulting clip can be edited in the normal way. This works well with a collapsed Submaster effect (see later).

Vertical effects

To add an effect such as a Title, Picture-in-picture, or Superimposition, add a video track or tracks (Clip menu) and patch the source video to the desired track. To apply

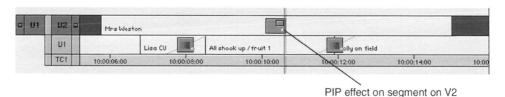

PIP effect on segment on V2

Figure 10.28 Multiple video tracks

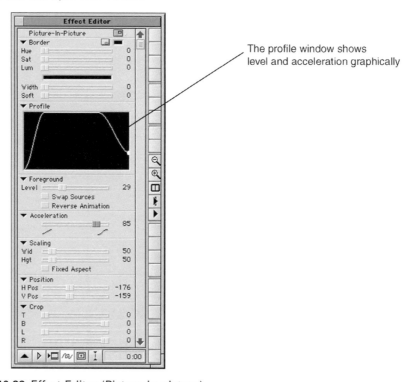

The profile window shows
level and acceleration graphically

Figure 10.29 Effect Editor (Picture-in-picture)

an effect, drag it from the Effect Palette on to a segment (Source/Record mode) or double-click if one or more segments are selected in Effect mode or Source/Record mode. To view the effect, set the video monitor (track panel) to the highest track. Avid monitors the tracks from above and the effects are displayed. Clips on higher tracks are viewed as foreground objects over clips on lower tracks (background). The system will preview all effects present if Render on the Fly is on but won't play more than two video streams without some rendering (Figure 10.28). Figure 10.29 shows the Effect Editor with parameters for a typical 2D vertical effect – Picture-in-picture.

Many Transition effects may be applied to segments (for instance a horizontal or vertical wipe gives a split screen).

To re-order elements on multiple tracks (change foreground and background priority) use Segment edit Lift/Overwrite (you may need to add an extra video track to temporarily store one of the clips).

Rendering multiple effects

If all the segments line up, a simple approach is to render the top layer only. This is efficient in terms of rendering time and disk storage – all effects on lower tracks are included in the rendered media. The elements on the lower tracks must remain in place (take care with trimming later). Place the video monitor on top track and play. It is not necessary (and counter-productive) to render all the segments individually; it takes too long and too much media is created. If the effect on the highest segment is real time, it is possible to render the track below the top track and let elements on the top track play in real time; in Figure 10.28, for example, the two transition effects on V1 could be rendered, letting the PIP on V2 play in real time. Alternatively, mark I/O and use ExpertRender from the Clip menu (see earlier). ExpertRender may occasionally be beaten by an expert editor: in Figure 10.30, for example, it is more efficient to render the dissolves although ExpertRender suggests rendering the Resizes, which will take longer and create more media (Figure 10.31).

To render segments that don't align, add an extra track above. Place an Add Edit in the filler on the empty track to line up with the beginning of the first segment and

Figure 10.30 Clips highlighted by ExpertRender

Figure 10.31 ExpertRender dialogue box

the end of the last segment. Now apply a Submaster effect (Image category of the Effect Palette) to the newly defined segment of filler and render. The video monitor must be placed on the highest track and the elements below the submaster must remain in place after rendering (Figure 10.32).

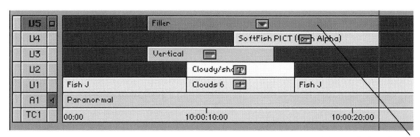

By rendering the Submaster effect, all the effects will play

Figure 10.32 Rendering with Submaster

Video Mixdown

A Video Mixdown creates a new clip with one linked media file of a complex effects section. Render the effects first, then set the compression using the Compression Tool or Media Creation Tool (⌘+5 [Ctrl+5]), depending on version. Now mark I/O around the section to be mixed and set the monitor to highest track (track lights aren't required). Select Video Mixdown from the Special menu (Clip menu on Xpress). It is possible to mix down at a different resolution from your source material, although this may take much longer.

Video Mixdowns can also be used to play back parts of sequences with a very high cut rate or to make one clip that can be reused in other sequences. It is also possible to apply a motion effect to a Video mixdown.

A disadvantage is that it is not possible to modify the contents of the mixdown or to use Match Frame to return to the source clips; for this reason make a subsequence or save a template with source before doing the mixdown.

Nesting effects

Avid allows you to step inside a segment effect to manipulate the contents – a technique known as nesting. At its simplest, this means that more than one effect may be added to the same clip (for instance a colour effect or a resize inside a mask). It is also possible to add tracks inside a nest – allowing a title to move with a picture-in-picture, for example. There are two ways to view the contents of a nest.

Viewing a nest – method 1

Click on the down arrow at bottom of Timeline window (Figure 10.33) to step in to a selected segment (only Media Composer and Symphony). This reveals the contents of the effect allowing editing within. Click on the up arrow to step out. This method allows the contents of a nest to be played without rendering the whole thing, as monitoring is done within the nest.

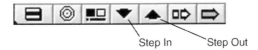

Figure 10.33 Step In and Step Out buttons

Viewing a nest – method 2

Double-click on a segment in Effect mode and the Timeline displays the contents of the nest above the video track (Figure 10.34). This method works on all versions. Double-clicking also works in Source/Record mode after selecting with one of the segment editing buttons. Media Composer and Symphony users can also option

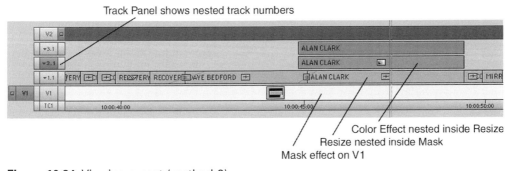

Figure 10.34 Viewing a nest (method 2)

[Alt]+click the step-in button in Source/Record mode. This method lets you see all the tracks inside and outside the nest but monitoring is always done outside the nest so some unrendered elements may not play. There are advantages and disadvantages to each method. Method 2 is useful when adjusting parameters of an effect deep in a nest (perhaps adjusting a resize inside a mask) as it is possible to see the results of all the applied effects together.

If you step into a multi-track effect such as a Superimposition or a Picture-in-picture, an empty Track 1 can be seen in the nest. Leave this track empty or the lower tracks outside the nest will not be visible.

Extra layers can be added within the effect, with more clips and more effects – these are processed before the effects outside. This is useful for adding a title on a picture-in-picture, for example. Adding tracks in this way gets around the limited number of tracks on some Xpress models. To edit to tracks inside a nest, patch the source video to the chosen nested track as normal.

Nested effects are not represented in an EDL. If you use nesting in an offline edit, you'll need to deconstruct the effects and make them into normal layered video tracks before making an EDL. See the section on the Collapse command for a method of extracting the contents of a nest.

Editing inside titles and graphics

It is possible to step into a title or graphic clip with an alpha channel and replace the graphic fill with moving video or another graphic. This is a very powerful technique as the effect will still play in real time, although the DSK will be disabled (see Chapter 12). Three tracks are visible inside a title or graphic (Figure 10.35): V1 is an empty track (and should not be used); V2 is known as the Graphic Fill – in the case of a title this is the colour of the text and border and so on; V3 is the Alpha Matte, or Alpha channel. The Alpha channel defines which parts of the title object are visible (black) and which are transparent, revealing the background (white). The matte is locked and cannot be manipulated within the nest although advanced users can copy the matte to the Clipboard and use it in conjunction with the Avid Matte Key effect (see later).

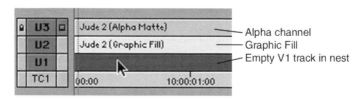

Figure 10.35 Tracks nested inside title clip (viewed by method 1)

Autonesting

Autonesting is a variant of nesting that adds an effect outside an existing effect; i.e., it places the existing effect within a new nest. To autonest, option [Alt]+drag (for one segment) or option [Alt]+double-click the second effect to autonest on top of the selected effect(s) in the Timeline. The option [Alt]+double-click method must be used if more than one segment is to be autonested. There need not be an effect already in place on the selected segments so autonesting is useful for adding an effect to a whole sequence – for example, every clip will be nested inside the new effect.

Collapse

This command 'collapses' selected tracks so that they become nested elements within a Submaster on the lowest selected track. To collapse a section: select adjacent tracks, mark I/O, and press Collapse (this is only found on the full Command Palette in Media Composer and Symphony, but is in the Composer fast menu in Xpress – Figure 10.36). An advantage of Collapse is that real-time transition effects can easily be added at the beginning and end of the collapsed segment (Figure 10.37). If this is done it is important to allow for 'handles' at each end – i.e., to make the collapse long enough to include the planned transition effects, which should be starting at the head and ending at the tail. If this is not done, the timing of the collapsed elements will be changed. Collapsing simplifies other editing – for instance single-sided trimming can be done upstream without unrendering the contents of the nest. Option [Alt]+dragging the Submaster icon from the Effect Editor back to a bin will save the Submaster and its nested contents as a template with source. This can then be edited as normal. The template can be reused many times; simply step into the nest and replace some of the clips as required.

Figure 10.36 Collapse button

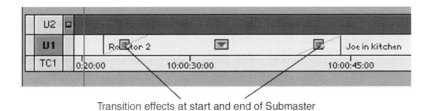

Transition effects at start and end of Submaster

Figure 10.37 Effects collapsed into Submaster on V1

Undo will reverse a collapse but there is no specific uncollapse command. It is best to make a subsequence before collapsing if you may need to use the elements later. To extract the contents of a collapse, step in, mark I/O, select the tracks and copy the contents to the clipboard from where it can be edited. If you wish to store the contents as a subsequence in a bin, first edit the segments into a sequence in the Timeline, then subsequence. If a subsequence is made straight from the Source monitor in some versions, the Avid may freeze if the subclip is used. It is not possible to subsequence directly from within a nest. This 'copy to Clipboard' technique must be used to extract the content of any nest, not only those created by the Collapse command.

Special cases

Most of the foregoing information is common to a number of Avid effects. Below are several special cases, including the Color Effect and the key effects.

The Color Effect

The Color Effect is a segment effect allowing adjustment of luminance and chrominance, colour balance and the addition of some colour styles. On Meridien systems, Color Effect is in addition to the two streams of video; on ABVB systems, processing the Color Effect takes up the real-time capacity so that a dissolve (for example) into a Color Effect needs to be rendered. Some ABVB users may find that the whole Color Effect will need rendering – on some systems the effect ends one field early, showing a visible flash on screen. As the effect modifies the playback of the original media, it is important to work with an external waveform monitor and vectorscope, to stay within the legal range for broadcast.

PAL: Keep luminance under 1v and above 0.3v in the waveform monitor (range 16–235 digital).
NTSC: Keep luminance under 100 IRE and above 7.5 IRE in the waveform monitor (range 16–235 digital).

As a rough guide, do not allow chrominance to exceed the 'safe zone' (the outside circle) in the vectorscope. For broadcast it is important to use and understand professional waveform monitors and vectorscopes. The Media Composer Video Input tool can be used on Mac ABVB systems but a) it only reads one scan line at a time and b) it doesn't respond in real time when playing from disk, but it can help pinpoint a problem area. On Meridien systems the Input tool does not respond at all when editing.

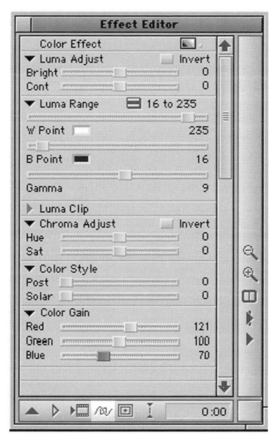

Figure 10.38 Effect Editor – Color Effect

Color Effect controls

Note that the luminance adjustments take place before luma clipping is applied, so the image will stay within the legal broadcast limits of 16–235 (digital) if Luma Clip is set to the default. Luma Range and black level clip are not available on Xpress v3 and earlier. Figure 10.38 shows the Color Effect parameters on Media Composer and Symphony.

Luma Adjustment: the contrast adjustments can push the signal outside broadcast limits, so watch the waveform monitor unless Luma Clip (below) is set to the default 16–235.

The **Luma Range** is normally set to 16–235. By clicking with the eyedropper on the image it is possible to reset the white and black points on a segment – anything above the white point and below the black point will be clipped. The Gamma control allows mid-tones to be adjusted without affecting the extremes. It is possible to expand luma range to 0–255 – which is useful if a clip is being prepared for use with the Luma Key effect (see later). Luma Clip will also need to be changed to 0–255 for this to be effective.

Luma Clip is set to 235 and 16 as a default. This means that simply applying a colour effect to a clip will clip the luminance to legal levels but that this clipping is done before any colour gain or special effects are applied (see below). Thus it is possible to exceed legal levels by adding colour gain.

Chroma Adjustment: the hue control moves values around a colour wheel; +180 or –180 has same effect. Watch your vectorscope when adjusting saturation.

Style: posterization removes gradations in tone – watch that luminance doesn't drop below the legal black level. Solarization gradually inverts the luminance levels, starting with brightest.

Color Gain: This is useful for grading shots. To keep overall luminance close to the original, adjust the levels of all the sliders – i.e., if you add red, take out some green and blue. If you wish to apply a tint to a clip, remove all chroma saturation before adding colour back with Color Gain. This way, you can save the effect as a template, and it will then be consistent on all clips.

There are no keyframes in the Color Effect on ABVB systems. To make a change over time on these systems, split the clip with Add Edit, adjust the two segments and place a rendered dissolve on the transition.

Chroma Key

The Avid Chroma Key Effect allows the keying of actors and presenters shot against a blue or green screen over a new background. The effect requires two video tracks. The new background (weather map, scenery or whatever) is edited on to V1, while the foreground (the person or object shot against the blue screen) is edited on to V2. There are a number of considerations for lighting and shooting chroma key footage successfully but, by the time the editor gets the tapes, it is usually too late. The editor should discourage directors and producers from using DV formats and encourage the use of formats such as Digibeta or Betacam SP.

When digitizing, always use the Component or SDI input where possible; digitizing using composite will be much less effective. Use as high a resolution as possible (AVR77, 2:1 or uncompressed if available) if the show is to be finished on the Avid.

There are a number of combinations of hardware and software that users will encounter when attempting to finish programmes using the Avid Chroma key effect:

1 ABVB (Mac) 2D MC1000 and Xpress. The 2D Chroma key effect found in the standard Effect Palette was designed for use with a 2D Avid with the ABVB fitted. This can be used reasonably successfully with care.

2 ABVB (Mac) with 3D option and 3D Meridien systems up to Media Composer v9, Symphony v2 and Xpress v3. If an external (ABVB systems only) or internal 3D board is fitted, it becomes difficult to use the 2D Chroma key effect (although there is a partial workaround). The usual advice is to use the 3D Chroma key effect (see the section on the 3D interface) although some users prefer the appearance of the 2D keyer. Xpress with the 3D option does not include a 3D keyer.

3 Media Composer v10 systems with the 3D option and Symphony v3. In these software versions, additional controls appear in the 3D interface giving more control of the effect. Symphony v3 users will have the real-time Ultimatte keyer which offers dramatically improved results. Use this in preference to the Avid effect (this effect is not covered here).

4 Media Composer 1000XL systems on Meridien hardware without the 3D option. These systems, even though they don't have the 3D effects enabled, do have the 3D board inside the Meridien box (it is installed as standard). This means that the 2D Chroma key effect cannot be used successfully and there is no 3D alternative available. 3D Meridien Xpress systems suffer from the same problem. A solution to this dilemma might be the installation of one of several suitable AVX plug-ins such as the Ultimatte keyer or Boris FX, which will offer good results. These plug-ins, however, are non-real-time.

Using the 2D keyer

Edit the foreground and background layers as described (foreground on V2 and background on V1). Apply the Chroma Key Effect from the Effect Palette to the clip on V2. Depending on the colour used when shooting, a partial key may take place. Make sure you are in Effect mode and take a look at the Effect Editor. In addition to the usual controls such as Foreground (level, etc.) there are three new parameter panes: Key, Secondary key and Spill Suppression (Figure 10.39).

Key is the main key colour to be keyed out to reveal the new background. Secondary Key can be used if there is considerable variation in the tonal range of the key colour. Spill Suppression is used to clean up edges between the foreground and background, where the key colour may reflect back on to the subject.

If you have an evenly lit background, select the key colour by first setting the Key Gain slider to zero. Now click with the mouse in the colour sampler bucket and drag over the screen image in the monitor. Try to find a representative area. Once the colour is selected, increase the Key Gain slider until the new background begins to appear. Use the cursor keys on the keyboard for fine control. The transition between the subject (V2) and the background (V1) can be softened or eased by judicious use of the Soft control. Don't overdo this or the subject will begin to become transparent.

Background image

Foreground image

Figure 10.39 Effect Editor and Effect mode – Chroma Key

If blue or green background is uneven, use the Secondary Key control. For best results, set this before setting the main key. The Secondary Key will need to be activated (click the small button next to the colour sampler – it is pink when on). Make sure the main Key Gain control is at zero so the entire foreground is clearly visible then click in the Secondary Key sampler bucket and sample the chosen area. Now adjust the Secondary Key gain slider as described above. At this point the main key colour can be chosen and adjusted; the main and secondary key controls will interact so some experimentation will be needed.

Apply Spill Suppression after the main area is keyed out (click the activation button or you won't see any effect). You may need to magnify the monitor to see clearly the edge between the foreground and background. If there is any fringing, sample the problematic pixels and adjust gain and softness. Take care not to increase the gain too much as the Spill Suppression desaturates the selected pixels. The 'Show Alpha' button in the foreground parameter pane displays the key generated by the effect, making it easier to spot problem areas (Figure 10.40).

The effect is real time if only the main key control is used; once Secondary Key and Spill Suppression are activated, the effect becomes non-real-time (blue dot) and will need to be rendered. It is also not possible to promote this effect to 3D if Secondary Key and Spill Suppression are used (see Chapter 11).

Figure 10.40 'Show Alpha' display

If you have an ABVB system with the 3D board and wish to use the 2D Chroma Key effect, it will prove very difficult unless the 3D board is temporarily disabled. To do this, quit from Avid and, as you relaunch the application, hold down the 'f' and 'x' keys on the keyboard. A message will ask if you wish the effects board to be enabled or disabled; choose 'Disabled'. Now adjust the effect as described earlier and render the effect. If you now quit and relaunch, the 3D board will be enabled again and your rendered effects will still play.

The Luma Key effect

The Avid Luma Key effect is applied in much the same way as a Chroma Key. Once again, the foreground object (with a super white or sub-black surround) is edited on to V2 and the new background on V1. The Luma Key effect is in the key category of the Effect Palette and is applied in the same way as a Chroma Key. The adjustments are simple. Use the bucket and eyedropper to sample the area to be keyed out and raise the gain parameter in small increments (often a value of 2 or 3 is sufficient). A small degree of softness may be added to improve the edge. This is a real time effect.

The Avid Matte Key effect

This effect requires three video tracks and a specially prepared black and white matte that matches an object on the foreground video track – this could be an animated logo for instance. Once again, the new background is edited on to V1, the foreground video on to V2 and the matte on to V3, carefully synchronized with the

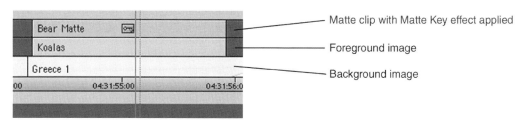

Figure 10.41 Avid Matte Key effect

clip on V2. Apply the Avid Matte Key effect from the key category of the Effect Palette on to the clip on V3 (Figure 10.41). Make sure the video monitor (track panel) is on V3 and the effect can be previewed. It is non-real-time and will need to be rendered if constructed in this fashion. If the matte you are given does not key well, step in to the Matte Key effect and apply a Color effect to the matte clip (see the section on nesting); use the Color effect to adjust the black and white points of the matte clip.

In Media Composer v10, Symphony v3 and Xpress v4, if a Quicktime movie with an alpha channel is imported it will play as a matte key effect in real time (make sure the Quicktime has no audio). If you are not dealing with an animated image, it is faster to import and edit a still graphic with an alpha channel (see Chapters 12 and 14).

Managing effect media

Media files are created whenever an effect is rendered, a title is created or a graphic is imported and it is important to keep a track of them and delete unwanted Precomputes (rendered effect files). The Precomputes are linked to the media files. See Chapter 13 (Files and Media) for information on media management.

11 3D video effects

This chapter should be read in conjunction with the chapter on 2D effects. All the information regarding layering, nesting and rendering apply equally to 3D effects and these things need to be understood before using the 3D interface.

There is not space here to cover every 3D feature but this should give users a head start.

Media Composer may have 3D effects as standard (MC8000, 9000, 9000XL) or as an option (MC1000 and 4000 and 1000XL). All models of Symphony have 3D as standard. There is a 3D version of Avid Xpress but the feature set is much reduced (some of the techniques described here will not work on an Xpress).

On an ABVB system, the hardware may be external (a Pinnacle Aladdin, colloquially known as the pizza box), which connects to the computer via two cables, one to the Mac's external SCSI port and one to the JPEG board or internal (Genie) board, which occupies one of the slots on a PCI system. On Meridien systems, an internal 3D board is always used. One technical point – if you are using a system with the external 3D box, it is internally terminated and needs to be the last device in the SCSI chain. Any devices such as Zip or Jaz drives need to be placed between the Mac and the 3D box.

All current Media Composer and Symphony systems have the 3D hardware installed in the Meridien system, although the 3D option may not be enabled (for example on a standard Media Composer 1000XL). This has an impact on effects such as Chroma Key (see Chapter 10) and titles and graphics that do not use the Downstream Keyer (see Chapter 12).

The 3D effect offers the ability to move an image in an illusion of three dimensions. With normal 2D effects a picture-in-picture (for example) can only be scaled, moved left and right or up and down. With a 3D effect, the PIP can also be moved towards or away from the viewer and can be rotated around one of the three 3D axes. In addition, there are a number of useful effect shapes, such as page turns and waves, which can be applied to segments or transitions. There are extra border parameters, shadow and defocus effects, highlight effects, real-time trails and corner pinning (not Xpress). There is also a stamp buffer (not Xpress), allowing real-time static logos and images to stay on screen without using a second video stream or the DSK. All effects available through the 3D interface are real time, within the normal constraints of two streams of video.

Applying the effect – Media Composer and Symphony

Unlike the 2D effects, the 3D Warp effect on a Media Composer or Symphony is undefined until it is applied to a transition or segment. You'll find the 3D Warp effect in the Blend category of the Effect Palette. To apply the effect, simply drag the 3D Warp icon on to a transition or segment (or double-click in Effect mode). No change will be seen until entering Effect mode and modifying one or more of the 3D parameters. By default, on a transition, the 3D effect always manipulates the incoming video relative to the outgoing video, so in the case of a transition there will be a cut to the incoming shot at the beginning of the effect (Figure 11.1). By adjusting parameters on the first keyframe (say crop, position, scale or rotation), the incoming shot can be brought on to the screen as desired. To fly off the outgoing shot, click 'Swap Sources' in the Foreground parameter pane and all the settings will apply to the outgoing image.

V1
V2
V1
TC1
Whizz
oud montage
10:01:08:00
10:01:10:00
10:01:12:00
10:01:14:00

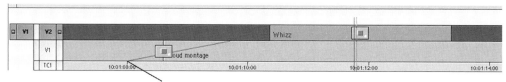

An undefined 3D transition effect will cut to the incoming clip here

Figure 11.1 3D effect icons in Timeline

If you plan to move a sequence from a Media Composer or Symphony to an Xpress, there is a special category of Xpress 3D Effects in the Media Composer and Symphony Effect Palette (Figure 11.2). These effects will work on all systems.

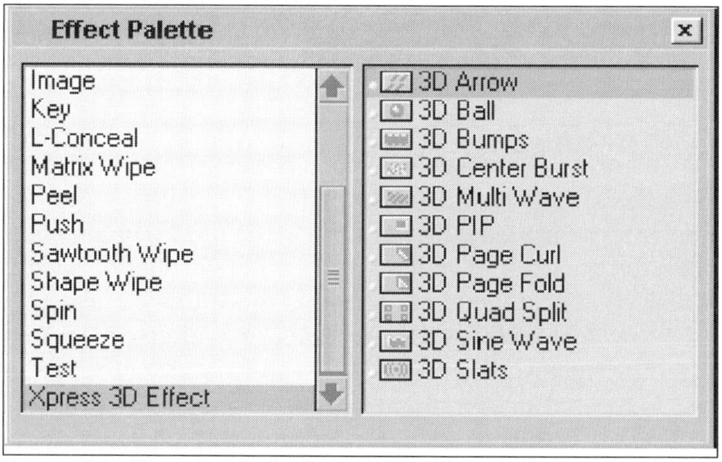

Effect Palette
Image
Key
L-Conceal
Matrix Wipe
Peel
Push
Sawtooth Wipe
Shape Wipe
Spin
Squeeze
Test
Xpress 3D Effect
3D Arrow
3D Ball
3D Bumps
3D Center Burst
3D Multi Wave
3D PIP
3D Page Curl
3D Page Fold
3D Quad Split
3D Sine Wave
3D Slats

Figure 11.2 Xpress 3D effects in Media Composer Effect Palette

Applying the effect – Xpress

The Xpress Effect Palette has a number of preset 3D effects (Figure 11.3). Once one of these is applied, the 3D parameters can be used (see below). An alternative (all versions) is to promote a 2D effect to 3D. If this is possible, a small '3D' button is visible at the bottom right of the Effect Editor (Figure 11.4). This cannot be reversed, except by using Undo. Titles and imported graphics may also be promoted to 3D.

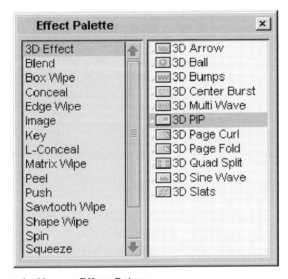

Figure 11.3 3D effects in Xpress Effect Palette

Figure 11.4 Promote to 3D button

Which way is up?

While the 2D effect controls refer to horizontal and vertical adjustment, the 3D controls refer to the X, Y and Z planes. X is horizontal, Y is vertical and Z is towards and away from the eye. Be sure what you are about to do – moving the object in X (left–right) is not the same as rotating the object around the X axis, nor is it the same as moving the axis in X, prior to a rotation (Figure 11.5).

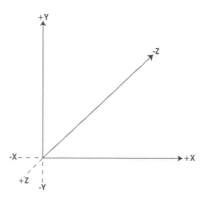

Figure 11.5 3D controls for position, scale and axis

When rotating, clockwise is positive, anticlockwise is negative. It is possible to make two complete rotations (720°) in either direction (Figure 11.6).

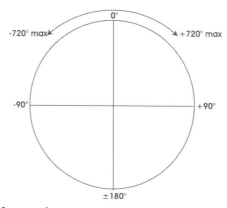

Figure 11.6 3D controls for rotation

3D parameters in the Effect Editor

The Effect Editor has many more parameters for 3D effects than for any of the pre-defined 2D effects. Figure 11.7 shows the parameters for Media Composer and Symphony; Figure 11.8 shows parameters for Xpress. Don't forget the useful trick of option [Alt]+clicking on an open triangle to close all open parameter panes! A useful addition to most parameter panes is the small enable button on the top right of each pane. This allows the user to set parameters but to temporarily turn them off without having to remember the default settings. This is particularly useful when saving effect templates – just turn on and off the parameters required after applying the template. Additionally, is possible to reset a parameter pane to the default by option [Alt]-clicking the enable button.

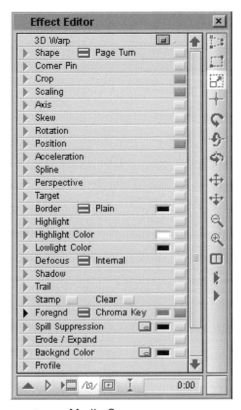

Figure 11.7 3D effect parameters – Media Composer

The image manipulation buttons

When using the Effect Editor for 2D effects, the only things that can be changed by direct manipulation (dragging) in the monitor are scale and position. In the 3D interface, the following can be adjusted by dragging:

- Corner Pin (not Xpress)
- Crop
- Scale
- Axis
- Z Rotation
- X Rotation
- Y Rotation
- X & Y Position
- X & Z position (Not Xpress)

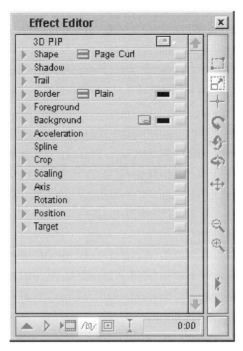

Figure 11.8 3D effect parameters – Xpress

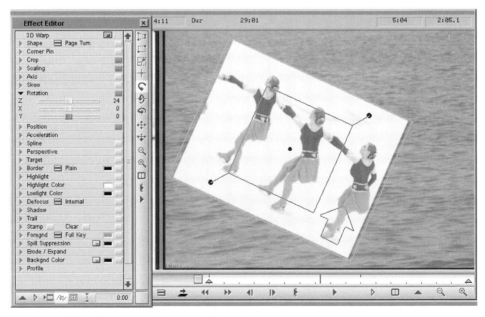

Figure 11.9 Effect Editor and image – Z rotation

Figure 11.10 Back of image, upside down

The buttons to enable these functions are arrayed down the right-hand side of the Effect Editor (Figures 11.7 and 11.8). When a button is active, an appropriate wireframe, with handles, is overlaid on the image in the monitor (Figure 11.9). When in wireframe view, the image has an outline arrow pointing upwards in the bottom right corner of the wireframe. If you are viewing the back of the image, the arrow is solid; if the image is upside down the arrow points down (Figure 11.10). When manipulating in the monitor, keyframes are added automatically under the right circumstances, as in 2D (see Chapter 10).

The hierarchy of parameters

If you take a look at the order of the parameter panes in the 3D Effect Editor (Figure 11.7), you'll notice that with the exception of Corner Pin (which was added later), they start with Crop (a simple 2D control), move on through such 3D parameters as Rotation and Skew (not Xpress), and end with Target, which is rather grandly referred to as a 'Post-Transformational' effect (Target allows you to pick up the entire effect you have built and scale it or offset it from where it started).

Even though you may apply any of these parameters in any order you wish, it makes sense to do the lower hierarchy items first – it is difficult to crop, for instance, if the image is rotated edge-on. Likewise, if the position of the axis is moved after rotation has been applied, the image may jump off the screen.

In summary:

Crop: if cropping the blanking, do it early, with all keyframes on and do it when you can see all the edges!

Scale: a 2D effect that may also give the illusion of moving the image closer or further away.

Axis: sets the point around which rotation will take place, so move axis before applying rotation.

Skew: simply distorts the image, like changing the shape of a parallelogram.

Rotation: apply after the axis position is set to rotate the image around any of the three axes.

Position: places the image in 3D space.

Acceleration: works as in 2D, giving an ease in/ease out to and from keyframes. Acceleration is on or off for all keyframes.

Spline: also modifies motion between key frames but changes the path to a curve. To see the effect of Spline, turn on Outline/Path. Like Acceleration, Spline applies to all key frames but it is possible to adjust the Spline parameters from keyframe to keyframe on a Media Composer or Symphony. Simply applying Spline applies a curve to the path even with all parameters set to zero (Xpress users cannot adjust Spline). The spline parameters are as follows:

- *Tension* governs how sharply the curve bends at a keyframe and also gives a dynamic ease in/ease out effect, similar to acceleration. Maximum Tension gives a linear path but considerable dynamic change.
- *Continuity* controls the amount of direction change at a keyframe. Minimum Continuity gives a path similar to maximum Tension, but without the speed changes. Maximum Continuity makes the path overshoot at each keyframe.
- *Bias* alters the emphasis on incoming and outgoing motion so that most or all of the direction takes place before or after the keyframe.

Perspective simulates a change in the viewpoint; as in real life, an object may appear differently, depending on the angle and distance of the viewpoint. Imagine looking up at a tall building and looking at the same building from a great distance.

Target moves the entire 3D path after the other parameters have been set. Target is useful for having one image track another image. Simply save the first effect as a template, apply it to the second image and offset it with Target.

The **Corner Pin** parameter (not Xpress) offers controls to map the foreground image on to the background in a specific way – a new image on to a television screen or billboard, perhaps, on the background shot (Figure 11.11). This is easily done by clicking and dragging on the handles in the monitor with the Corner Pin

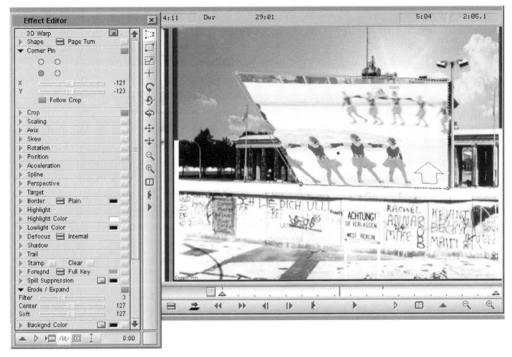

Figure 11.11 Effect Editor and image – Corner Pin

button active, although each corner can be set using X and Y controls in the Corner Pin parameter pane. The active corner is highlighted in the parameter pane. The 'Follow Crop' option resets the pin handles on the edge of the cropped image, if crop is applied.

The preset shapes

At the top of the Effect Editor when working in 3D is a fast menu marked 'Shape'. This offers a number of preset shapes, some of which are useful for transitions and some are more suitable for segments. Figure 11.12 shows choices for Media Composer and Symphony; Figure 11.13 shows Xpress shapes. They can be divided into a number of categories: Page Turns, Waves, Ball, Offset shapes and Scaling shapes. As each shape is chosen, appropriate controls appear in the parameter pane. Note that on an Xpress, these effects may applied from the Effect Palette (Figure 11.3).

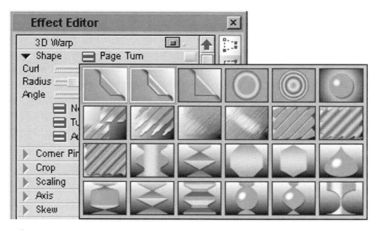

Figure 11.12 3D preset shapes – Media Composer and Symphony

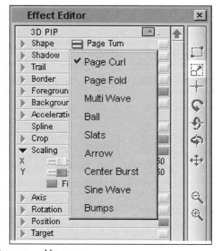

Figure 11.13 3D preset shapes – Xpress

Page turns

The page turns are mostly used for transitions. The Curl parameter moves the effect across the field of view; it works in conjunction with the Radius parameter so experiment with the values at the start and end of the effect (0 and 100 aren't always the best values). Following the logic of the 3D interface, Page Turn brings on the incoming clip; to give the impression of the outgoing clip being removed, click 'Swap Sources' in the Foreground parameter pane. If this is done, the values at the first and last keyframes will need to be swapped, too.

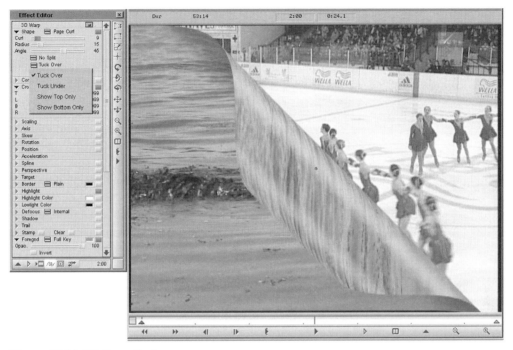

Figure 11.14 3D Page Curl

Another fast menu offers variations on the standard page turn – double and quad splits, for example. The next fast menu sets whether the top, bottom or both sides of the page turn are visible (the default is to show back of the image as the page is revealed). These choices, which are not available on Xpress, can be used to layer another effect on top of the transition, so that a different clip is seen on the back of the page turn.

The final fast menu defaults to 'Auto Highlight' (several effects can display a highlight). Other choices are 'Manual' and 'Reverse Manual' highlight. Whichever choice you make, you'll need to turn on the Highlight enable button, further down the Effect Editor (not Xpress). Figure 11.14 shows a 3D Page Curl with highlight.

The next effects to be encountered are 'Wave' and 'Multiwave', which simulate the effect of a pebble being thrown into water. The Frequency slider governs the number of ripples, while Amplitude controls the depth between each ripple. The position of the centre can be adjusted, as can the aspect ratio and the angle. These effects are very attractive but don't work too well as transition effects by themselves (the incoming video is clearly visible from the first frame of the transition). Try using a rendered dissolve to make the transition and layer or auto-nest the wave

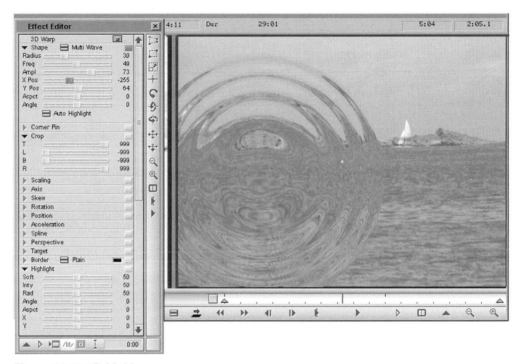

Figure 11.15 3D Multiwave

effect over the dissolve. Judicious use of Amplitude and Frequency over time with keyframes can create an animated splash effect. Figure 11.15 shows a Multiwave, offset in X and Y.

The Ball shape (top right of the palette) wraps video around a ball, either over a coloured background (set this with the Background parameter), or a video background. In this case, apply the 3D Ball effect to a clip on V2, layered over a background on V1.

The next seven shapes are known as offset shapes and weave foreground and background (or incoming and outgoing) video together in a series of slats, arrows or bursts. In a transition effect, Amplitude can be used to bring on the incoming clip. Frequency adjusts the number of slats or other elements.

Finally, there is a selection of shapes: hourglass, goblet and so on. The foreground video is forced into a shape that can be modified by the control sliders.

When working with different shapes close together in the Timeline, some effects may unexpectedly display a green (conditional) dot. The 3D hardware needs at least 5 seconds to reset itself to a new shape, so not all effects will play in real time; some will need to be rendered. Sometimes a green dot will display but the effects will play fine.

Other parameters

Border

The 3D Border control has a fast menu offering some designs other than the flat 2D border.

Highlight

The Highlight control (not Xpress) was mentioned earlier. It needs to be on (click the enable button) for the Shape Auto Highlight to work. It may be also used as a manual highlight on any clip, title or graphic. The default Manual highlight is a bright soft-edged semi-transparent circle (see the Highlight parameter pane in Figure 11.15). The shape, size, opacity, position and so on may all be adjusted with the parameter sliders. A Reverse Manual Highlight is also available. This darkens the area around the highlight, making it useful for highlighting text in a document or isolating a face in a crowd. Oddly, to enable Reverse Highlight, the fast menu in the Shape parameter pane must be used. Unfortunately, when applied, the default shape (page turn) appears, so adjust the Amplitude control to zero on all keyframes so that the shape is not visible.

Defocus

Early 3D systems have a limited Defocus control (not Xpress). This is augmented in Media Composer v10 and Symphony v3 by extra controls supplied by the new Copperhead board. The original Defocus is now called 'Internal' in the fast menu. Other choices (that give a greater degree of defocus) include 'Foreground' (the only one available for normal clips), Foreground and Key, Key and KeyBlur (for Matte Key effects). KeyBlur blurs an area of the foreground based on the opacity of the matte. These controls will have no effect unless the system has the correct hardware installed.

Shadow

Shadow adds a shadow of variable opacity, offset from the clip (there are X and Y controls). Shadow cannot be used in conjunction with Trail or Stamp (see later). There is also a limitation in that if the main clip moves off the edge of the monitor, the shadow cuts off early, too. A workaround is to use a black clip with the foreground level set to show some transparency, with a soft edge. Save a template of the parameters of the original clip and apply it to the black clip. Now use the Target parameters to offset the black clip from the main clip and render. Your custom shadow will faithfully follow the main clip as it moves.

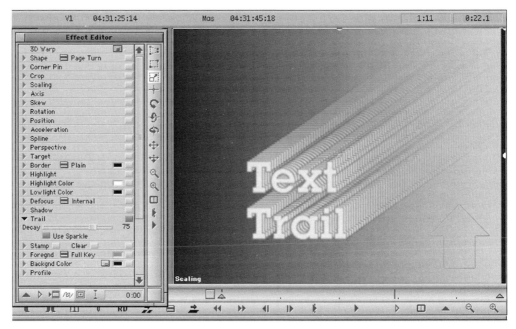

Figure 11.16 3D Trail

Trail

The Trail effect is real-time only (i.e., it cannot be rendered). It leaves a trail behind a moving clip or title on the monitor (Figure 11.16). To avoid the trail suddenly cutting off at the end of the effect, either use keyframes to stop the moving clip well before the end of the segment, or adjust the decay parameter.

Stamp and Clear

The 3D Stamp buffer (not Xpress) can hold a number of still frames (either normal clips, titles or graphics) that have been 'stamped' on the screen at various points. Like the Trail effect, Stamp is real-time only; when playback is stopped, the stamped items vanish. To stamp a clip (say a title, for example), edit the clip as normal on to V2 over a background on V1. The duration of the clip may be very short as it only needs to be long enough to encompass the fade-up or move that brings the clip on to the screen. To fade up a clip that will be stamped, use the normal Foreground Level control with keyframes; the Stamp Level parameter controls the opacity of items already in the buffer. At the last keyframe in the effect, click on the Stamp button in the Stamp parameter pane. When the sequence is played, the stamped frame remains on the screen as play continues. When play stops, the stamped frame or frames (as several frames can be stamped) will vanish.

Normally, the contents of the stamp buffer stay in front of any other objects that are layered later in the sequence. The 'Foreground on Top' button sets the stamped element behind any incoming foreground clips.

There is a slight delay in the way the stamp buffer reads the frame you wish to stamp. To see this, try bringing on a clip using Z Rotation (i.e., at the head the clip is rotated, but at the last keyframe it is perfectly aligned). Now stamp the last keyframe and play. You will see that the image does not settle correctly into position and it appears as though the wrong frame has been stamped. The fix is to copy the final keyframe (⌘+C [Ctrl+C]), move back one frame (two fields) in the effect, add a new keyframe and paste the parameters from the final keyframe on to this new keyframe. Now the image will sit correctly when played.

To remove images from the stamp buffer, use the Clear parameter. It is not possible to remove just one stamped image, the whole buffer is emptied. You needn't use an existing clip – you can apply a 3D effect to filler to clear the buffer. Move to the chosen point in the sequence and put two Add Edits into filler on a video track. As long as the second Add Edit is at the point where you wish to clear the buffer, the duration is unimportant, unless you wish to fade off the images. In this case, make the duration between the two cuts the duration of the fade. Add a 3D effect to the new segment, move to the final keyframe and click the Clear button in the Stamp parameter pane. To fade down the stamped images before clearing, click on the last keyframe and adjust the stamp opacity slider to zero. Now set Clear on the final keyframe and everything will fade off before clearing.

The 3D Chroma Key effect

If your system has the 3D option, you can use the 3D Chroma Key effect (not Xpress). Edit the layers as described for the 2D effect (Chapter 10) and apply a 3D Warp effect to the foreground image on V2. Go into Effect mode and move to the Foreground parameter pane. Click in the fast menu (normally reading 'Full Key') and choose 'Chroma Key'. Open the foreground parameter pane (Figure 11.17) and using the key colour bucket, sample the foreground clip as described for the 2D effect. This should give you a starting point. To achieve a good key, adjust the H Tol. and S Low sliders; H Tol. (hue tolerance) controls how wide a tonal range is keyed out relative to the tone you originally sampled. S Low (saturation low) deals with areas of low saturation colour that may have reflected off the blue screen background on to the subject. H Soft (hue softness) will ease the edges between foreground and background.

The L Tol. and L Soft controls are not usually needed. Luma Range may need adjustment in current versions. The Invert button will swap the key areas. As with the 2D effect, 'Show Alpha' (not all versions) displays the matte that is generated

Figure 11.17 3D Chroma Key parameters

by the effect making it easy to spot areas that are not keying correctly (Figure 10.40). 'Swap Sources' will apply the key effect to the clip on the other track.

Symphony v3 and Media Composer v10 may offer two further parameters that are of use when fine-tuning the key: Spill Suppression works in a similar way to the feature described under '2D Chroma Key'. 3D Spill Suppression, however, allows the user to define the replacement colour for the spill areas (Replace Color). The 2D effect always replaces with grey. 'Erode/Expand' adjusts and softens the boundary of the area that is keyed out. If the Center control is reduced, the keyed area is eroded (reduced); if the value is increased, the keyed area expands. The 'Soft' control will soften the boundary, while 'Filter' widens the area around the edge that is being adjusted. All these controls can work in conjunction with one with another, all in real time (Figure 11.18).

Figure 11.18 3D Spill Supression and Erode/Expand parameters

As mentioned at the beginning of the section on the 2D key, success will depend to a large extent on how well the footage has been lit, shot and digitized. If you have a Symphony v3, the real-time Ultimatte keyer will give markedly superior results to the Avid Chroma key effect.

12 The Title Tool and the Downstream Keyer

The Title Tool

The Avid Title Tool lets the user create 2D titles to key over video (the default) or over a coloured background. Titles are created and saved as uncompressed graphics with alpha channels and will display at high quality using Avid's Downstream Keyer. Fonts used by the Title Tool are those already installed on the computer. Mac users will need to have Adobe Type Manager running to use Postscript fonts with the Title Tool. Figure 12.1 shows the Title Tool and tool bar from Media Composer v10, Symphony v3 and Xpress v4. Earlier versions have a slightly different layout.

To start work, choose 'New Title' from the Clip menu (all versions) or Title Tool from the Tools menu (Media Composer v9, Symphony v2 and Xpress v3 and later). When the Title Tool launches, the current frame in the Record monitor is used as a reference background (to change the frame, move to a different position in the sequence and the frame will update when the Title Tool is reselected). This frame is not part of the title – any title can be used in any sequence. If the Title Tool vanishes behind the Composer window, use the Windows menu to get it back. To change to a coloured background, press the green 'V' button in the toolbar; click 'Bg' to see a pop-up palette for background colour (Figure 12.2).

Adding text

The default text is 48 point white Geneva [Arial], ranged left, bold. The simplest way to work is to select the text tool (T) and begin typing. When the text is correct, select it with the Selection Tool (the arrow icon) and adjust colour, style, shadow and so on. To change the default for the current editing session, make adjustments while the selection tool, not text tool, is highlighted and with no objects selected in the Title Tool.

'KeyCaps' (in the Apple menu on a Mac) allows access to special characters and correct left and right inverted commas and so on. Use the shift and option keys to see alternative characters. Not all characters are available in all fonts. Either use

Figure 12.1 Title Tool

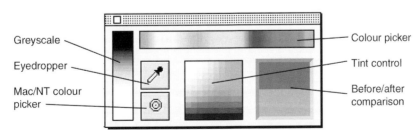

Figure 12.2 Color Palette

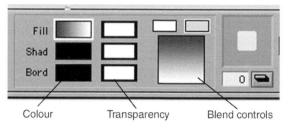

Colour   Transparency   Blend controls

Figure 12.3 Colour and Transparency selection

Keycaps to make a note of the required keystrokes, or copy and paste text from Keycaps into the Title Tool. On NT systems, use the Windows Character Map (Start /Programs/Accessories) to see extra characters; copy and paste the characters into the Title Tool. Special characters can also be typed straight into the Title Tool by holding down Alt and typing a number on the numeric keypad on Windows systems. Check the Character Map for the code for a particular character.

Text can be copied from a text editor (⌘+C) [Ctrl+C] and pasted into the Title Tool (⌘+V) [Ctrl+V]. Use plain text only. It can save time if title text is prepared away from the Avid.

To colour a selected text object, click on the Fill button (Figure 12.3) – a colour palette appears (Figure 12.2). Either choose a colour or use the eyedropper to sample from the background (on Meridien systems prior to Media Composer v10, Symphony v3 and Xpress v4, the eyedropper didn't sample accurately). The small circle icon brings up the Mac or Windows colour picker. Click on the boxes below Fill (Figure 12.3) to set colours for Border and Shadow if these have been applied. The second set of large boxes (to the right of the colour boxes) allow the setting of transparency. The smaller pair of boxes (right again) offer a choice of a second colour or a second level of transparency, giving a blend. The blend direction (45° increments only) is set by clicking and dragging in the large box below the small blend boxes.

Aligning and adjusting text

When a text object is selected, a bounding box with six handles appears on the monitor. Choose an alternative font from the pop-up, and a point size either from the pop-up or by typing a number in the box and pressing Enter. If you click on the point size box, the up and down cursor keys allow fine adjustment. One annoying feature of the Title Tool is that if a smaller point size is chosen, the text bounding box contracts to match. If a larger size, or a different font is then chosen, the bounding box has to be manually resized by dragging on one of the handles. It is not possible to distort text by dragging in this way.

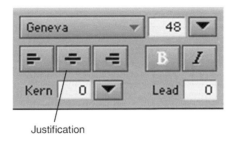

Justification

Figure 12.4 Text options

Alignment Help   3:2(
        Align To Frame Left
        Align To Frame Right
        Align To Frame Top
        Align To Frame Bottom ⇧⌘Z

        Center in Frame Horiz. ⇧⌘C
        Center in Frame Vert.

        Align Objects Left
        Align Objects Right
        Align Objects Top
        Align Objects Bottom

        Distribute Left to Right
        Distribute Top to Bottom
        Distribute First to Last

        Show Alignment Grid
        Align to Grid

Figure 12.5 Alignment menu

To align text, first justify the text within the bounding box using the buttons in the toolbar (Figure 12.4), then position the box in the video frame using the Alignment menu that appears when the Title Tool is active (Figure 12.5).

Pair kerning is on by default but the default kerning may not be appropriate for larger point sizes. Place the cursor between a letter pair and option [Alt]+click with left and right cursor keys to adjust pair kerning. The kerning control in the toolbar is more like a tracking control, applying the adjustment to the whole text string. Either type a plus or minus number in the box, then press Enter, or use one of the kerning presets from the pop-up. Bold or italic styles can be applied by pressing the 'B' or 'I' buttons.

Leading (line spacing) defaults to 120 per cent of point size but can be adjusted; type a plus or minus number into the Leading box followed by Enter.

Graphic shapes

Straps and other simple graphic shapes can be made using the rectangle, oval and line tools (Figure 12.6). The shapes can be resized by dragging the handles and a selected shape can be coloured in the same way as a text object (Figure 12.7). Hold down the shift key while creating an object to constrain the shape to a square or circle. To rearrange the priority of objects (i.e., to put a strap behind text), use the options in the Object menu (Figure 12.8). Rounded corners can be added to rectangular shapes and arrowheads added to lines by clicking the Corner button (Figure 12.9).

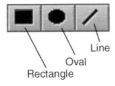

Figure 12.6 Shape tools

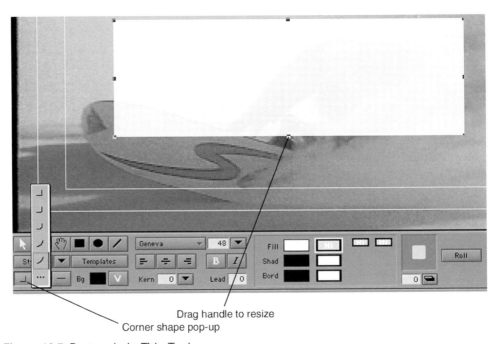

Figure 12.7 Rectangle in Title Tool

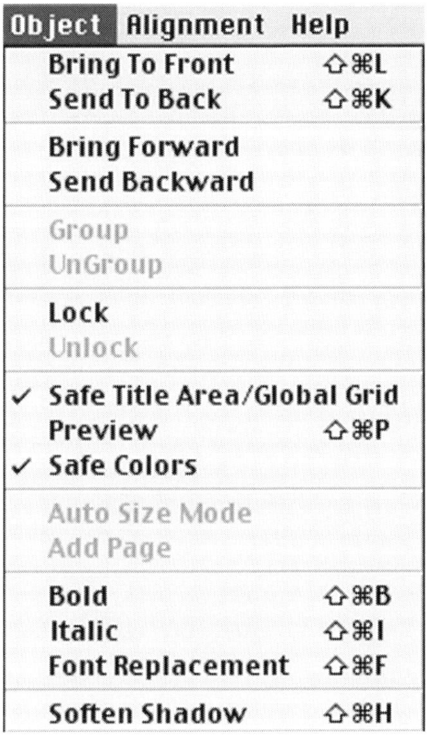

Object	Alignment	Help

Bring To Front	⇧⌘L
Send To Back	⇧⌘K
Bring Forward	
Send Backward	
Group	
UnGroup	
Lock	
Unlock	
✓ Safe Title Area/Global Grid	
Preview	⇧⌘P
✓ Safe Colors	
Auto Size Mode	
Add Page	
Bold	⇧⌘B
Italic	⇧⌘I
Font Replacement	⇧⌘F
Soften Shadow	⇧⌘H

Figure 12.8 Object menu

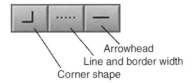

Arrowhead
Line and border width
Corner shape

Figure 12.9 Corner button

Borders and shadows

To add a border to text or a graphic shape, click the button with the dotted line (Figure 12.9). This doubles as a border width and line width tool. Preset or custom width borders can be added. Colour the border by clicking the Border Color picker (Figure 12.3).

Drop shadows can be applied to a selected object (text or shape) by dragging the shadow button (Figure 12.10). Offset and direction are set simply by

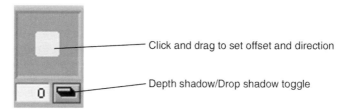

Figure 12.10 Shadow adjustments

dragging; offset can also be set using the numeric entry box. In Media Composer Mac v8, NT v9 and later, Symphony v2 and Xpress v3 and later, a soft shadow can be applied from the Object menu – Shift+⌘+H [Shift+Ctrl+H] is the shortcut. To add a glow (a soft edge without an offset), type in a figure for the soft edge without setting the shadow position. Colour the shadow by clicking the Shadow Color picker (Figure 12.3).

Saving titles

Save your title using the File menu; the Save dialogue box (Figure 12.11) offers choices for destination bin, media drive and video resolution. Make sure that the video resolution chosen is the same as, or compatible with, the resolution of the clips in the sequence (normal rules about playing back mixed and incompatible video resolutions apply to titles). Consider saving at the highest resolution compatible with the background video. The 'Fast Save' option saves the title clip to the bin without creating media (title media can be created or recreated at any time

Figure 12.11 Save Title dialogue

from the Clip menu). A title clip can be used in any sequence by recreating the media (see below).

It is possible save a Title Style (left of tool bar), which records font, size, colour, etc. These are saved as part of the User settings and can be used in other projects. To use a style, select an existing text string and choose a style from the pop-up (Figures 12.12 and 12.13). If the Save Style window appears on the monitor and promptly vanishes, use the Windows menu to bring it to the front; this is an anomaly on some systems.

Style pop-up   Template pop-up

Figure 12.12 Style and Template pop-up

Figure 12.13 Pop-up Style palette

Media Composer v10, Symphony v3 and Xpress v4 and later have a Template button in the tool bar (Figure 12.12). A Template can be made recording graphic shapes, colours, fonts and styles as a basis for future titles. If a template is reused, only the text can be changed, with other characteristics being locked.

Editing with titles

To edit your titles over video, add a second video track, patch source V1 to record V2, mark I/O in the Timeline and overwrite the title on to V2. Each title as made has a default length of two minutes (only a small amount of media is created; a single frame is saved and loaded into RAM as each title is required). To avoid problems if you decide to trim back later, move in a few seconds from the start of the title in the source monitor before you edit the clip. To quickly add a fade up and fade down, use the Fade Effect button in the fast menu (Figure 12.14). Park on the

Figure 12.14 Fade Effect button

title, press 'Fade Effect' and enter durations for the fade up and fade down. This is a quick way of adding keyframes to the title effect and fading in and out but doesn't always give a clean result. With some combinations of shadow size and transparency on Meridien systems, a more acceptable fade may be achieved by using 'Add Dissolve' at the head and tail of the title. These dissolves will need to be rendered.

It is possible to modify existing titles in a sequence by entering Effect mode and clicking on the grey 'Other options' button (top left in the Effect Editor – Figure 12.15). Adjust the title, close the Title Tool, click 'Save' when prompted and a modified title appears in your sequence bin with an incrementing number such as 'Main title.01'. Alternatively Ctrl-double-click (both platforms) on a title clip icon in a bin (in text view only in Media Composer v7 and Xpress v2) to load the clip back into the Title Tool for modification. This way you can do a 'Save Title As' from the File menu – very useful to base a new title on an existing title.

Figure 12.15 Other options button

Rolling and Crawling titles

To create Rolling (vertically moving) titles, click on the 'R' or 'Roll' button and begin typing, with a Return at the end of each line. The text will scroll as you type. When finished, save the title and load it into the source monitor. Mark In/Out in the sequence – the duration between the marks is the time that the title will take to move up the screen. Now edit the entire title into the sequence; if marks are set on the source side, only part of the title will be used. To stop and hold the roller at the end, enter Effect mode and add a keyframe at the position where you'd like the title to stop. Now copy this keyframe and paste the parameters on to the final keyframe. To fade the title off the screen, move back from the final keyframe by the number of frames you'd like the fade to take and add a keyframe. Now move to the final keyframe and set Foreground Level to zero. Don't use 'Fade Effect' in this case as your other keyframes will be removed or modified.

Crawling titles (ABVB only) are made in a similar fashion: click 'C' and choose a small point size (say 24 pt). Start typing at the top left of the screen – it will not scroll automatically but this is fixed in the next step. When the text is correct, click 'Make Crawl' in the Object menu and the text string is extended along the bottom of the frame. Adjust and save as before. Crawling titles will be available on Meridien systems from Media Composer v10.5, Symphony v3.5 and Xpress v4.5.

Xpress users will need to render rolling and crawling titles.

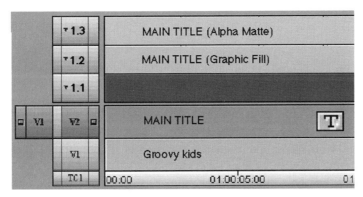

Figure 12.16 Nested tracks in title clip

Changing the graphic fill

Step in to a title segment in the Timeline and the nested elements are revealed (Figure 12.16). See Chapter 10 for more on nesting. V1 is an empty track and shouldn't be modified. V3 is the Alpha Channel and is locked (the alpha channel defines which parts of the title object are visible (black) and which are transparent, revealing the background (white)). V2 contains the Graphic Fill (i.e., the text colour) and this can be replaced by another graphic or moving video. The shape of the new contents is defined by the alpha channel. The Downstream Keyer (see below) will be disabled if this is done and a warning given in early versions. To move the nested video relative to the shape defined by the alpha channel, apply a resize or 3D effect to the clip on V2, adjust and render. This is best monitored using the second nesting method. These techniques can be applied equally well to imported graphics with alpha channels.

Saving a title move

Dragging the Title icon from the Effect Editor in Effect mode to a bin (as with effect templates) saves the title text and any keyframes and parameter changes. Option [Alt]+dragging the Title icon saves just the keyframes and parameters. You can apply this template to a new title by dragging the template on to the monitor window when the new title is selected in Effect mode. If the destination title is larger than the original, adjust the crop parameters to show all the title. If the Downstream Keyer (see below) was off in the source title, it may need to be turned off in the destination title before the contents become visible.

Recreating title media

If you need to change the video resolution of an edited title (after you redigitize, for example), use 'Recreate Title Media' in the clip menu. Either park on one title or mark I/O then select the correct video track(s). This will strip out any nested edits, however (see earlier). To keep the nested video, copy the contents to the clipboard (see the section on Collapse in Chapter 10) and load into the source monitor. After recreating the title media, the nested video can be edited back. Titles made at the wrong compression and keyed over video are not visible in the Record monitor; however, if a title is the first clip in a sequence, and the compression doesn't match the following video, then all the video clips will display 'Wrong Format'. Change the title resolution and all will be well. If you take your offline sequence to another computer for the online, see the warning about missing fonts in Chapter 15 (Redigitizing).

The Downstream Keyer

The Downstream Keyer is a third, uncompressed, real-time graphics channel in addition to the two real-time video streams on all systems with the exception of some Xpress models prior to v4. 'Downstream' means that the graphics are keyed over the video after the two video streams are mixed together. Static and rolling titles and imported graphics with alpha channels automatically use the DSK on Media Composer and Symphony. Clips using the DSK play in real time, even over unrendered real-time effects on lower tracks, although the only effect control available on Meridien systems will be Foreground Level and Acceleration (Figure 12.17). ABVB systems also offer Position and Crop controls with the DSK active. Crawling titles on Media Composer v7 use the DSK.

When a title is made, or a graphic is imported, two lots of media are created; one uncompressed (that is normally used), and a second, compressed set of media that

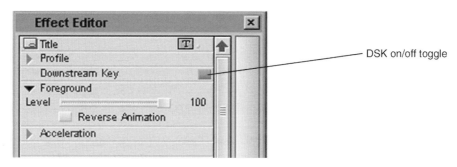

Figure 12.17 Effect Editor (Title) DSK on

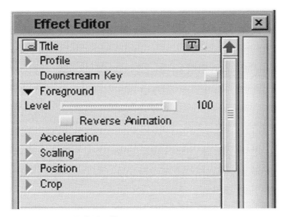

Figure 12.18 Effect Editor (Title) DSK off

is used if the DSK is disabled or the clip needs to be rendered. If a title or graphic is promoted to 3D, the DSK is again not used. On a 2D system it is possible to resize a title or graphic only if the DSK is turned off – press the pink DSK button in the Effect Editor and parameter panes for Scaling, Position and Crop appear (Figure 12.18). On some systems, the clip will then become non-real-time, with a blue dot, and will need rendering. If the graphic fill of a title is changed for video, the DSK is also disabled and the compressed media is used. For this reason, it is important to set an appropriate resolution when saving titles or importing graphics. A good trick is to always use the highest resolution compatible with your digitized video; for instance if the video is AVR75, use AVR77 for the titles and graphic imports.

Rolling and crawling titles normally use the DSK but may be rendered if necessary. On ABVB systems, it is possible to use a hard- or soft-edged crop on the moving title. Meridien systems do not have this feature.

As a general rule, try to keep all titles and graphics with alpha channels playing in the Downstream Keyer – the quality will be higher and less rendering will be needed. You may choose to reserve a high video track for all your DSK clips.

13 Files and media

- Saving your work
- Retrieving bins from the Attic
- Backup to floppy
- Deleting media and the Media Tool
- Consolidation
- Relink and Unlink

Saving your work

As you work, Avid saves the bins in your project at timed intervals. Because your clips and sequences are stored in bins, this means that all your work is regularly saved. It is also possible to save a bin, or the whole project, manually. Select a bin and in the file menu is an option for 'Save Bin'. Select the Project or Composer windows and the file menu option changes to 'Save All' – in this case your settings are saved, too. It is worth doing this before leaving the edit suite, even for a few moments.

The Bin Setting (Project window) allows the editor to set the autosave interval (the default is 15 minutes). Note the references to the Attic. The Attic folder contains copies of recently saved bins and the user can choose how many bin copies are retained. When any bin is saved (either automatically or manually), a backup copy is placed in the Attic folder with an incrementing number. If your bin is called 'Main Sequences', then the Attic copies will have names such as 'Main Sequences.bak.07', and so on. The idea of the Attic is not to be a genuine backup but rather to be a safety net if the original bin is mistakenly deleted or a sequence becomes corrupted.

Retrieving a bin from the Attic folder

On Mac systems, the Attic folder is at the top level of the Avid (internal) drive. Inside the Attic folder is a folder for each project on the computer. This means that folders from old projects in the Attic will build up and need to be regularly trashed (when each project is completed for instance).

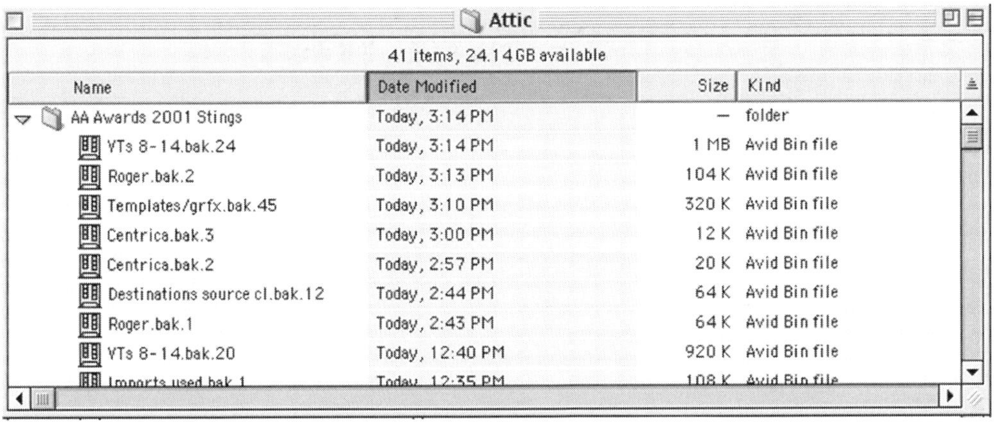

Figure 13.1 Old files (bins) in Attic folder

On NT systems, the location of the Attic folder depends on the original installation. You may find it in D:\Avid\Attic, or D:\Avid\Media Composer\Attic or even D:\Program Files\Avid\Media Composer\Attic. (Replace 'Media Composer' with 'Symphony' or 'Xpress' as appropriate). You may possibly find the application and the Attic folder on the C: drive. Find out where it is before you need it!

If you delete a sequence by mistake, or your sequence becomes corrupted, you can copy a bin (file) from the Attic folder into your Project folder. Avid will only allow one version of the same bin to be open at any one time; even if your backup is renamed, so first close your problem bin. Now, follow these steps:

1 Quit the Avid application (your project will be saved).
2 Double-click on the icon for the internal drive and open the Attic folder, and the Project folder. You will then see the list of backed-up bins, with names such as 'Sequences.bak.12'. These should be displayed in date/time order; if not, change the window to a list view and sort to show the newest files at the top of the list (Figure 13.1).
3 Look at the list of files until you see an earlier version of your bin (usually not the most recent, as that will be a copy of the problem bin, made as it was saved).
4 Open your project folder then, on a Mac, option/drag your earlier bin from the Attic folder into your project folder. This makes a copy of the bin (file). You cannot open the backup bin directly from the Attic. On NT, right-click on the .bak bin in the Attic folder and choose 'Copy'. Now move to your project folder, right-click and paste. Alternatively, on NT, Ctrl+drag the attic bin to your project folder.

5 Relaunch Avid and you should see the backup bin listed in the Project window. If not, choose 'Open Bin' from the file menu, navigate to your project folder and open the bin. Earlier versions of your clips will be in the bin. Make a new bin, drag any clips you need into this new bin and close and delete the backup bin.

If you have merely deleted a bin by mistake, you don't need to quit Avid while you copy the bin, but if the bin or sequence is corrupted, it is best to do this.

Backing up your work

As the Attic folder is on the same drive as the Projects folder, it should not be regarded as a true backup. After each day's editing it is advisable to back up your project folder on to either a floppy disk or some other medium such as a Zip cartridge. As the project information is just the data about your clips and sequences and does not contain any media, quite large projects can be copied on to one 1.4 MB floppy. If the project becomes too large, either backup selected bins (there is no need to carry on backing up bins that are not changing from day to day) or use a file compression program such as Compact Pro (Mac) or WinZip (NT).

To copy your project to a floppy or Zip cartridge, insert the disk and copy your Project folder on to the disk. Remove the floppy and take it home with you (or at least don't leave it in the computer!). If something should happen to the system, you can restore your project by copying the backup folder into the Projects folder on a different system. If the master tapes are safe, then work can continue after redigitizing.

Digitized media is not often backed up – the original tapes are the ultimate backup here. Sometimes media may be copied onto other drives or a tape streamer so that the project can be put on hold. See 'Consolidation' below.

Deleting media

At some point, it will become necessary to delete some or all of the media from your external drives. Let's start with a simple case, where one editor has been working on the system and there is only material from one project on the drives. If the job is finished and the system is needed for the next project, then the OMFI MediaFiles folder on each drive or partition can be deleted at desktop level. This may seem drastic but it is effective and means that the next project starts with drives that are completely empty, rather than having an assortment of files scattered about, leading to drive fragmentation.

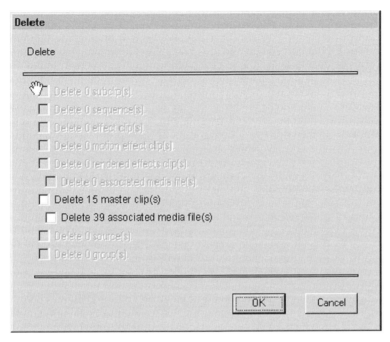

Figure 13.2 Delete from bin dialogue

Deleting from a bin

It is possible to delete master clips and media from a bin. Select the clips in the bin and press 'Delete'. You are now given the choice of deleting the clips, the media or both (Figure 13.2). Unless the clips have been wrongly logged, it is worth hanging on to them even if the media is deleted. That way, they can be redigitized later. Note that when deleting media from a bin, it is not possible to distinguish between audio and video media files. To do this, use the Media Tool and 'Select Media Relatives' (see below).

Effect clips, titles and so on can also be deleted from a bin, but prior to Media Composer v10, Symphony v3 and Xpress v4, there was no option to delete the associated media. Again, use the Media Tool and 'Select Media Relatives'.

Using the Media Tool

If other projects have media on the system, then the Media Tool can be used to isolate the media from the current project, leaving other media alone. In v8 (Mac), v9 (NT) and later, Symphony v2 and later and Xpress v2.5 and later, the Media Tool has options to search by specific project and to search specific drives; in earlier versions, all drives are checked and the choice is simply 'Current' or 'Other' projects (see Figures 13.3 and 13.4).

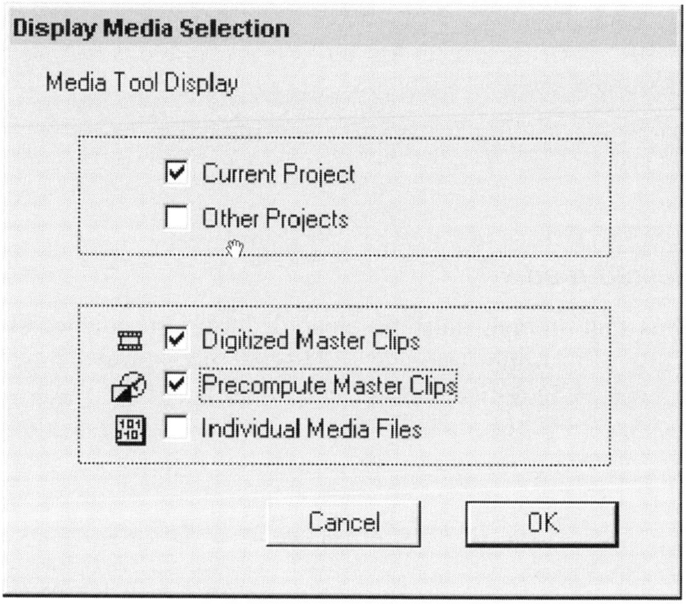

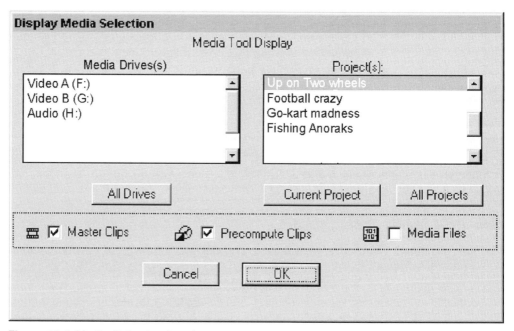

Figure 13.3 Media Selection (old)

Figure 13.4 Media Selection (new)

To delete all media from the current project, select the Media Tool from the Tools menu, select 'Current Project' and check all three categories of file: Master Clips, Precomputes and Individual Media Files. Now press Delete and you get one last chance to change your mind. Click OK and the media is gone. Even though one of the categories is 'Master Clips', the Media Tool only deletes the associated media files; the original clips are safe in their bins.

Deleting selected media

It often happens that storage must be cleared during an edit to allow for more digitizing. Let's look at an approach that will list the media associated with a specific sequence or sequences. This media can then be kept or deleted, as desired.

Let's assume that the current sequence does not use all the clips originally digitized, but that anything not in the sequence is not required and that media can be deleted. Take the following steps to remove this media: open the Media Tool, select Current Project/Master Clips, choose the appropriate drives (current versions) and click OK. Now select the current sequence in its bin. In the Bin menu, choose 'Select Media Relatives'. Now, any other clip in any open bin (including the Media Tool) that is linked to or associated with the selected sequence, will be highlighted.

In the Media Tool fast menu choose Reverse Selection. Now, all those clips in your project *not* associated with the sequence (and thus not required) will be highlighted in the Media Tool. Make a final mental check and delete the media (Figure 13.5). This technique can also be used to delete unwanted Precomputes (the effect files created by rendering or associated with titles or graphics clips; these

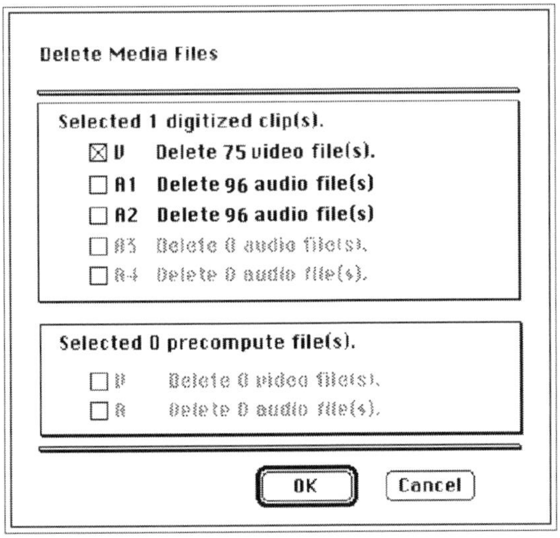

Figure 13.5 Deleting from Media Tool

build up over time). If there is more than one sequence to be checked, move them into the same bin and select both before selecting Media Relatives. The clearing of unwanted Precomputes is an important regular housekeeping task – many users forget to do this and wonder why their drives gradually fill up!

Consolidation

Sometimes simply being able keep or delete media already on the system is not enough. The editor may wish to copy or move media, or copy selected parts of media files in order to reduce storage requirements. The Consolidate command in the Clip menu (Media Composer and Symphony) or Bin menu (Xpress) will do this. It is possible to consolidate master clips, sequences and subclips. In Media Composer v8 (Mac), v9 (NT) and later, Symphony v2 and Xpress v2.5 and later, video and audio media may be sent to different volumes, offering greater flexibility in the consolidation process.

1 Consolidating master clips

The media for a master clip may be copied to a different drive or partition and the original media deleted. To do this, select 'Delete original media files when done' in the Consolidate window. When this is done the original clip is automatically relinked to the new media after copying. This is useful for gathering together media scattered over several partitions. Select a drive (all versions) or drives (current versions) from the list (Figure 13.6).

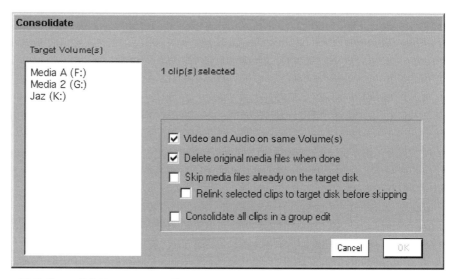

Figure 13.6 Consolidating master clips

It is also possible to copy media files associated with a master clip (to the same or a different volume) and retain the original media. In this case deselect 'Delete original media files when done' and a new master clip will be made to go with the new media. If the new clip is to be associated with the new media, the new clip has a .new extension to the name (i.e., 'Black cat.new').

It may be that the original clip needs to be linked to the new media; if so the new clip will be called 'Black Cat.old' and will be linked to the original (old) media file, while the original clip is relinked to the new media file. A dialogue box appears offering these choices.

2 Consolidating a sequence

Consolidating a sequence is a useful technique as it will delete media not used in the sequence by copying just the parts required and clearing the rest. It is important to duplicate the sequence before consolidating – rather like redigitizing (see Chapter 15), new clips will be created that will be linked to the new (shorter) media files. In case there is any possibility of going back and redigitizing the original clips, retain a copy of the unconsolidated sequence, which of course is linked to the original master clips.

To consolidate, select the duplicated sequence in its bin and choose Consolidate from the Clip (or bin) menu. It is possible to add handles to each of the new clips that will be created – a good idea if the sequence is only at the rough-cut stage. Choose a drive or drives (click and shift+click) from the list available. In early versions, only one drive can be chosen; if there isn't enough space available, either add more storage or consider splitting the sequence in two. If you do this (or you have been editing with a 'Part 1' and a 'Part 2') then *do not* select the 'Delete original media when done' option, if any material appears in both parts of the programme. Wait until everything is consolidated and then delete the original media. Newer versions of the software allow video and audio media to be sent to different media volumes (Figure 13.7). Media Composer v10, Symphony v3 and Xpress v4 also offer the facility of converting the audio sample rate during the consolidation process; any audio not at the rate set in the Audio Project setting will be converted.

If you are having to consolidate on to a volume that contains some of the original media, and you aim to gain some storage space, then deselect the option 'Skip media files on target disk' or some of the media will not be consolidated.

You may wish to consolidate just the audio from your sequence prior to moving to an online Avid to finish the project, leaving the offline video behind. In this case, make a subsequence of just the audio tracks and carry on as before. Consolidate to either a spare fixed drive or a Jaz drive that can be taken to the online system; take the offline sequence and the audio subsequence with you and copy the consolidated

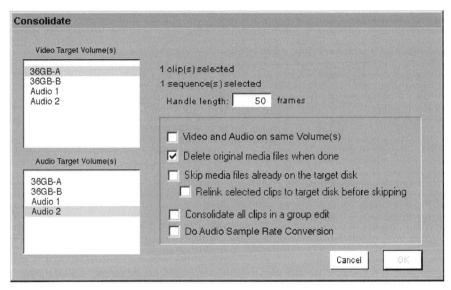

Figure 13.7 Consolidating a sequence (new)

media on to the online system – it will relink as Avid is launched. See Chapter 15 for information on redigitizing.

3 Consolidating subclips

This technique can be a great time saver if you have digitized long master clips with short sections of good material interspersed with sections of rubbish. It can be faster to digitize a whole tape (say) and make the final selection on the computer. When finished, the system will have made new master clips based on the subclips that were consolidated.

Load the source clip and make subclips as described earlier. Do not bother renaming the subclips yet. Select all the subclips and choose Consolidate from the Clip menu. You will be asked if you want handles on your new clips. If you have been generous in making your subclips, you can choose zero frames. Choose a media volume for the new media files and click OK. The new media will be created by copying the old media so that you need a volume with enough space. The original media files can be deleted automatically at the end of the process or you can do this later. Note the warning earlier about clips that have been used elsewhere before allowing automatic deletion.

When the consolidation is finished, each original subclip will have: a) a new master clip the length of the subclip plus the handles and b) a new subclip linked to the new master clip (Figure 13.8). The simplest thing to do now is to delete all

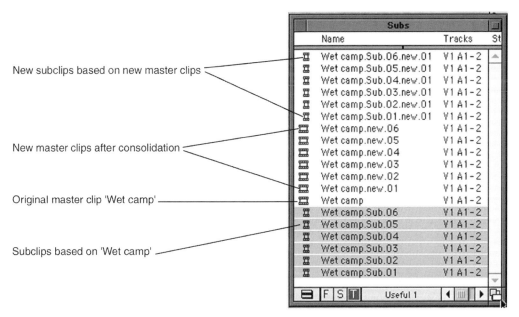

New subclips based on new master clips

New master clips after consolidation

Original master clip 'Wet camp'

Subclips based on 'Wet camp'

Figure 13.8 Bin with consolidated subclips

the subclips and the original master clip and media, leaving a number of new master clips in the bin that reflect exactly your choice of material. These clips can now be renamed. It is best to do this before editing any of the clips concerned. If parts of the original master clips have been used in a sequence, the sequence will need to be relinked to the subclips.

Relink and Unlink

The Relink command in the Clip menu (Media Composer and Symphony) or Bin menu (Xpress) is designed to allow the relinking of Master Clips, Subclips and Sequences to media files. Relink can be simply used to get rid of the Media Offline message that sometimes appears in the Composer window, or in a bin in frame view (Figure 13.9), or to force a particular clip to link to media on a particular drive or of a particular resolution.

Normally, during the digitizing process, media files are created to go with the master clips that have been logged and there is never a problem with clips becoming unlinked from the media. Occasionally, however, we may be sure that media exists but still see a 'Media Offline' message. Here are some relinking scenarios (the degree of control over the process varies depending on the version of the software in use).

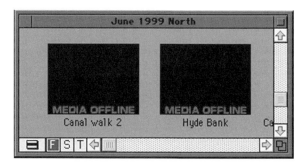

Figure 13.9 Bin showing offline clips

In Media Composer Mac v7, NT v8, Symphony v1 and Xpress v2, the choices are fairly restricted when it comes to relinking. Let's start with an attempt to relink a number of master clips to media files that we think exist on our drives. Select the clips in their bin and choose Relink from the Clip (or Bin) menu. The dialogue box (Figure 13.10) appears. To relink master clips, click in the appropriate check box and click OK. The drives are searched for media files that will link with the clips you selected. The system will only link if the media files have the same source (tape) name and identical start and end timecodes as the clips selected for relinking. The Volume pop-up allows for a search to be made of all drives, or selected drives.

If a sequence shows some frames as Media Offline, the entire sequence may be relinked. In this case select the sequence in the bin, deselect both check boxes in the Relink dialogue box, and press OK. This is sometimes successful when an attempt to relink master clips has failed, as the system only looks for the start and

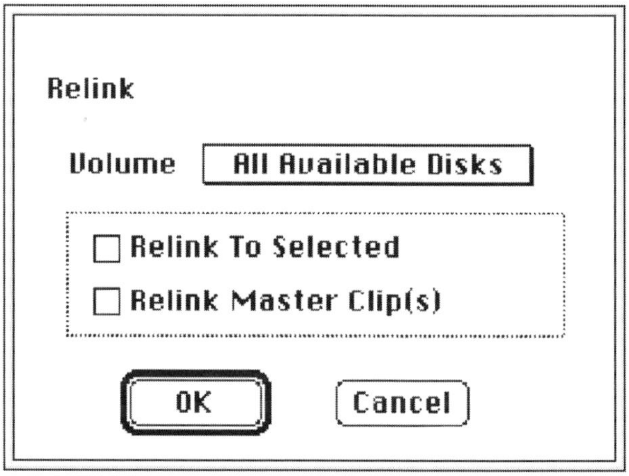

Figure 13.10 Relink dialogue (old)

end timecodes of the parts of master clips actually used in the edit during the relink.

A third choice is Relink to Selected. This is designed to let the user link sequences and subclips to media files associated with specific master clips. Say version 3 of your sequence has been consolidated, but that later you decide to return to version 1. Version 1 displays Media Offline in the Composer window. Temporarily move version 1 into the same bin as the consolidated master clips from Version 3, select both the sequence and the master clips and choose 'Relink to Selected' when the Relink dialogue box appears. This will force your sequence to link to the selected master clips if possible. It is a good idea to duplicate the sequence first.

This choice is particularly useful if media files of different video resolutions exist on the same system. If one sequence has been redigitized at high quality, and another, different, sequence has been offlined but contains some material common to the first sequence, then move a duplicate of the second sequence into a bin containing the high resolution clips you have already digitized, and do 'Relink to Selected'. A proportion of the high resolution clips may relink, thus saving digitizing time and drive space. Once this is done, decompose or redigitize the sequence to make new master clips of the offline material and digitize that. Note that the system ignores video resolution and audio sample rate when relinking normally, so 'Relink to Selected' narrows down the process to the specific clips and media you choose.

In later Avid versions, the Relink dialogue box has more choices (Figure 13.11). The option 'Relink offline non-master clips to any online items' will attempt to relink sequences and subclips to any online media files. 'Relink all non-master clips to selected online items' will carry out the same task as 'Relink to Selected' as described above. The third choice is 'Relink offline master clips to online media files'. In all cases, this enhanced dialogue box offers the choice of searching for tape names while matching or ignoring case, and restricting the search to media files associated with the current project.

A final sanction to take in attempt to get stubborn clips to relink is the force the system to rebuild the media file databases. In each OMFI MediaFiles folder on the media drives, are a couple of files that keep track of where all the media files for that volume are located. If these are deleted, Avid will rebuild them from scratch when it is relaunched or becomes the active application.

To delete the databases, quit the Avid application. Now, open each of the media volume icons on the desktop (or in 'My Computer') in turn and open the OMFI MediaFiles folder inside. Now look for two files with names commencing msm; on Media Composer v7 or Xpress v2 they'll be called msmOMFI.mdb and msmMac.pmr while on later systems they are called msmFMID.pmr and msmMMOB.mdb. Delete these two files and when you relaunch Avid, the databases will be rebuilt.

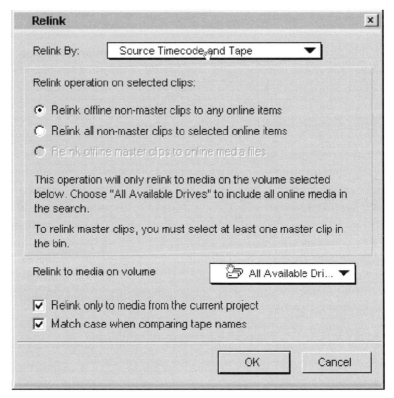

Figure 13.11 Relink dialogue (new)

Unlink

The Unlink command is hidden in the Clip (or Bin) menu – it is only revealed if Shift+Ctrl are held down while accessing the menu. Why use the Unlink command? There are several reasons. If we log and digitize clips from a particular tape and later realize that the logged timecodes could be applied to clips from a different tape (say on a multicamera shoot, or an associated DAT tape), we can save some time by avoiding relogging. Simply select all the clips of interest and duplicate them (Edit menu or ⌘+D [Ctrl+D]). Drag the clips into a bin of your choice and, with Shift+Ctrl held down on the keyboard, choose Unlink. All links these clips had with any media are now broken and to all intents and purposes they have returned to the status of having just been logged but never digitized. This means that the tape source and tracks can be modified (Clip or Bin menu again) and they can be digitized as desired.

This command can be also be used to remove unwanted tracks from clips – say, for example, that 10 minutes of narration had been digitized from a tape but the video track had inadvertently been digitized, too. Even if the video media file is deleted, the video track will still exist in the clip and a Media Offline message will be displayed. Once a clip has been digitized, it is not possible to change the tracks (even if all media is offline), so to get rid of the video track and media do the following.

Select the clip (or clips) in their bin and open the Media Tool. Set the media display to show Master Clips from your project. Back in the bin with the selected clips, choose Select Media Relatives from the fast menu – your clip will be highlighted in the Media Tool. Now click on the title bar of the Media Tool and press Delete. Delete only the video media file(s) (take care). This leaves you with clips that have an unwanted video track. Unlink these clips (see above) and modify the tracks (Clip or Bin menu) leaving just the audio tracks. Now, relink all the selected clips (use Relink Master Clips) and the audio media will come back online. Finally, a word of warning; be careful with the Unlink command. In particular, don't carry out the last described procedure if any of your clips have been edited into a sequence.

14 Importing graphics

Increasingly, an editor who is finishing programmes on the Avid will be faced with importing graphics that have been supplied by a graphic artist. Before running through the import options, it will be useful to consider the best way of preparing graphics for video. Of particular importance are the frame size and the pixel aspect ratio.

Frame size and pixel aspect ratio

The native video frame size used by Avid (PAL) is the ITU-R 601 standard of 720 × 576 non-square pixels, for the standard 4:3 aspect ratio. A little arithmetic will show that 720 × 576 does not equate to an aspect ratio of 4:3. This is because the pixels are not square but, in PAL, are slightly wider than they are high, thus displaying the normal 4:3 image on the video monitor. A similar situation exists in NTSC, but the frame size in that standard is 720 × 486 non-square pixels.

Even though a video monitor will display your non-square pixel image correctly, a computer monitor displays square pixels. This means that if the graphic artist creates the image to look correct while working in Photoshop (or whatever graphic application is used) some thought needs to be given as to the size of the original image and to how it will be saved prior to importing into Avid.

The simplest route is to create the image at a convenient size that gives a 4:3 aspect ratio when working in Photoshop (please delete and insert the name of your favourite graphic application). The usual starting point for PAL is an image of 768 × 576 pixels; NTSC users can start with an image of 648 × 486 square pixels. 720 × 540 square pixels can be used as a basis for both standards. Once the image is complete, then we can either a) resize the image to 720 × 576 (PAL) or 720 × 486 (NTSC) in Photoshop or b) leave it as it is and have Avid do the adjustment during the import process (described below). The import process deals well with the resizing and adjustment, although for the very best results you may choose to do the adjustment in Photoshop.

If the size adjustment is made in your graphics application, the image will look distorted but will appear correct when imported into Avid. In Media Composer v6 and Xpress v1.5 (the only earlier versions to work with the ABVB) it was important to do the resize prior to import for acceptable results.

Graphics levels

Avid allows the user to deal with the luminance of the graphic image so as to keep within legal limits for broadcast. A graphic file will have luminance levels somewhere within the digital scale of 0–255. Inside Avid, a legal black level (0.3v PAL; 7.5 IRE NTSC) equals 16 on this scale, while a legal white level (1.0v PAL; 100 IRE NTSC) equals 235. When importing the graphic, there are two main choices:

1 RGB Color levels – this should be used when the graphic has been created in a graphics application but no adjustment has been made to the graphic levels (do not confuse adjusting the levels with adjusting the pixel aspect ratio). This is the default choice and it will map graphic white to 235 and graphic black to 16; thus the imported image will be legal for broadcast. This is shown as 'RGB Graphics Levels' in some versions.
2 '601 Color levels' assumes that the levels have already been set correctly prior to import and will make no adjustment. This is the appropriate setting if importing colour bars from the Test Patterns folder (see Chapter 16) or if re-importing a frame that has previously exported from Avid using 601 levels. This is also the correct choice if the main areas of your image are adjusted to fall within the 16–235 range but parts are at either 0 or 255 so that an Avid Luma Key effect can be applied later. This choice is shown as 'CCIR 601' or 'ITU-R 601' in some versions.

File formats

Your graphic files may be saved in a number of different formats (for a complete list see the Avid Input and Output guide) but some widely used formats include PICT, PCX, JPEG, Photoshop, TIFF and Targa. Some of these formats support alpha channels and some do not. If your graphic includes an alpha channel, use a suitable format such as PICT or TIFF. An alpha channel is a fourth greyscale channel inside the graphic that contains transparency information allowing the image to be keyed in real time over video, in the same way as an Avid title. To see what an alpha channel looks like, create a title, edit it into a sequence and step in (see the section on nesting in Chapter 10).

A good choice for moving images is the Quicktime format (available on both Mac and Windows). Avid provide specific Codecs (compressor/decompressor) for rapid export and import of Quicktime movies. These are fast and efficient and allow the video resolution to be set. If you are specifying Quicktime criteria, make sure you state your desired video resolution. If this is set incorrectly, or a non-Avid codec is used, import will be very slow.

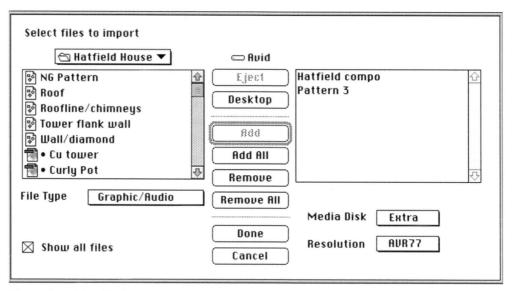

Figure 14.1 Mac file import dialogue

Importing the files

You may be given your graphic files on a Zip cartridge, a CD ROM or even on
a floppy disk. In all cases, copy the files on to one of your hard disks (probably
the internal drive); the import process will be faster and go more smoothly. This
will also help if files need to be re-imported later. Once the files are on the
system, open a bin (perhaps make a new bin for imports) and with the bin
selected, choose Import from the File menu. The import dialogue boxes vary.
Figure 14.1 shows the Mac version. Navigate to the drive and folder where your
files are stored. The default File Type is Graphic/Audio. When you can see the
files click Add or use Add All. It is not possible to click and shift+click. The files
are added to a list on the right-hand side of the window.

On NT, select a bin, choose 'Import' from the file menu and navigate to the
drive of your choice. Click and Ctrl+click on the files you wish to import
(Figure 14.2).

On both systems, choose a media drive and a video resolution from the pop-
ups. It is worth choosing the highest resolution compatible with your digitized
video. If you are doing an offline edit and have many such graphics, consider
importing them at 2:1 or AVR77 and using 20:1 or AVR12 as your offline
video resolution. In Media Composer Mac v8, NT v9 and later, Symphony v1
and later, and Xpress v2.5 and later, it is possible to batch re-import later (see
Chapter 15).

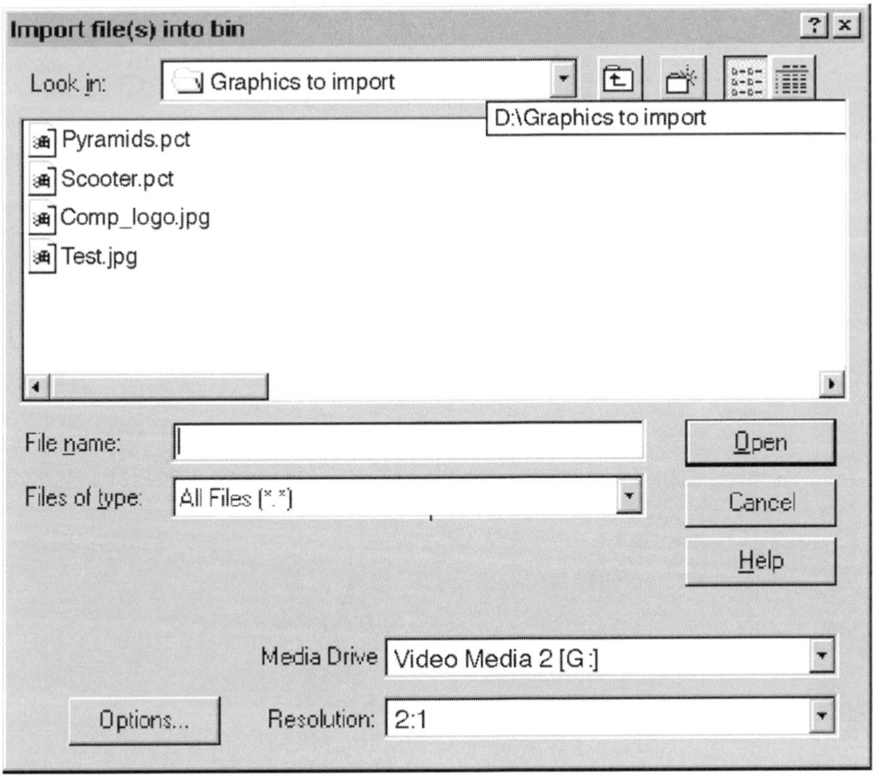

Figure 14.2 Windows file import dialogue

Import settings

Now it is time to check the import Options. In all the versions of Avid covered, the options can either be set on an 'as needed' basis or adjusted and saved as user settings. Figure 14.3 shows import options for Media Composer v10 – some of the descriptions vary in earlier versions.

In the Aspect Ratio, Pixel Aspect panel, '601 non-square' will import correctly either files that have been resized in Photoshop (described earlier) or files with square pixels of the correct image aspect ratio (i.e., 768×576 in PAL or 648×486 in NTSC). If the size of the image you import does not match either of these criteria, the image will be squashed or stretched to fit the video frame. This option is shown as 'Force to Fit', 'CCIR non-square' or 'ITU-R 601 non-square' in earlier versions.

'Maintain, non-square' (v10 only) will take an image containing non-square pixels and display as many of them as will fit into the standard video frame. Any pixels outside the frame dimensions (i.e., more than 720 or 576 in PAL)

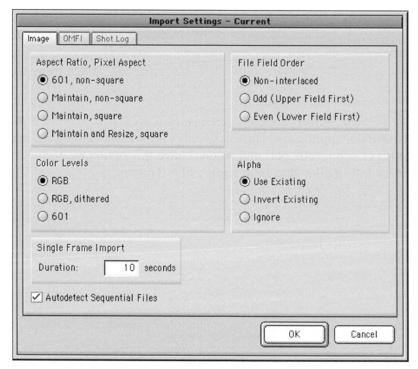

Figure 14.3 Import settings (image) Media Composer v10

will be cropped. Images smaller than the frame size will appear surrounded by black.

'Maintain, square', is designed to take small images with square pixel aspect ratio and place them in the video frame surrounded by black.

'Maintain and Resize, square', is similar to the previous choice but will stretch or compress the longest image dimension until it fits the video frame, scaling the other dimension in proportion.

The two main choices in the Color Levels panel (RGB and 601) are fully described at the beginning of this section. The third choice, 'RGB dithered', is designed to improve import of images with very fine gradations of tone and to avoid banding. The 601 option is shown as 'CCIR video levels' or 'ITU-R 601 video levels' in some versions.

In addition to setting the duration of the clip that will be created, ABVB systems have two options for the method of creating the media – this is set in the Single Frame Import panel. The default is to make a single frame's worth of media, which is loaded into RAM and played out in real time, just like an Avid title. This is always the case if your imported file has an alpha channel. This is a good choice for graphics without an alpha channel, too, as the import is fast and little disk space is used. The alternative, which you may see on some versions, is to import as a media file. This creates a normal media file, which means the clip may play back more reliably in conjunction with other real-time effects. The downside is that more disk space is used and the import time is longer.

The option 'Autodetect Sequential Files' is designed for importing PICT, Targa or other sequences – a sequence of files that will have been exported from After Effects or a similar application. These sequences have incrementing file names such as 'image01.pct', 'image02.pct' and so on. Leave this option off if you have been given folders full of files that have names like 'Graphics1', 'Graphics2', or Avid will only see the first folder!

Leave File Field Order set to Non-Interlaced for most still files created in a graphic application. The other choices are used when importing moving image files. If specifying criteria for the preparation of Quicktime movies in other applications, make yourself familiar with Avid field ordering requirements as once the movie is created, the field ordering cannot be changed.

The alpha channel choices are fairly self-explanatory. Invert allows the user to invert (swap white for black) in the Alpha channels of imported clips. The Avid way has always been to regard black as defining the foreground object and white as being transparent to reveal the background when the clip is keyed over video. The only exception is Quicktime movies with alpha channels being imported into Media Composer v10, Symphony v3 and Xpress v4 or later. In this case, white must define the foreground object and black is transparent.

In Media Composer v10, Symphony v3 and Xpress v4 or later, not only can the import settings be duplicated in the Project window and modified as desired, but several preset templates are also included. It makes sense to define your own settings once, then select them prior to import, rather than adjust everything every time.

When everything is set, on a Mac system click Done and the bin fills with the logged clips. On NT, click Open and the selected files are imported.

Editing with imported clips

Imported files without alpha channels appear as normal clips in a bin and can be edited as usual. Files with alpha channels are imported as Effect clips and have names such as 'Matte Key: Logo (with alpha)' (Figure 14.4). These can be dealt with and manipulated in the same way as titles created in Avid (but of course 'Recreate Title Media' won't work). Media Composer v10, Symphony v3 and Xpress v4 or later support fast import of Quicktimes with alpha – a great time saver. The only way to deal with a moving image with a matte in earlier versions was to use the Avid Matte Key effect (see Chapter 10). Figure 14.5 shows a real-time matte key clip in the Timeline.

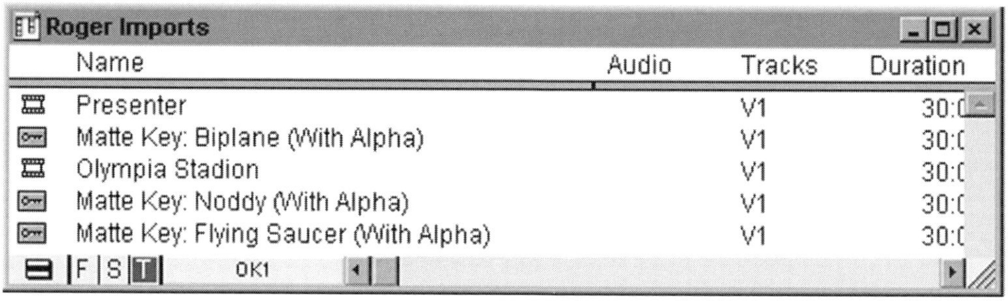

Roger Imports			_ □ ×
Name	Audio	Tracks	Duration
Presenter		V1	30:0
Matte Key: Biplane (With Alpha)		V1	30:0
Olympia Stadion		V1	30:0
Matte Key: Noddy (With Alpha)		V1	30:0
Matte Key: Flying Saucer (With Alpha)		V1	30:0

F | S | T   OK1

Figure 14.4 Bin containing graphic clips

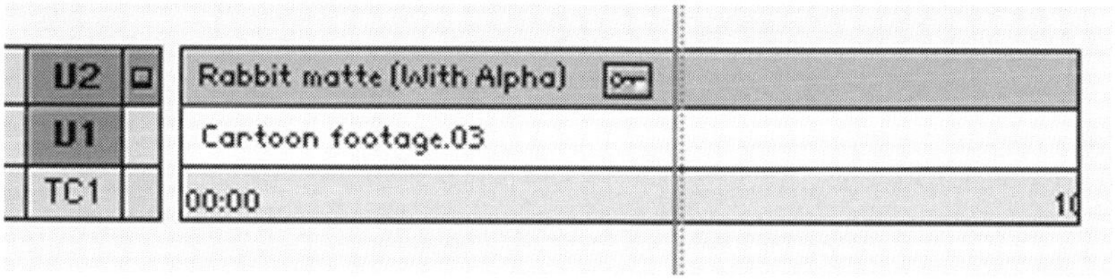

U2	□	Rabbit matte (With Alpha)	
U1		Cartoon footage.03	
TC1		00:00	1

Figure 14.5 Real-time matte key clip in Timeline

15 Redigitizing

1 Redigitizing original master clips

There are several reasons why redigitizing may need to be done; some media may have been deleted for reasons of storage space or a project may need to be put on one side for a period before editing resumes. An old project may need to be revived for a re-edit or parts of a sequence may need to be incorporated into a new programme. In most of these cases, the original clips may well be digitized as they were logged. This means that if media is ever deleted, it is good practice to keep a copy of the original bins and clips; this does not take up much space (floppies or Zip disks can be used) and it will save much time later.

If most of the material for a project needs to be redigitized, simply open the bins and batch digitize the master clips. If a sequence needs major re-editing, it is useful to discover exactly which master clips were used. This can be easily done – in the bin containing the sequence, click on the fast menu and choose Set Bin Display (Figure 15.1). Now choose 'Show Reference Clips' and click OK. The bin will now fill with all the original master clips used in that sequence and digitizing can begin.

2 Redigitizing sequences

Many times a programme will be offlined on an Avid and the online or finishing will be done on the same or a different Avid. In this case the only media needed will be just that required to play the sequence and no more. If redigitizing is to be done at 2:1 or uncompressed, storage space may well be tight, so it is best not to digitize any more material than is needed.

There are two main ways to redigitize a sequence, with some variations (although only the first method is available to Xpress users). Whatever method is chosen, it is important to duplicate the sequence before starting. This way, there will be a copy of the original sequence (that is linked to the original master clips) if any major re-editing is needed or if anything goes wrong. First name your sequence something like 'Offline final' and duplicate it (Edit menu or ⌘+D [Ctrl+D]). You will now

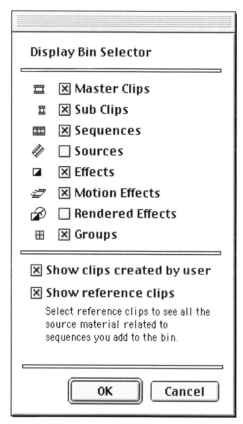

Figure 15.1 Set Bin Display

have a new sequence called 'Offline final copy.01'. Rename this (something like 'Ready for High Res'), move the new sequence to a new bin, and close down the bin containing the original offline sequence.

The first method is to simply select the sequence in its bin, choose Batch Digitize and force the system to redigitize the material required for the sequence. This is simple, although not very flexible. If this is to be done, decide whether you will keep the audio used for the offline. If a lot of mixing and balancing has been done, and particularly if much audio has been imported or digitized without timecode, then this is a good plan. If the offline was done on a different Avid, consider consolidating an audio-only subsequence of your offline, and moving the audio clips to the online Avid via a Jaz cartridge or spare hard disk (see Chapter 13). Copy the media files into one of the OMFI MediaFiles on the finishing system at desktop level, then launch Avid. The media should link to the audio subsequence you brought from the offline.

Figure 15.2 Delete from Media Tool

If you are working on the Avid used for the offline and you are happy deleting the low-resolution video media, then go ahead and do this. Open the Media Tool and display the master clips from your project (see Chapter 13). Select all the clips and press Delete. Now stop and take the next step slowly: *deselect* the check boxes next to the entries 'Delete xxx audio files?' so that when you press OK, you will only delete the video (Figure 15.2). Get this wrong and you are in for a lot of extra work. When done, close the Media Tool.

Next, move to the bin containing your new sequence and open the Digitize Tool. Choose the new resolution, select the sequence, choose Batch Digitize and make sure that you leave 'Digitize only those clips for which media is unavailable' selected. The system will now detect that audio media exists and only digitize new video. If you did not delete any original media, then no new media will be created as the system detects media that will link with the sequence and thinks that the job is finished (the resolution is ignored). If you deselect 'Digitize only . . .', new media will be created regardless, both audio and video.

During the digitizing process new clips will be created to go with the new media. If you have used an original clip called 'Office GV' several times in the edit, then you will end up with new clips called 'Office GV.new.01' and 'Office GV.new.02'

Figure 15.3 Batch Digitize dialogue (sequence)

and so on. Before the redigitizing commences you have the chance to set handles (extra material at the head and tail of each new clip) so that some minor changes (trimming or adding transition effects) can be done after redigitizing (Figure 15.3). Take care, though; the default handle is 2 seconds at each end of each new clip. This will add around 36MB per clip at 2:1, which may mean that you run out of storage space. If everyone is happy with the cut, then make the handles shorter.

Once the batch digitize is under way, you will be prompted to insert the tapes as needed. If the Video Input tool was adjusted for each tape at the offline stage, then it will reset to the saved setting for each tape. If the sequence has been brought from a different Avid (using a different VT), then don't use on the Video Tool settings. If any clips need individual adjustment then this is difficult and the second method (see below) is more appropriate.

When the job is finished, the bin will have filled up with new clips and the sequence will display the new clip names in the Timeline. One final step remains: any titles will need to have their media recreated at the new resolution. Simply select the track(s) on which the titles are placed, set a Mark In and Mark Out around the titles, check that the correct resolution is selected in the Compression Tool or Media Creation Tool, and choose 'Recreate Title Media' from the Clip menu. A caution appears warning that any video nested in the graphic channel of the title will be lost as the titles are recreated. See the notes on nesting in Chapters 10 and 12 for a solution to this.

Note that if the offline edit was done on a different system, then the appropriate fonts will need to be on the online system or the titles will not look correct. If an attempt is made to recreate title media on most versions, and a required font is missing, a dialogue box appears inviting the user to choose an alternative. Prior to Media Composer v10, Symphony v3 and Xpress v4, if none of the installed fonts is chosen, and you press 'cancel', the title is converted to the default font (Geneva) [Arial], whether you like it or not. It is best to keep a copy of the sequence, as a precaution. If the required font is later installed, Avid relaunched, and the title is viewed in the Title Tool (for instance by clicking the 'Other Options' button in the Effect Editor), then the correct font will be displayed. To force a save with the correct font, make a minor change (such as typing in a space) and close the Title Tool. You will be asked if you wish to save the change and the correct font will be displayed in the sequence. In current versions, you are given the choice of not recreating the title if the required font is missing.

Decomposition

This second method of redigitizing a sequence is broadly similar to the first, with the difference that the new clips are created before the digitizing starts, rather than as the digitizing proceeds. Decomposition is not available on Xpress. Decomposition gives the editor more control – clips from a particular tape that fall within the limits indicated by the colour bars can be done as a batch; other clips (too bright, or with a colour cast, say) can be isolated and redigitized with the TBC controls on the VTR set to manual. This process uses a command called Decompose in the Clip menu.

To decompose, duplicate your sequence, as before. Now select the new sequence and choose Decompose from the Clip menu. The choices regarding media and handles are made here (Figure 15.4). After clicking OK, if any media exists for the sequence, an alert appears in Media Composer v10 and Symphony v3 stating that the selected sequence will be linked to new offline clips. In earlier versions the message reads 'Selected clips will go Offline'. This means that any links the sequence had to old media will be broken, prior to the new clips being made (this is why we duplicate the sequence). Press OK and the bin fills with new clips. These can now be selected in batches or individually for digitizing. At this stage, any clips that have been reshot or are not required could be discarded.

If you are finishing on the Avid used for the offline and wish to use the original audio but have the space to keep the low-resolution media on the system, take the following steps. Duplicate the sequence as before and make a subsequence of just the video track(s). Now decompose this, deselecting the 'Decompose only . . .' option. New video-only clips will be created that can then be digitized. When finished, edit the high resolution video sub-sequence on top of your existing audio. Deal with any titles and the job is done.

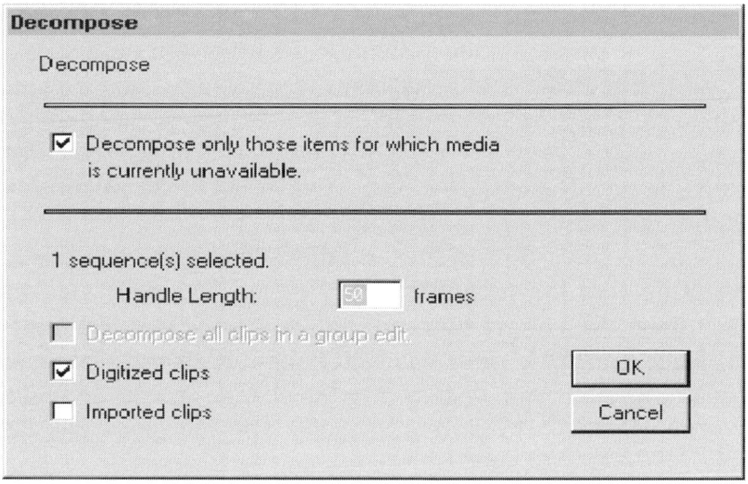

Figure 15.4 Decompose dialogue

Whichever method you use for redigitizing, watch out for timecode problems on your new clips. If you were careful to avoid timecode breaks at the offline digitizing stage and then add handles to your clips prior to redigitizing, you may cause the VTR to attempt to roll back over a timecode break that didn't cause a problem earlier.

Graphics considerations

If any graphics have been imported into the offline sequence (see Chapter 14), then these must be dealt with if the other video in the sequence is to be redigitized at a higher resolution.

Media Composer v7 and Xpress v2 (ABVB)

It is not possible to batch re-import graphics into these versions, so another approach must be taken. If the offline editing can be done on the online system, then a good plan is to digitize the offline material at AVR12, and import the graphics at this stage at AVR77 or the chosen finishing resolution. AVR12 is a two-field resolution that is compatible with AVR70, 75 and 77. When the editing is done, delete the AVR12 media (use the Media Tool and do a Custom Sift to find the AVR12 video) and redigitize a duplicate of the final sequence, with the 'Digitize only . . .' option selected. This way the AVR77 graphics will be ignored and only the missing (ex AVR12) clips will be redigitized.

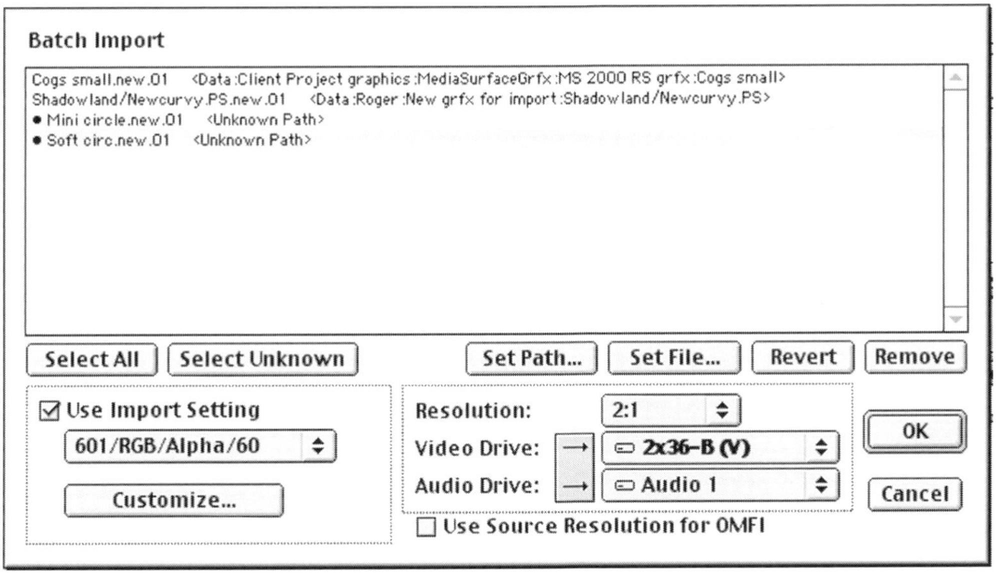

Figure 15.5 Batch Import dialogue (Media Composer Mac v10)

If the offline editing was done at AVR3s (say) on an ABVB system, and the graphics were imported at this resolution, the task is less simple. If there are only a few graphics, edited straight into the programme with few effects, then it may be easy to re-import the graphics at the finishing resolution and manually edit them into the final sequence. If the programme is heavy on effects, or some of the graphics are nested, then this will be a daunting prospect. There is a way of linking a particular batch of graphics (without alpha channels) to a particular sequence but it is tedious and time consuming and is not included here.

Later versions

In Media Composer Mac v8, NT v9 and later, Symphony v1 and later, and Xpress v2.5 and later, it is possible to batch import graphics at a different resolution. Choose 'Batch Import' from the Clip menu (Media Composer and Symphony) or Bin menu (Xpress) to re-import the clips at the finishing resolution. Figure 15.5 shows the Batch Import dialogue box on Media Composer v10 (Mac). Avid will remember the path to the folder from which the graphics were originally imported but this can be modified.

If storage space is not a problem, it is still easier to import the graphics at the finishing resolution from the start, and digitize the video at a suitable two-field offline resolution such as 20:1, as described above.

16 Output

Output from Avid is normally in the form of output to tape (Digital Cut) or an EDL (Edit Decision List) to transfer the information about the edit to a conventional online tape suite. Other methods of output or export are available: OMFI (Open Media Framework Interchange), Quicktime, and various graphic and text formats.

Digital Cut

Outputting to tape for a broadcast master may be the ultimate goal of the editing process, or the tape dump may merely be a low resolution reference copy with timecode or a VHS tape for assessment by a producer or director.

Assuming that the tape copy is to be of high quality, check that all the audio levels are OK and that the video levels are within limits. It may then be necessary to put colour bars, line-up tone and a clock on to the beginning of the programme. You'll need your own clock but it is possible to use the colour bars used by the Avid Video Output Tool – these exist in the form of PICT files and can be imported and used as a clip provided that the correct graphic import settings are used.

To import these bars, select a bin and choose Import from the file menu. Click on 'Options' and choose Pixel Aspect Ratio: '601 non-square' and Color Levels: '601'. The wording in the file import options varies from version to version (see Chapter 14 for more details). Now navigate to the Test Patterns folder, inside the Supporting Files folder, inside the Avid application folder. Select the file 'Colorbars' for full-field bars (NTSC users may choose SMPTE bars). See Chapter 14 for illustrations of the Mac and NT Import dialogue boxes. Choose a duration, choose 'Import as a slide' (ABVB only) and choose an appropriate video resolution. Click 'Done' (Mac) or 'Open' (NT) and a new clip appears in your bin.

To generate audio line-up tone, open the Audio Tool and click on the 'PH' button on the right-hand side (Figure 16.1). Choose Create Tone Media and select a duration, frequency and level (–18 dB or –20 dB digital is probably suitable). Choose a bin and a target drive, click OK and you will have a line-up tone clip in your chosen bin. Current versions allow generation of more than one track at once; earlier ones didn't (Figure 16.2).

Figure 16.1 Audio Tool Peak Hold menu

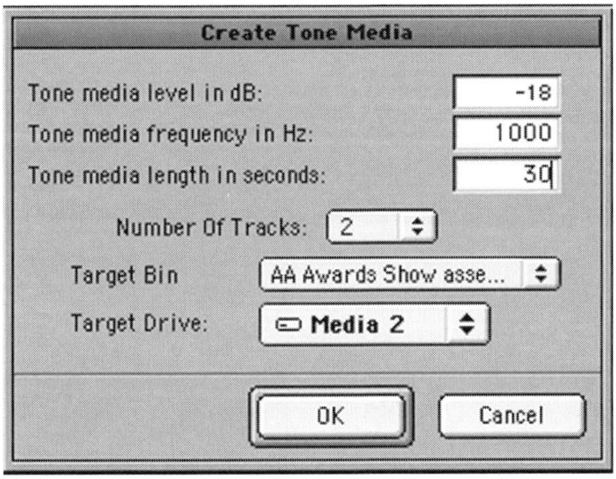

Figure 16.2 Create Tone Media dialogue

Once you've edited your bars and tone on to the front of the sequence and possibly added a clock, you may need to load some filler between these elements and the start of programme material. On Media Composer and Symphony, click on the current clip name in the Source monitor to bring up the monitor menu and choose 'Load Filler'; Xpress users can find this in the Clip menu. Once the filler is edited in place, you'll need to reset the start time of the sequence so that your desired master programme time matches the first frame of picture. In all versions, click on the Record monitor and press ⌘+I [Ctrl+I] for Clip Info and a box appears allowing the renaming of the clip and the setting of the start time. Subtract the amount of material you have edited into the sequence prior to the actual programme start from your chosen start time and modify the start time in the Info box. For instance, if you have 1′30″ of bars, tone and clock, and the show should start at

10:00:00:00, set the start time to 09:58:30:00. NTSC users can also change a
sequence from non-drop to drop-frame by simply typing a semi-colon in the 'Start'
box.

In Media Composer v10, Symphony v3 and Xpress v4 and later, this method can
be used to change sequence start time but you can also simply click on the current
start time of your sequence in its bin, and overtype with a new start time.

If any of your audio clips have an incorrect sample rate, this is the last chance
you have to change them. Select the clips in a bin and choose 'Change Sample
Rate' (Figure 16.3) from the Clip menu (Media Composer v10 and Symphony v3)
or the Bin menu (Xpress v4).

Figure 16.3 Change Sample Rate (Media Composer and Symphony)

Output without timecode

Once these preparations are done, Media Composer and Symphony users should
choose Digital Cut from the Output menu; Xpress users find this in the Clip menu.
Figure 16.4 shows the Digital Cut Tool from Media Composer v7 and Xpress v2;
Figure 16.5 shows a current version, with extra features. To output the whole
sequence, select 'Entire Sequence'; if this isn't done, only the section from the
position indicator or between In and Out marks will be output. To record to a deck
not supporting timecode, deselect 'Record to Tape' (early versions), put the deck
into record and press the large red Start button in the Digital Cut window. To stop
the Digital Cut, press the Spacebar, or the blue button in later versions. In later
versions, choose 'Local' for deck control. 'Record to Tape' really means 'Record
to Tape with timecode' and is a rather confusing term.

Output with timecode

To record to a tape deck with timecode, a striped tape will be needed with at least
a few seconds of timecode at the head. All systems covered will carry out either an
assemble edit or insert edit when outputting to tape (insert editing replaces video
and/or audio on a continuously striped tape; assemble lays down new timecode as
well as picture and sound).

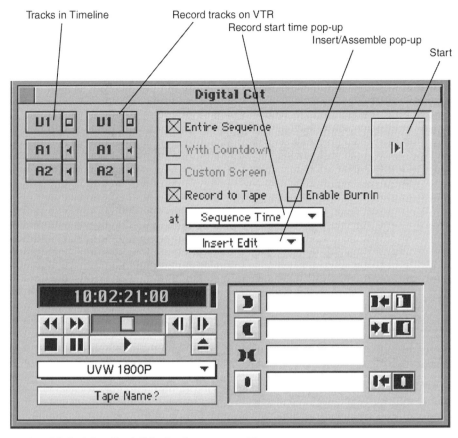

Tracks in Timeline
Record tracks on VTR
Record start time pop-up
Insert/Assemble pop-up
Start

Figure 16.4 Digital Cut Tool (Media Composer v7)

If an assemble edit is required, enable this option in the Deck Preferences setting (Project window – Figure 16.6), then choose 'Assemble' from the pop-up in the Digital Cut tool. This will not be visible unless the Deck Preference has been set. Make sure the timecode settings on your deck are set to 'Regen' and 'Rec-Run' for an assemble edit. The Avid system itself does not output timecode.

If the target tape has been striped with timecode that matches the sequence (or at least enough to enable an assemble edit), then choose 'Sequence Time' from the pop-up. Other options are 'Record Deck Time' and 'Mark In Time'. Record Deck Time will take the point at which the tape is parked as the starting point of the recording (a pre-roll will take place, however). Mark In Time will begin recording at the tape timecode set by the Mark In button in the Digital Cut window. This is very useful for adding an item to the end of a compilation tape or replacing a section of sound or picture on an existing tape. If you plan to do the latter, make sure that

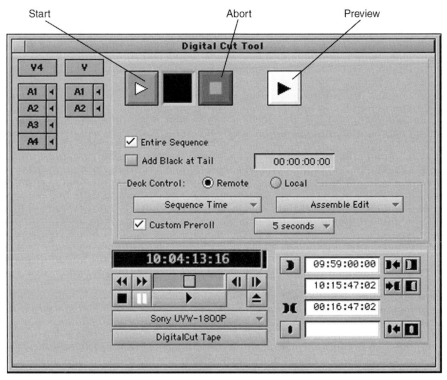

Figure 16.5 Digital Cut Tool (Media Composer v10)

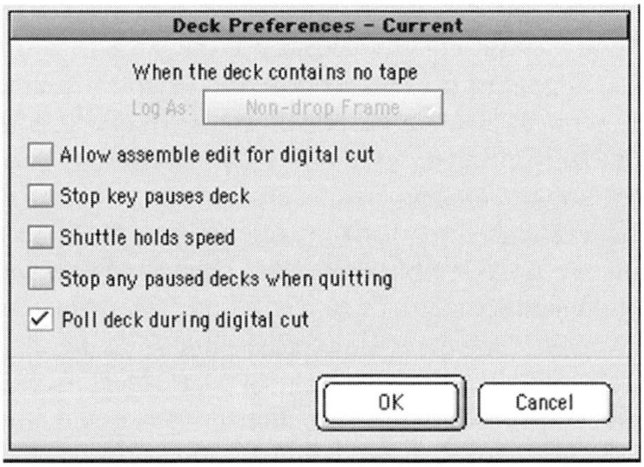

Figure 16.6 Deck Preferences

the position indicator is parked at the correct point on the sequence in the Timeline, or that an In and Out are set. If 'Entire Sequence' is deselected, the sequence only plays from In to Out, or from the position indicator if no marks are set. The deck controls are useful for cueing up the VTR. Note that the deck output cannot be seen through the Avid when cueing up – it will need to be directly routed to a video monitor.

The chosen tracks of the sequence to be output need to be selected in the left-hand panel at top left of the Digital cut window. Don't use the Timeline track panel. All desired audio tracks need to be selected but select the highest video track if all effects and titles are to be recorded.

The right-hand part of the panel can be used to turn on and off the destination tracks in the recorder – useful for replacing a section of just video or just audio. Note that the destination track panel does not appear unless Record to Tape (early versions) or 'Remote' (later versions) is selected.

Now check the audio record levels on the VTR; either play the calibration tone from the Audio Tool (in the PH menu) or play the tone at the beginning of the sequence. To lay black on the tape beyond the end of your sequence, choose Add Black at Tail but beware – if you are replacing a section in the middle of a recorded tape, black will be laid after the section you plan to record, possibly obliterating material you cannot replace. This feature is missing in early versions; see below.

When all is set, press the red Start button. You will then be prompted for the tape. If there is a tape in the deck when you choose Digital Cut, or you insert one before being prompted, you may see the 'What tape . . .?' message. It's no good typing 'DigitalCut tape', as you'll be prompted again later anyway! Just click 'Cancel'. After clicking 'OK', the system will check the timecode on the tape and wind back in preparation for a pre-roll (you must take the pre-roll time into account when you stripe the tape). If you encounter error messages, check that the deck pre-roll is not too short, that the cassette does not have the record protect tab set or that the deck doesn't have record inhibit on.

If a problem arises during playout, press the spacebar to stop (all versions); on later versions, there is also an Abort button. When you've fixed the problem, set the position indicator at some suitable point prior to the break, rewind the tape a little way (essential if you are doing an assemble edit), deselect Entire Sequence and go again. The system should pick up cleanly at the chosen point. Unless you can monitor the audio and video output from the recorder, it is best to record a few seconds output, then stop and check that the signals are getting through, before outputting a long sequence.

You may wish to lay black on the end of the sequence on a system lacking the 'Add black at Tail' feature. This is a good idea if you plan to record over existing material on a used tape, or are using Assemble edit. It is not possible to add filler to the end of a sequence, so a bodge must be employed. One way is to use an imported black graphic file or a black title frame, and another is to edit a few seconds of audio on to the end of the sequence and take the level down to zero using the Audio Mix Tool.

Making an EDL

Although many programmes are finished directly from the computer, there are a large number of offline Avids out there and a good EDL is the key to a trouble-free tape online.

A standalone program called EDL Manager is used to make EDLs from an Avid sequence. EDL Manager can be launched from the Media Composer and Symphony Output menu and (provided the system has enough RAM) can be run alongside Avid, enabling sequences and lists to be transferred backwards and forwards. On Xpress systems, it will be necessary to launch EDL Manager independently and open the sequence from the File menu (see later).

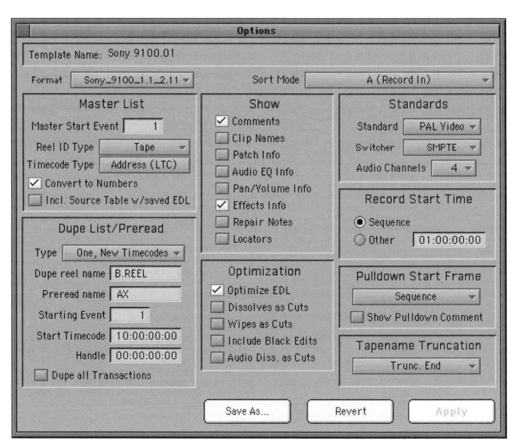

Figure 16.7 Options window (EDL Manager v10)

When EDL Manager is launched, click on the Options button (early versions) or choose 'Options' from the Windows menu and you will be faced with a bewildering number of choices (Figure 16.7). Before we run though the options, let's look again at tape naming.

Tape numbers

Try to think ahead to the online or conform early in the project. If the show is definitely going to be conformed, it is worth talking to the online editor at an early stage as they may have some constructive suggestions to make regarding the list format (which has an impact on tape numbering).

As suggested in Chapter 3, it pays to take care with tape numbers. Even though Avid allows long names for tapes, many edit controllers will only accept numbers and even those that accept alphanumerics have limitations on tape name length. If the person who logged or digitized the tapes hasn't used a sensible numbering system, how does EDL Manager deal with unacceptable tape names?

If the list format requires it, versions of EDL Manager prior to v10 will attempt to convert tape names by assigning a number based on any number that it finds in the tape names. Thus, TAPE20 becomes 020 or 20; 130297FRIDAY becomes 297 in a Sony 9000 list or 97 in a Paltex list. 123FRED456 becomes 456 or 56. If your source tapes contain such horrors as Rushes-1, Graphics-1 and Music-1, and the edit controller will only accept numbers, these older versions will strip out the letters and be left with conflicting numbers. New numbers are then assigned, which of course don't match those on the tape boxes! The recourse here is to the Source Table, a list of tape numbers assigned in the list, alongside the tape names used at the digitizing stage. It is well worth taking a printout of the Source Table to the online session, but save the Source Table separately, rather than appended to the main list.

EDL Manager v10 allows any tape name to appear in any list format (but see the section on 'Convert to numbers', below). Version 10 also has some other options for translating unsuitable tape names – see Figure 16.8. If tape library numbers have to

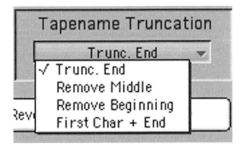

Figure 16.8 Tape name truncation options (EDL Manager v10)

be used, what happens to tapes 991000111 and 992000111? Depending on the version you are using, either temporarily renumber one of these tapes or set tape name truncation appropriately.

EDL Manager options

List format

The list format is chosen from the Format pop-up (Figure 16.9).

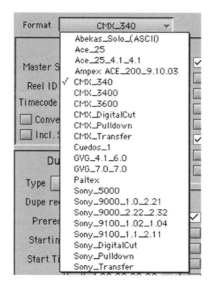

Figure 16.9 Format choices (EDL Manager v10)

Master list

'Master Start Event' sets the number for the first event in the list – normally 1. If you make separate lists for different video tracks (essential), then you can reset the Start Event number for each list so that there is no confusion. If you have 179 events in your main list for V1, for example, then make the first event in the V2 list 200. 'Convert to Numbers' will force a conversion of all tape names to numbers regardless of list format. Users of EDL Manager v10 will need to use this with some list formats if unsuitable tape names have been used.

Dupe List/Preread

What is a Dupe List? When the EDL requires the edit controller in an analogue suite to carry out a dissolve or wipe between two shots, this can be done by putting one source tape into one player and the second source tape into the second player, and

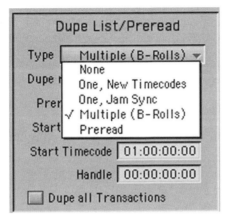

Figure 16.10 Dupe List choices

laying the effect onto the record VTR. This works fine if the two source clips come from different reels but what if they are from the same source reel? In this case one of the shots needs to be duplicated on to a new tape – thus Dupe reel. The Dupe List is a list of all the shots in the programme that need to be duped. The dupe reel will get its own new number – what this is depends on the list format.

There are several options for the Dupe List format (Figure 16.10). One in common use is 'One, New Timecodes'. This gives a list enabling a dupe reel to be made that has new continuous timecode. This new timecode is then referred to in the main list whenever a dupe is needed. Other options include 'Jam Sync', which is simply a list of discontinuous source timecodes in both the player and recorder columns of the list – in this case the online editor needs to know exactly where to look for each dupe. The 'B roll' option assumes that every source tape from which a dupe is needed has been duplicated and the main list simply refers to '45B' or whatever, depending on list format, when a dupe from reel 45 is needed. Getting the Dupe list format is vital – ask the online editor what is preferred. If you have no guidance, do a list with the None option, too, as this will at least reference the original timecodes correctly.

Digital formats can use the Preread option. In this case, there is no dupe reel as such. The outgoing shot is laid over length on the record machine and the incoming shot is cued up in the player. The wipe is made by the recorder simultaneously reading the outgoing shot from itself and combining it with the incoming shot and re-recording the combination of the two. Don't use this unless you are certain that the online system can handle it. For Sony edit controllers, make the Dupe reel name and the Preread name identical (say, *record*) for a successful preread list. You may find that EDL Manager cannot make a preread list in C Mode. If you have problems, make an A mode list instead and mention it to the online facility – problems can often be fixed by using other list management programs.

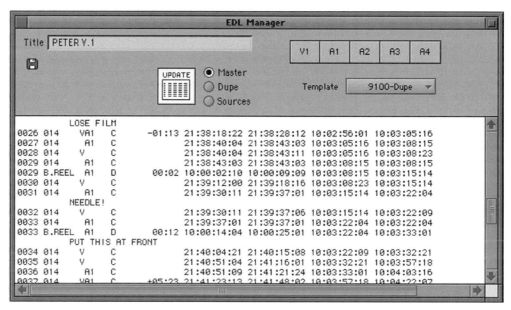

Figure 16.11 Comments displayed in list

Show . . .

This section (just named 'Comments' in earlier versions) allows you to append comments to events in the EDL. The first option, 'Comments', refers to comments added to your sequence. To do this, highlight a segment in the Avid Timeline (not Xpress), using one of the segment buttons, and click on the current sequence name over the record monitor. Choosing 'Add comments' opens a dialogue box where your comment can be typed. The comments can be shown in the Timeline and in the EDL. 'Patch Info', 'Audio EQ Info' and 'Pan/Volume Info' adds comments about your audio edit to the EDL 'Repair Notes' indicates points where the EDL Manager has not been able to represent an event in the sequence. If you include comments, make one list without comments, for the edit, and a second list with comments that can be printed out. EDL Manager v10 allows the inclusion of Locator text in the list, too. Figure 16.11 shows comments included in a list.

Optimization

The option to optimize is normally on, and has the result of removing matchframe edits and simplifying the list by combining events (such as a simultaneous audio and video cut). One thing to be aware of is that the EDL Manager will not remove matchframe edits in audio tracks if any of the audio parameters (level or pan) are different on either side of the cut (see below). The option 'Include Black Edits' will specify a source for any sections of picture black in your sequence. If it is not selected, black sections are ignored – ask the tape editor for their preference.

Standards

For most jobs, set this to PAL video or NTSC video as appropriate. The option for switcher lets you choose a particular vision mixer, otherwise leave this set to SMPTE – this will assign industry standard numbers to your effects. Most list formats don't support more than four audio tracks, so choose that option unless advised to the contrary. See below for information on making EDLs with many audio tracks.

Sort mode

There is one final thing to consider – the Sort mode (Figure 16.12). This option is set by a pop-up at top right of the window. The common choices are A Mode, B Mode and C Mode. What are the differences?

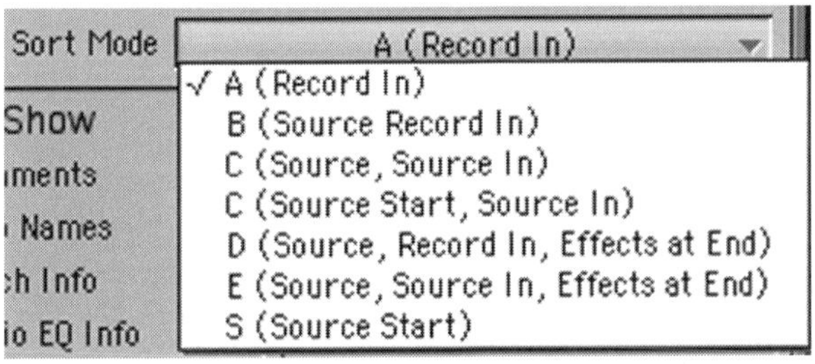

Figure 16.12 Sort mode choices

An **A Mode** list reflects the structure of your sequence closely in that the shots are listed in record machine order. This is at least simple and understandable and it is always worth taking a printout of an A Mode list to the online session. A Mode may not be the most efficient way of conforming the programme, however, as it may involve a lot of source tape swapping.

B Mode deals with each source tape in its entirety before moving on to the next, and does this in the order the shots appear in the programme. Thus, the play machine shuttles up and down between shots while the record machine proceeds steadily towards the end of the show as the shots are dropped in.

C Mode deals with the shots from each tape in source timecode order, so that each source tape moves from start to finish, while the recorder shuttles back and forth, to the required location of each shot. C Mode is a common choice but make an A Mode list too, as it is more understandable if anything goes wrong. If you don't know what the online house wants, make an A Mode list. EDL Manager v10 has an additional option that prepares a C Mode list using source timecode as a priority rather than tape number, as usual.

When you are finished, click 'OK' or 'Apply'. Once the options are set, EDL Manager comes back that way next time. If you are making lists regularly with differing requirements, you can make templates to be used again later (Figure 16.13).

Figure 16.13 Save Template dialogue

Making a list

We are now ready to make some lists (you may be asked for more than one). On Media Composer and Symphony, once EDL Manager is launched, press the arrow in the main window, pointing to the left. This will get the current sequence and generate an EDL using your settings. Xpress users should move or copy the final sequence into a bin by itself and call the bin something like 'Ready for EDL'. Now, choose 'Open' from the EDL Manager File menu, navigate to your project folder and open the bin containing your sequence. Select your sequence (which should be visible) and open it. If there is only one sequence in the bin, EDL Manager should open it automatically. Users of older Mac-based systems without much RAM may need to quit Media Composer or Xpress and open sequences in this way.

Dealing with Add Edits and dissolves

If you have been working without Audio Gain Automation, you may have split your audio clips with Add Edits and added dissolves between segments. It is unlikely that these fades and Add Edits will be needed in the EDL. It is best to remove all audio dissolves in the sequence, then to remove the match-frame edits. The command to do this (Clip menu – not Xpress prior to v4) will not remove match-frame edits if the audio levels have been altered on one side of the cut. They can be stripped out either by trimming the edits to one end of the clip, or replacing the whole audio segment with a continuous clip by using Match Frame.

Dealing with multiple audio tracks

Your EDL format may only support four (even two) audio tracks. How do you extract information from tracks five and six and so on? Make the first list and save as 'AUD14' or whatever. Now click on the boxes labelled A1, A2, etc., at the top of the EDL Manager window and switch them to A5, A6, etc. (Figure 16.14). You can now extract the data from tracks 5 and upward in groups of two or four. Your list will still refer to them as A1–A4 so name your list (say 'AUD58') and point this out to the online editor. On some versions of EDL Manager it is important to reload the sequence each time you change your track selection (do another 'Get' or 'Open' rather than 'Update'), otherwise the list will still display the tracks loaded previously. Check this on the version you are using. Before EDL Manager v10, always save the sequence bin after making any editing changes, before making another list.

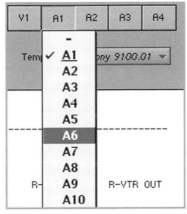

Figure 16.14 Track selection pop-up

Saving the EDL

When it comes to saving your list, what sort of disk do you use? The safest option is a double-density (720k) DOS floppy. Do not use a Mac-formatted disk and only use a high-density DOS disk if you know the online house will accept it. Mac-based Avids should be able to read, write and initialize (format) DOS disks as well as Mac disks. You may be asked for an RT11 disk. This is a format used by some Grass Valley and CMX systems. The EDL Manager can produce one of these if you insert a blank (unformatted) double-density disk and follow the prompts, while EDL Manager is active (Figure 16.15). Once formatted, you'll see a tiny disk icon in the corner of the EDL Manager window, but not on the desktop (Figure 16.16). In this case, use the 'Use RT11 disk' option when saving your file (Figure 16.17).

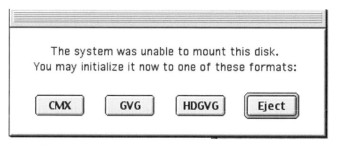

Figure 16.15 Format disk dialogue

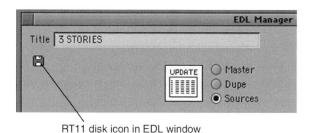

RT11 disk icon in EDL window

Figure 16.16 Disk icon

When you save the EDL, you must conform to DOS filename protocols. This means a maximum of eight characters (numbers and letters only) and no spaces, followed by a dot and a three-letter extension. This is nearly always .EDL and will be added to your filename by EDL Manager. Edit controllers using the RT11 format only accept six characters plus the .EDL extension, so if in doubt, stick to six characters. When you save from EDL Manager the default filename on offer is based on the name of the sequence from which you made the EDL, which led to illegal characters in some versions of EDL Manager. Current versions remove illegal DOS filename characters and use a six.three character protocol.

If your sequence is called 'Demo v.1', this will translate to 'Demov1' with the illegal space and dot removed. You must now change the filename, to something like COMBIN.EDL (for a combined list), VMAIN.EDL for a video only main list,

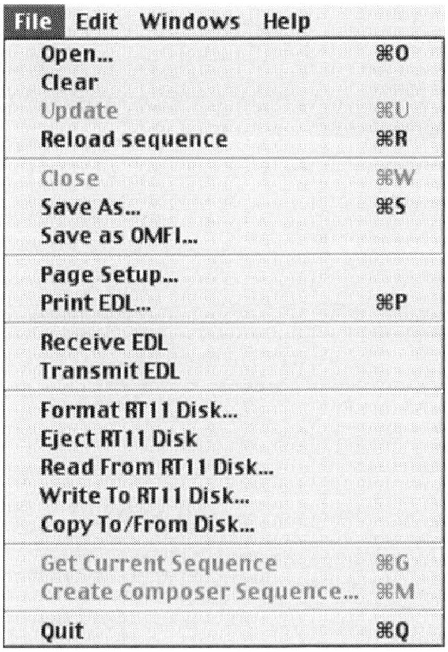

Figure 16.17 EDL Manager File menu

or VDUPE.EDL for a video dupe list. Try to describe the nature of the list as best you can using the few characters available. Don't forget to save the current list before generating a new one. To check that your list has been saved, use File/Open or go to the desktop and check that the file has arrived on the disk.

OMFI Export

Finally, a quick look at OMFI export. What is OMFI? It stands for Open Media Framework Interchange, a file exchange protocol developed by Avid and other companies. Think of it as a kind of Super-EDL that may include media and effects. Video and audio information from Avid sequences can be transferred to other systems, for video effects work or audio finishing for example. OMFI is often used to move audio to Digidesign Pro Tools, Avid AudioVision or other audio finishing systems – this is covered briefly below.

Preparing for audio transfer

As with EDLs, it pays to consult the people who will be working with the exported audio – they will be able to advise on the audio file format and the method of OMFI export. It is useful to set the audio media file format correctly for your Avid project from the start. This is done using the General setting (see Figure 3.2 in Chapter 3); choices will be SD-II, AIFF-C or WAVE, depending on your system. AIFF-C is usable on both Mac and Windows computers so is a good choice if you are not sure. After the editing is completed you will almost certainly need to consolidate the audio in your final sequence – if you don't do this, much more audio than you actually need is likely to be exported with the OMFI composition. Before consolidation, consider how the audio files will be moved to the audio finishing system. Typically, a Jaz cartridge or a spare media drive may be used; CD-Rs have been used successfully, too. Be aware of the maximum capacity of these devices – Jaz cartridges are either 1 or 2GB; CD-Rs are only 650MB.

It may be possible to consolidate the audio directly to a drive or it may be necessary to consolidate to one of your media drives first, then copy the files later. If you do this, try to find an empty partition or your consolidated media files will get mixed up with other existing media. Before consolidating, duplicate your final sequence and move it to a new bin. Strip off the video tracks and consolidate the sequence following the steps in Chapter 13. If you are forced to consolidate to a partition already holding some of your media, be sure to deselect 'Skip Media Files already on the target disk'. If you don't, some of your media may not be consolidated and the exported composition will include more media than you need. When done, you are ready to make the export.

OMFI settings

Depending on the system you are using, you may find preset OMFI export templates in the settings in the Project window. Either choose one of these, or make your own. Open the export setting and choose OMFI (Figure 16.18), after which the OMFI options will open (Figure 16.19).

OMFI Version 2 will transfer more information from your sequence than OMFI Version 1, but check with the people who will use your export and be guided by them. In both cases, it is possible to create a Composition (which refers to and plays back the media you consolidated) or a Composition with Media (in which case the media is embedded in the composition). Sometimes you can use either, other times it will be essential to choose one or the other (a composition with embedded media is a way of successfully exporting audio media to a system that normally would not support that format). Avid's 'Input and Output Guide' covers most scenarios. The choices (Figure 16.19) marked 'Link to . . . Media' are used for a 'Composition only' export. The choices marked 'Embed . . . Media' are used for a 'Composition with Media' export. Bear in mind that embedding your media in the composition may result in a very large file that exceeds the file size limit on your system or exceeds the space available on the drive used for the transfer. Making a composition

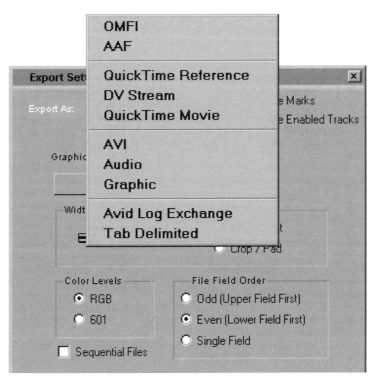

Figure 16.18 Export Settings – OMFI

that is linked to the media offers more flexibility as the media files can be split across more than one drive, cartridge or CD.

The 'Use SD2 format' option is only needed when the audio is going to a system that uses Digidesign's Sound Designer II format and your original audio is either WAVE or AIFF-C. If you originally chose SD2 as the audio file format for your project, you don't need to do this. If you are exporting for an AudioVision session, select 'AudioVision Compatibility', too.

Exporting the composition

When everything is set, select the sequence in the bin and choose 'Export' from the File menu. Click 'Options' to make sure you really have chosen OMFI as the export setting, navigate to your chosen drive and click 'Save'. If you have exported directly to a Jaz cartridge or large removable drive, that's it – remove the cartridge (or the drive, after shutting down) and hand it over to the audio person. If you need

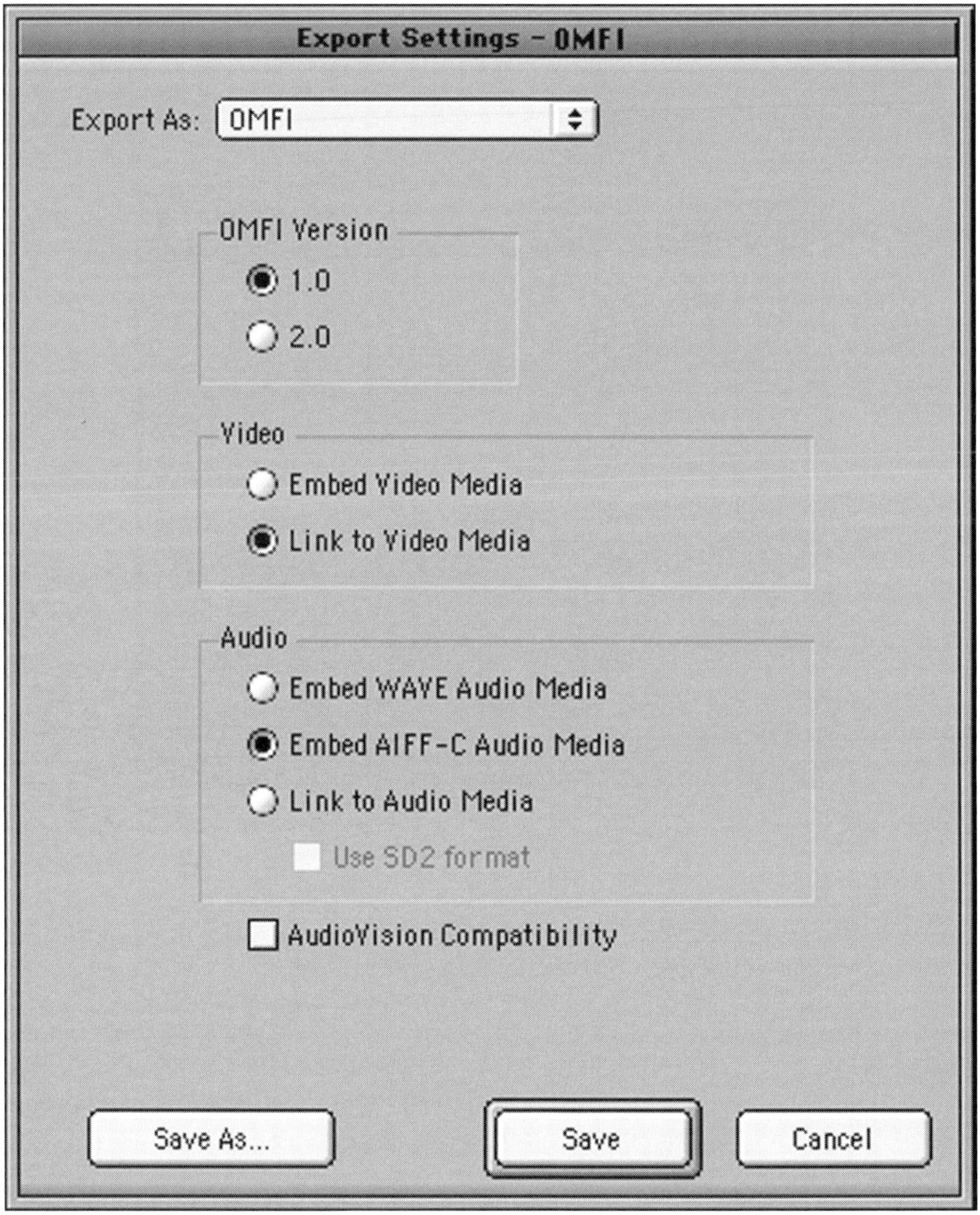

Figure 16.19 OMFI options

to copy the media files to another drive from one of your media drives, you can identify the consolidated files inside the OMFI MediaFiles folder by sorting the window by date.

Appendix A

Some Avid history

What version?

Media Composer is the longest-running Avid application and several versions are in regular use – here is a brief summary:

v5.6 and earlier

Version 5 of Media Composer ran on PowerMac and earlier Apple Computers fitted with the NuVista+ video board (which had a lower resolution than the current systems). These computers used the older NuBus internal expansion slots, rather than the current PCI slots. The highest video resolution available was AVR27, a two-field resolution roughly equivalent to the later AVR71. Single-digit resolutions (i.e., AVR1–AVR6) are single-field and double-digit resolutions (i.e., AVR25–AVR27) are two-field resolutions.

Typical computers are Quadra 650, Quadra and Power Quadra 950, 8100 with expansion chassis and the AMP (Avid Media Processor). This version is still used, mainly for offline, but is not covered in this book.

v6.0–6.5

Version 6 software was introduced to support the Avid Broadcast Video Board (also known as the ABVB or Studio board) that offered the CCIR 601 video frame size of 720×576 non-square pixels (PAL). A number of new features also appeared at this time. Different versions were released, to support the ABVB on both older (NuBus) and newer (PCI) Macs. Video resolutions changed and were described differently (AVR2s–9s and AVR70–77). The ABVB on NuBus Macs only supported resolutions up to AVR75. Typical computers are Power Quadra 950, AMP and PPC9500 and PPC9600. This version is not specifically covered here but many of the techniques can be used.

v7.0–7.2

Version 7 was a major upgrade offering many new features. It only runs on Apple PowerPC computers with PCI slots. Typical computers are PPC 9500, 9600 and G3 with an expansion chassis.

v8 (NT)

This was released for a short time and supports the Meridien board set on a PC with the Windows NT operating system. Features are broadly similar to v7.2 for Mac. The computer usually supplied is an IBM Intellistation.

v8 (Mac)

This version supports the Meridien hardware on Apple computers. There are some feature changes from v7.2 and they are detailed in this book. Typical computers are 9600 and G3 or G4 with expansion chassis.

v9 (NT)

This version supports the Meridien hardware on a Windows NT computer and is broadly similar to v8 (Mac) but with some extra features. The computer usually supplied is an IBM Intellistation.

v10 (Mac and NT)

This version supports the Meridien hardware on both MacOS and Windows NT. Many new features were introduced together with a large number of useful improvements. Typical computers are Apple G4 with expansion chassis and IBM Intellistation.

v10.5 (Mac and NT)

Released in the summer of 2001, this upgrade introduced a number of new features and improvements. See Appendix C for a summary of these features.

Appendix B

Grabbing tracks directly from an audio CD

Prior to Media Composer v10, Symphony v3 and Xpress v4, it was not possible to import audio tracks directly into a bin. Below is the import procedure for these earlier versions.

Mac systems

- Hide Avid if it is running (option-click on the desktop).
- Insert the audio CD into the computer.
- Find the Apple Quicktime Movieplayer application (if it isn't in the Apple menu or doesn't appear as an alias on the desktop, type +F and type 'Movieplayer' in the search field).
- Launch Movieplayer and choose 'Open' from the File menu.
- Navigate to the desktop and open the desired track from the CD.
- Click 'Convert' in the dialogue box. Now choose 'Options'. Set the options to 44.1 kHz/16 bit/Stereo. Don't worry if you are using a 48 kHz sample rate in Avid; the file will be resampled when imported.
- Choose a destination for your converted AIFF file (create a folder or use the desktop) and save the file.
- When done, return to Avid, select a bin and choose Import from the File menu. Make sure that the import file type is set to Graphic/Audio then navigate to your file with the box above the left-hand window. Select the file or files, and click 'Add'. Ignore the video resolution and options buttons as they are not needed for audio import.
- Select a media volume from the pop-up and click 'Done'. The files are imported and appear as clips in your bin.
- (Optional) Many directly imported audio files come in at a very high level so it is worth loading each one into the source monitor and adjusting the level using the Audio Mix tool.
- Delete the intermediate AIFF files when done.

Mac users might try Adaptec's Toast Audio Extractor or the Freeware Track Thief as alternatives to Movieplayer.

NT systems

- A shareware program called WinDAC32 is included on the system and can be started from shortcut on the desktop. WinDAC32 will generate files from the CD, which can then be imported into the Avid. If you are using WinDAC32 for the first time, here are the steps to follow:

- Make a folder in which to store your converted files – the best place is probably in the root level of the Avid drive.
- Start WinDAC32 (usually from a shortcut on the desktop).
- From the DAC menu, choose Settings; in the General setting, choose Output file and select the new folder you created for your files.
- In the WAV setting (still in general settings) make sure you are creating 44 100 Hz, 16 bit stereo files. If you need a mono track, choose Mixed Mono from the channels sub-menu.
- Insert the CD and play the tracks, if you need to (the play controls are in the menu bar). You will only hear the sound from the computer speaker at a low level at this stage.
- Click on the track number you wish to copy (Ctrl+click to add more) and choose 'Copy track' from the Actions menu. When copying is finished, close WinDAC32.
- Return to Avid, select a bin, and choose 'Import' from the File menu. Navigate to the folder you stored the files in, select the files and choose 'Open'. Ignore the video resolution and options buttons as they are not needed for audio import.
- When done, you will have a number of new clips in your bin. Load each clip in turn into the source monitor and check the audio level. Directly imported clips often come in at a very high level so adjust them with the Audio Mix window before editing. Rename the clips if required.
- Delete the intermediate WAV files when done.

Appendix C

Media Composer v10.5, Symphony v3.5 and Xpress v4.5

In mid-2001, Avid released 'point five' upgrades to Media Composer, Symphony and Xpress, too late for details to be included in the main text. There are a number of new features and modifications of existing features. Some of these features appeared in an interim release, 10.1, 3.1 and 4.1. A summary of the main features follows.

The editing interface

Avid have changed the appearance of the editing interface over the years but users have had little control over it, other than changing the shade of background grey or changing the buttons. Now users can change button shape, spacing and shading, and change the background colours of various windows. These changes are made from the Interface setting (Project window) (Figure C.1). Interface appearance templates may be saved and applied also.

The Timeline now acquires an optional toolbar along the top edge (Figure C.2); this can be displayed from the Timeline settings (Project window). The buttons can be modified in the usual way, using the Command Palette.

Media Creation Tool

The Media Creation Tool replaced the simple Compression Tool in Media Composer v10, Symphony v3 and Xpress v4. It allows the user to set storage drive and resolution defaults for digitizing, creating titles and so on. Two new tabs have been added in this release: 'Drive Filtering' and 'Motion Effects'. The Drive Filtering tab allows the user to prevent digitizing and rendering to the computer's

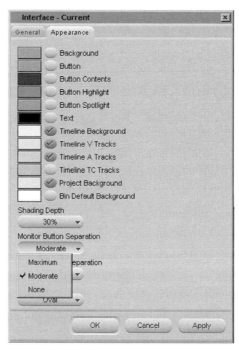

Figure C.1 New interface choices

system drive and the drive or volume from which Avid is launched (Figure C.3). 'Drive Filtering based on Resolution' has been moved here from the General setting.

Digitize settings

A new tab has been added to the Digitize settings – 'Media Files'. The 'Switch to emptiest drive' option can now be found here as can 'Digitize to a single file, 2GB limit' and 'Digitize to multiple files; Maximum (default) digitizing time . . .'. These are similar to the options previously found in the 'General' tab.

Figure C.2 The Timeline toolbar

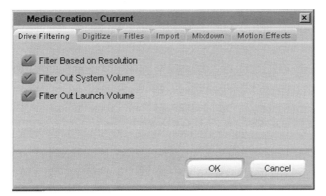

Figure C.3 Drive filtering in the Media Creation Tool

Batch digitize

The old option 'Digitize only those items . . .' has been changed to 'Offline media only'. A new option has been added: 'Extend handles beyond master clip edges'; when deselected this is designed to prevent problems when batch digitizing sequences with handles if timecode breaks are encountered on the tapes. A similar option has been added to the Decompose dialogue (not Xpress).

Title Tool

ABVB users have the benefit of real-time crawling (horizontal) titles. This feature is a welcome addition for Meridien systems with this release. Crawling titles can be applied as described in Chapter 12 but must be rendered on Meridien systems.

Changes to effects and Effect Mode

Monitor display

The Effect monitor window has a new appearance in this release, in addition to the interface changes mentioned above. Some of the buttons previously found on the Effect Editor (Split Screen, Add Keyframe, Wireframe Play, Magnify and Reduce) can now be found under the monitor.

Creating real-time moving mattes

If a three-layer Avid Matte key effect is constructed as described in Chapter 10, it can be converted into a real-time matte key effect in this new release. After the

Figure C.4 The new Fit to Fill button

effect is built, select a bin and choose 'Make RT Moving Matte' from the Clip menu. A new effect clip is created and placed in the bin; this clip can then be edited as required. This feature is not available on Xpress.

It is also possible to recreate matte media, in a similar way to recreating title media (the 'Recreate Title Media' option in the clip menu has been changed to 'Recreate Media', to cover both eventualities).

'Fit to Fill' button

'Fit to Fill' has been a feature of the Motion Effects dialogue box; it now gets its own button (in the Edit tab of the Command Palette) (Figure C.4). When the button is used, a motion effect will be created to fit the marked footage in the source monitor into the marked section in the Record monitor. The motion effect parameters set in the Render settings and the drive selected in the Media Creation Tool will be used.

Index